D0687290

BeBOP
and
NOTHINGNESS

FRANCIS DAVIS

BeBOP
and
NOTHINGNESS

Jazz and Pop at the End of the Century

SCHIRMER BOOKS
AN IMPRINT OF SIMON & SCHUSTER MACMILLAN
NEW YORK

PRENTICE HALL INTERNATIONAL
LONDON MEXICO CITY NEW DELHI SINGAPORE SYDNEY TORONTO

Schirmer Books
An Imprint of Simon and Schuster Macmillan
1633 Broadway
New York, NY 10019

Library of Congress Catalog Card Number: 95-24545

Printed in the United States of America

printing number
1 2 3 4 5 6 7 8 9 10

Design and text composition by Ellen R. Sasahara

Library of Congress Cataloging-in-Publication Data

Davis, Francis
    Bebop and nothingness : jazz and pop at the end of the century /
Francis Davis.
        P. cm.
    Includes index.
    ISBN 0-02-870471-1
    1. Jazz musicians—United States—Biography. 2. Jazz—History and
criticism. 3. Singers—United States—Biography. I. Title.
ML394.D36 1996
781.65'092'273—dc20   95-24545
                                                                CIP
                                                                MN

For Bill Whitworth—

not just the most skillful editor

a writer could ask for,

but the most perceptive reader.

Contents

■ Contents ■

Introduction

B_ebop and Nothingness_, the title a pun on Sartre you should think about in light of what follows, but not take literally, is my third collection of essays on jazz and tangential musics, following _In the Moment_ (1986) and _Outcats_ (1990). A unifying theme in _Outcats_ was the alienation of jazz musicians and their followers from mainstream culture. Despite a number of pieces that attempt to make the points they have to make in humorous fashion, this new collection is just as moody. Its unifying theme might be my growing disenchantment with contemporary jazz.

I once likened myself to a beat reporter, but I no longer feel as compelled to keep up with current developments in jazz as vigilantly—no, as _doggedly_—as I did just a few years ago, because keeping up has ceased to be fun. I guess it happens to all jazz critics sooner or later. It happened to Whitney Balliett, whom I once mocked (in my review of his _American Musicians_ for _The Times Literary Supplement_) for seemingly preferring deceased musicians to living ones and "pining for the days when giants supposedly huddled on the bandstand." It even happened to Amiri Baraka, a revolutionary in deed as well as in rhetoric whom I accused of "yearning for the [sixties,] when men were men and took forty-minute solos," in my review of his 1987 collection _The Music_ for the _Washington Post_. And now, as I burrow deeper into middle age, it seems to be happening to me. In my case, however, age isn't really the problem. Unless I flatter myself, it's jazz that's failed to keep up with me.

Forty years ago, in his introduction to _The Sweet Science_, A. J. Liebling explained that he had given up his post as _The New Yorker_'s press critic to go back to writing about pugilists and their promoters because "the longer I criticized the press, the more it disimproved." I know the feeling. The deadening same-

ness of most of what I was hearing on records and in clubs
began to get to me about five years ago—not coincidentally
around the same time that *The New York Times Magazine* ran a
long piece in which the writer Tom Piazza enthused about a
flock of musicians under the age of thirty who had recently
been signed by major labels eager to find the next Wynton
Marsalis.

Piazza opened with a look at the trumpeter Roy Hargrove
wowing his elders on an unnamed Charlie Parker tune at
Bradley's, a club in Greenwich Village. "Ten years ago, you
could have stopped into every jazz club between Bradley's and
Yankee Stadium and not found any 'youngsters' playing this
way," Piazza claimed. "For a long time, young musicians were
taught to play a hybrid form that was jazz in name only, often
heavily electronic, with large infusions of funk and rock in it."

This was published in 1990, so "ten years ago" was 1980, a
blink before Wynton and Branford Marsalis, when the most
talked-about young musicians in Manhattan were Anthony
Davis, George Lewis, Craig Harris, David Murray, and the
like—nominal avant-gardists busy collaborating with poets,
choreographers, and painters in a game attempt to erase the line
that had traditionally separated jazz from the other performing
arts. They had more on their minds than a Columbia Records
contract and a week at the Village Vanguard. You didn't hear
them at Bradley's, but maybe that spoke badly about Bradley's,
not about them.

A few months later in 1990, *Time* ran a cover story on Wynton Marsalis (they were only seven or eight years late in getting
around to him), with sidebars on most of Piazza's tadboppers.
The whole package was headlined "The New Jazz Age," and a
spate of such articles have followed in the years since. They're
still coming.

The problem with such "trend" pieces, quite apart from
their refusal to consider that there might be young musicians
shunned by major labels for not fitting the desired mold, is that

they perpetuate the neocon myth that jazz evolved from bebop to aberrant fusion to bop again, with thirty-plus years of free and its offshoots not even counting as jazz. They also foster the illusion that nothing much was happening in jazz until the arrival of these neophobic youth, proof of which is that you hardly read a word about jazz in these magazines since the last time they published trend pieces on "the swing back to tradition" or whatever.

But if *Time* and the *New York Times* say that jazz is experiencing a renaissance, it is. That's how it works. So why am I yearning for the Dark Ages? I bear the younger musicians in question no malice. Though some of them are unworthy of the hype, many of them are very worthy indeed. But they're not the real story. The real story is the commodification of youth.

"In jazz, the Negro is the product," Ornette Coleman once sagely observed. But not anymore, or not exactly. Race still matters to jazz people; it's often all they seem to talk about. But the new "product" in jazz is youth. Look around the next time you go to a club. The youngest people in the room figure to be on the bandstand. In pop, youth is a market. But the target audience for a Nicholas Payton or a Joshua Redman isn't people their own age or slightly younger—it's people my age. More specifically, it's people in their forties and older who've stuck with jazz through the decades even though they haven't much liked anything they've heard since around 1965, when Miles still had his band with Herbie and Wayne, and before Coltrane went too far out.

As I suggest later in these pages, this drooling infatuation with youth is itself a sign that jazz is beginning to show its age. Years ago, *Down Beat* used to review reissues in a column headlined "Old Wine, New Bottles." Given the current emphasis on classic repertoire and fresh young faces, most of today's new releases could be listed under "Old Blood, New Bodies." Youth doesn't signify anything else in jazz the way it does in pop. Never mind that what it now signifies in alternative rock is cheap, inherited, merchandisable despair—at least it signifies something. Those of us who dote on jazz are expected to be thrilled that men and women young enough to be our children are playing it. But are appreciable numbers of them listening to it? Not to judge from the young people I encounter, including the students who take my course in Jazz and Blues at the University of Pennsylvania.

I'll grant that jazz is in far better shape commercially than it was when I began writing about it close to twenty years ago. If not more popular than it's ever been (not by a long shot), it's more popular than it's been since the early 1960s. For the first time in recent memory, every major U.S. record company is bringing out both jazz reissues and new jazz releases. Instrumentalists are no longer required to plug in or to record with strings in order to land a contract with one of the majors; they're encouraged to play in the studio more or less as they do in clubs. Another sign of health is that along with the middle-aged stags you've always seen at jazz clubs, you now occasionally spot dating singles in their late twenties or early thirties. Jazz still being very much a guy thing, *he's* usually trying to impress her with the depth of his knowledge and getting everything wrong. But the mere presence of such couples is proof that jazz has reclaimed its place alongside movies, rock concerts, and comedy clubs as a viable Saturday-night recreational option: a prelude to a kiss.

It's a far cry from a time not so long ago when the musicians on the bandstand occasionally outnumbered the people at the tables and we all concluded that jazz was doomed to be free. No one wants to return to those days. But many of us who were drawn as youths to jazz by what we took to be its premise that rules were meant to be broken can't help feeling that this increased acceptance has come at too great a cost—the codification of jazz into bebop, Ellington, Armstrong, and nothing else.

Free and everything that evolved from it (paradoxically

including many through-composed works) used to strike unreceptive ears as masturbatory noise. The current party line—handed down by the Lincoln Center troika of Wynton Marsalis, Stanley Crouch, and Rob Gibson, and repeated by their mouthpieces in the *Times*—is that jazz that doesn't swing in a prescribed manner is "European" and therefore not jazz.* Years ago, jazz fans used to insist that their music belonged in the university curriculum, and that the works of its greatest composers should be performed by institutionally housed and/or municipally funded orchestras, just like those of Beethoven and Mozart. Both of these desires have been fulfilled, but their fulfillment has proved to be a mixed blessing insofar as jazz pedagogy and the most solvent of our repertory orchestras (including the one directed by Marsalis at Lincoln Center) have combined to provide artistic narrow-mindedness with a quasi-intellectual rationale. Jazz repertory ought to encourage reassessment and periodically trigger revelation. In addition to slavish homage to already venerated composers and bandleaders, it ought to be forcing us to change our minds about supposedly minor or peripheral figures, as the New York Philharmonic did about Mahler and Charles Ives in its glory years under Leonard Bernstein. Loren Schoenberg's band occasionally does this in its modest way, and under the direction of John Lewis and Gary Giddins, the more ambitious (and now defunct) American Jazz Orchestra gave it a noble try. But reassessment apparently isn't defined by Marsalis, Crouch, and Gibson as part of the Lincoln Center Jazz Orchestra's mission.

Meanwhile, it says all you need to know about the tenuous place of jazz in academia (it entered through the back door, as part of Black Studies) that jazz instructors including myself are

---

* (It's distressing to see Marsalis and Crouch, both of whom have argued eloquently against narrow interpretations of black life, play such a discredited race card.)

busily formulating a canon at a moment when the validity of canons is being questioned elsewhere on campus. From one point of view, the mere introduction of jazz or any other form of black music into academic life rights a long-standing wrong. But isn't it late in the game for us to go on defining jazz in opposition to European classical music? At this point, "inclusion" should mean acknowledging the contributions of white musicians, including actual Europeans.

"Tradition" has been a buzzword in jazz since at least the late 1970s, when it briefly became the rallying cry of a handful of historically conscious avant-gardists who saw their music and Jelly Roll Morton's as part of the same continuum. The word amounted to a way of pinpointing excellence beyond superficial concerns of era and style. It meant improvising on *jazz itself*, using acknowledged masterpieces and near-misses as raw material for new works, in much the same way that earlier generations of musicians had utilized pop standards. As used today, however, "tradition" has become a rationale for conformity: outside the chord changes means outside the tradition, and let's hear nothing more about it. I doubt that I'm the only one who's beginning to wonder if this isn't yet another sign of how out of touch jazz is with serious contemporary discouse. Used to signify what it's now used to signify, "tradition" is an elitist, patriarchal concept. ("Custom" is another story, of course, and I would argue that the reason we don't hear many women babbling about "passing it on" is that they've "traditionally" been the ones faced with the task of doing just that. They're also the ones who literally "pass it on," by virtue of giving birth, and the gender with less vested interest in preserving the status quo.) And doesn't the premium placed on the most mechanical aspects of musicianship by Marsalis and younger players groomed in his image seem shortsighted in the wake of funding cuts that have all but eliminated musical instruction in urban public schools? Young jazz players will continue to emerge in the future, just as they always have, *Time* articles to herald their arrival or no. But black or white, they're soon going to be almost exclusively children of the middle class, just like their classical-music brethren. I'm not being completely ironic when I say that we're fast approaching a day when, despite the liberal piety that continues to surround it, jazz will be regarded as politically incorrect. But will it deliver the wallop we've come to expect of art and entertainment decried as such? I fear not.

At one extreme we have the museumlike approach of Jazz at Lincoln Center, at the other the bohemian posturings of something called "acid" jazz, in which both sampled and live snatches of bop are parts of an imagined jazzclub ambience, together with cigarette smoke, fingersnaps, and stylish duds. Acid jazz isn't much of an alternative, because as Theodor W. Adorno observed in his essay on museums, "When discontent with museums is strong enough to provoke the attempt to exhibit paintings in their original surroundings or in ones similar . . . the result is even more distressing than when the works are wrenched from their original surroundings . . . ."

> With music the situation is analogous. The programmes of large concert societies, generally retrospective in orientation, have continually more in common with museums, while Mozart performed by candlelight is degraded to a costume piece.

So acid jazz isn't the answer, and neither is "smooth" jazz, jazz plus hip-hop, or any other commercially motivated gambit that reduces jazz to mood-altering environment or vintage geezer cool. It's reached the point where a young writer calling himself Touré can go unchallenged on saying in an article in the *New York Times* that jazz is about mastery and hip-hop about innovation. Wasn't jazz once about both?

Jazz is simultaneously more popular than it's been in decades and in a state of crisis if it increasingly fails to engage a long-time advocate such as me. Yet I haven't given up on jazz—far from it, as the sheer volume of what I've written on the subject over the last five years should attest (a state of crisis might be an ideal climate for a critic). The musicians I gravitate to tend to be those on the well-populated fringes, not all of them left of the Lincoln Centerists. It isn't only experimentalists who have been marginalized by the new status quo. As a swing-based songplayer, Ruby Braff would probably be appalled by the music of a free player like Charles Gayle, and Gayle's cult following probably considers players like Braff to be hopelessly old hat. What I admire about each of them amounts to the same thing: audible individuality, the conviction of each that his way is the only way *for him*. The same goes for practically all of the musicians whose work I discuss in these pages—including Wynton Marsalis, who's hardly to blame that only one jazz musician at a time is allowed to be famous (and, therefore, to be synonymous with jazz in the public mind). To paraphrase Sartre, I guess that my philosophy as a jazz listener has become that any position is valid as long as it's extreme enough. It's worth considering that (unlike today's young traditionalists) the veteran musicians discussed here as mainstreamers didn't necessarily start off that way—they struck out in new directions, and the mainstream eventually absorbed them.

The clarinetist Don Byron once told me that what first appealed to him about Mickey Katz's brand of klezmer was its sense of "mischief." I guess I respond to the same quality in Byron's music, and mourn its lack in so much of the music sent to me for review. The third section here is titled "Mischief," and it weighs in on the side of fun—with more than a bit of mischief in the writing, too.

I realize that I might be the only one who enjoys the work of all of the jazz musicians included in the pages. All I ask of you as a reader is that you hear me out. This also applies to the pieces in "Words and Music," on pop and Broadway (the piece on Jack Kerouac mostly concerns itself with the music of his recorded voice). As a listener, I retain a craving for song that jazz doesn't always satisfy. Especially in the last few years, I've written more about pop than you might guess from what's collected here. In the interest of thematic unity, I've included only those pieces on pop that in some way reflect my primary calling as a jazz critic. The pieces about Broadway and singers of vintage pop are here for an obvious reason; this is where jazz used to draw much of its repertoire. The piece on rap might be harder to justify, and so might the piece on Prince and Michael Jackson. I sometimes tell people that I started writing about pop at the urging of Bill Whitworth, my editor at *The Atlantic Monthly*, who has long encouraged me to widen my horizons. Or I say, paraphrasing a critic in an old sitcom, "Just because I specialize in jazz doesn't mean I can't find fault with everything."

These are futile attempts at a simple answer. The complicated truth is as bebop becomes more entrenched and jazz as a whole consequently becomes more predictable, many longtime jazz listeners not content to limit themselves to their old Albert Ayler records for the rest of their lives are finding qualities to admire in pop or world music or experimental forms so new they don't have names yet. I grew up listening to pop, and it continued to fascinate me even during those years when I had little to say on it in print. At this point in my life, I don't exactly keep up with pop, and on some level, the very notion of "keeping up" with it strikes me as absurd—kind of like "keeping up" with sex. The great thing about pop music (and about popular culture in general) is that it's there for the taking, should you choose. I hear what I hear and I like what I like, though I suppose that my piece on rap demonstrates that the second half of this equation isn't always so clear-cut. What most interests me about pop at this point is that it's again becoming a generational battlefield, as it was in the 1950s, in the early years of rock and roll. With the arrival into middle age of the generation that three decades ago rewired popular culture into youth culture through the sheer force of its numbers (and forever politicized youth in the bargain), the nineties are going to be about age in the same way that the sixties were about race, the seventies were about gender, and the eighties were about money (this might be the one area in which jazz remains in touch with the times).

The pieces within each section are arranged by mood, seldom by musicians' birth dates or the order in which the pieces were originally published. Some of them are profiles and some are critical essays, but most of them are hybrids that afforded me the luxury of briefly becoming obsessed with people and issues that have preoccupied me for most of my adult life. I try to crowd even those pieces that begin as record reviews with what Dwight Macdonald, in his essay on Hemingway, described as "the subject matter of the novel: character, social setting, politics, money matters, human relations, all the prose of life" (you'll detect the influence of hard-boiled fiction, in particular).

Though I often joke that writers are gang-edited at *The Atlantic*, I try to make it clear that my pieces are improved by the process. The second voice you might sense in some of these pieces is that of Bill Whitworth, whose questions and comments inevitably lead me in directions I might have otherwise never explored. At *The Atlantic* I also benefit from working closely with Corby Kummer, who always seems to know what I'm trying to say even when I don't. Barbara Walraff and Martha Spaulding represent the last word on grammar and usage, and the magazine's fact checkers have spared me from embarrassment on more than one occasion. Thanks also to Avril Cornell, Bill's right hand, whom I frequently have to borrow as mine.

All of these pieces, with the exception of those on Bobby Previte and Loren Schoenberg, were first published in somewhat different form (often in vastly different form) in various newspapers and periodicals. For their careful work on them, I thank Don Shewey of the much-missed *7 Days*; Joe Levy of the *Village Voice*; Linda Hasert, Neil Goldstein, and Avery Rome of the *Philadelphia Inquirer*; Richard Cook and Mark Sinker of *The Wire*; Alex Kaplan and Julie Just of *Wigwag*; Cynthia Grenier of *The World & I*; and Holly Eley of *The Times Literary Supplement*.

A Pew Fellowship in the Arts, in the category of literary nonfiction, fattened both my savings account and my sense of self-worth as I began the task of revising and expanding these pieces. I was also fortunate to receive a Morroe Berger-Benny Carter Fellowship from the Institute for Jazz Studies at Rutgers University, and a very generous fellowship from the John Simon Guggenheim Memorial Foundation. I also owe large debts of gratitude to Mark Kelley for being my agent, Carl Apter for transferring many of my old computer disks, Leslie Saunders for making trips to the library when I was unable to, Dr. John F. Szwed for recommending me to Penn (and Dr. Dan Ben-Amos for overlooking my lack of academic credentials), Anne and Irving Gross for making me feel like one of the family, and Jonathan Wiener for signing me up at Schirmer (and twice extending my deadline). As always, my most sincere note of thanks goes to my mother, Dorothy Davis, and my wife, Terry Gross. I hope they never tire of hearing it.

Mainstreams

Mainstreams

Better with Age

Jazz is enduring a midlife crisis. What else are we to think? As in people, the telltale symptom is a drooling infatuation with youth. It all began with the success of Wynton Marsalis, who was just twenty when he released his first album, in 1982. Overlooking the fact that musicians as talented as Marsalis are rare at any age, the major record labels have since been signing untested young instrumentalists in the hope that lightning will strike twice. Not surprisingly, given the promotional effort of which these labels are capable, these young musicians are virtually the only jazz performers now receiving any notice. The subject of group profiles in magazines as diverse as *Time* and *Elle*, they are being treated as such a novelty that it's becoming difficult to remember that jazz was once assumed to *require* the vigor of youth.

For a reminder of the way things used to be, I recently reread an essay called "Why Do They Age So Badly?" by the French critic and composer André Hodeir. (Written sometime in the 1950s, it was included in Hodeir's 1962 collection *Toward Jazz*, translated by Noel Burch.) Lamenting that what lay ahead after middle age for any jazz musician who had achieved some degree of recognition was "an unremitting decline, an inevitable subsidence into complacency," Hodeir argued that "jazz has one thing in common with sports: it requires its performers . . . to be in first-rate physical condition." But whereas "the aging athlete is *obliged* to retire [Hodeir's italics]," jazz audiences permit older musicians to go on suiting up, as it were, until they drop. Hodeir cited, as an example of fans reluctant to repudiate their traditional idols, a Parisian audience that responded worshipfully to the trumpeter Roy Eldridge in 1950, when he was already "well on the decline."

In 1950, Eldridge was all of thirty-nine, with at least twenty-five more years of crackling solos ahead of him. What's aged badly is Hodeir's argument, although in fairness it needs to be acknowledged that he was one of the first to write about jazz with such candor, and that his essay dates from a period when bebop—then considered the ultimate in modernity—must have made the mature accomplishments of swing-era veterans such as Eldridge seem a little passé. Rereading "Why Do They Age So Badly?" in 1991, I find myself wondering what Hodeir would make of the alto saxophonist Benny Carter, who turned eighty-four last month, but whose powers as an improviser remain miraculously unimpaired.

The perseverance of elderly musicians is an open invitation to sentimentality, and Carter long ago reached the age at which an instrumentalist elicits admiration merely for playing his horn, no matter how shakily. But I really do believe that Carter, who aside from Lionel Hampton is the last surviving major figure of the 1930s, is still making vibrant contributions to jazz six decades later. In so doing, he offers present-day audiences a singular thrill—the chance to look back on history as it continues to unfold.

Carter has been around practically forever. Although the standard discographies show him to have made his recording debut with Charlie Johnson's Paradise Orchestra in 1928, Carter himself remembers participating in a session with the blues singer Clara Smith four years earlier. His first recorded arrangement (of "P.D.Q." Blues, for Fletcher Henderson) was in 1927, the same year he published his first composition ("Nobody Knows," co-written with Fats Waller). After working as a sideman with Henderson and Chick Webb, and serving as music director of McKinney's Cotton Pickers and leader of the Wilburforce Collegians, Carter formed the first of his own big bands in 1932.

These are dates selected almost at random from the detailed chronology included in Morroe Berger, Edward Berger, and

James Patrick's exhaustive two-volume *Benny Carter: A Life in American Music* (Scarecrow Press, 1982). Another piece of information might give a better sense of just how long Carter has been active in music. The album of his that's usually cited as his best is *Further Definitions* (MCA Impulse), from 1961. It reunited him with his fellow saxophonist Coleman Hawkins, whose path had regularly crossed his over the decades, most notably with Henderson in the twenties and on the four titles they recorded together with the guitarist Django Reinhardt in Paris in 1937. Two numbers were reprised from that 1937 session, with Phil Woods and Charlie Rouse taking the places of the French saxophonists André Ekyan and Alex Combelle. For the album Carter, whose trademark as an arranger is his rich saxophone voicings, also orchestrated Hawkins's emblematic 1939 solo on "Body and Soul" for four horns, and paid homage to Duke Ellington and Ben Webster by including the famous sax-section chorus from their 1940 recording of "Cotton Tail." *Further Definitions* was hailed as a latter-day triumph for Carter on its initial release—almost thirty years ago.

Carter has long inspired something approaching awe in his fellow musicians. He surpassed even Johnny Hodges as the primary influence on alto saxophone before the arrival of Charlie Parker in the 1940s. But he also plays credible trumpet (Dizzy Gillespie, who was in his brass section as a young musician, once said of him that "he was always the best trumpet player in his band"), and he might have become one of the greatest of jazz clarinetists had he not abandoned the horn in 1946.

Although one of only a handful of musicians to leave a mark on jazz as both an improviser and an orchestrator (Cab Calloway, Benny Goodman, and Artie Shaw were among the rival bandleaders who played his arrangements in the thirties and forties), Carter never succeeded in keeping an orchestra together for very long, and finally disbanded for good in 1946. What makes this so surprising is that Carter's first band enjoyed the services of Sid Catlett, perhaps the greatest of big-band drummers, and that Gillespie, Teddy Wilson, Chu Berry, Ben Webster, and Miles Davis were Carter bandmembers at one time or another. Carter's failure as a bandleader might explain why he has never achieved the public "name" recognition of a Goodman, Ellington, or Basie, despite the worship of his peers. It probably also hindered Carter that he was in Europe from 1936 to 1938, when America was catching swing fever, and in Hollywood, writing music for movies and TV, for much of three decades, after helping to orchestrate the music for *Stormy Weather* and playing on its soundtrack, in 1943.

Carter's best work for TV was his music for some thirty-five episodes of the crime series *M Squad* in the late 1950s. The four selections from this program included on *All of Me* (RCA Bluebird), a recent reissue, demonstrate Carter's ability to produce idiomatically convincing jazz within the framework of TV-genre conventions. By and large, however, Carter was underutilized and racially typecast in Hollywood: although he worked on over two dozen theatrical films, including *An American in Paris*, *The Sun Also Rises*, *The Guns of Navarone*, and *Red Sky at Morning*, his only complete scores were those for *A Man Called Adam*, a 1966 jazz movie starring Sammy Davis Jr., and *Buck and the Preacher*, a 1972 western with Sidney Poitier and Harry Belafonte.

Carter became a full-time jazz musician again around 1976. His stepped-up pace since then has created the happy illusion that he's playing better than ever, though the truth is simply that we now have more opportunities to hear him. Everyone I know who writes about jazz seems to have his own favorite recorded Carter solo from the last decade. Mine is his virtuoso turn on the standard "Lover Man," from his otherwise uneventful 1985 album *A Gentleman and His Music* (Concord Jazz). In addition to being the recent solo that best demonstrates Carter's undiminished instrumental command, it's also the one that best illustrates his confident embrace of contemporary rhythmic values. Hearing "Lover Man," you know at once that you're listening to Benny Carter, thanks to that enviably urbane intonation of his (which Hodeir, ever the naysayer, once characterized as "epicene"), and to that rococo approach to harmony he once shared with Coleman Hawkins. Still, this isn't a solo that you could imagine Carter playing fifty or even twenty years ago, because his asymmetrical double-time phrasing is so "modern" in conception—it's just short of abstract, despite his fealty to the melody.

Late last summer Carter shared a bill with the vibraphonists Milt Jackson and Bobby Hutcherson at Lincoln Center, just up the block from where the apartment house he lived in as a child once stood; the area was called San Juan Hill in those days, and it was known as a tough neighborhood. Jackson and Hutcherson each played a set accompanied by just a rhythm section; then they joined Carter and a big band for the premiere of a suite called "Good Vibes," which Lincoln Center had commissioned from Carter for this occasion. Although both of the featured soloists interpreted Carter's music with relish, neither had paid him the courtesy of performing even one of his tunes during the first half.

In a way, the evening was typical. The only Carter tune you're likely to hear during a jam session is "When Lights Are Low," which musicians usually know not from Carter's own recordings of it (the first was with the singer Elisabeth Welch in 1936, and the most famous was with Lionel Hampton on vibraphone, three years later), but from the version that Miles Davis recorded in 1953, without Carter's elegant bridge. For that matter, Carter himself is frequently guilty of not featuring enough of his own tunes when he plays nightclubs and festivals.

I asked about this when I spoke with him by telephone in his home in southern California late last year. "That's been because I've always felt that when people come to hear me, they want to hear me play songs with which they're already familiar," he told me in a tone that suggested this policy was the result of practicality, not undue modesty. "But you know, somebody else once asked me the same question, and I told him that I don't play many of my own tunes because the audience wouldn't know them. He pointed out that they never *will* get to know them if I don't play them. It's like the old question of which came first, the chicken or the egg. But I have started traveling with lead sheets of my tunes for the musicians I might play with who don't know them."

The proof of Carter's genius as a composer can be found on *Central City Sketches* (Musicmasters), featuring him with the American Jazz Orchestra, a New York repertory ensemble directed by the pianist John Lewis. This includes flawless performances of Carter compositions ranging in vintage from "Blues in My Heart" (1931), which would have been a perfect vehicle for Jackson at Lincoln Center, to the title suite, which Carter completed just in time for his concert with the AJO at Cooper Union a week or so before the recording session, in 1987. In addition to reviving interest in Carter, this concert, which was talked about for months afterward, supplied a rationale for the emerging jazz-repertory movement: it called attention to the existence of still timely music that wasn't likely to be heard in concert unless someone made a special effort to perform it.

Marian McPartland Plays the Benny Carter Songbook (Concord Jazz), with Carter augmenting the pianist McPartland's trio on six of eleven tracks, nicely compliments *Central City Sketches*, featuring as it does informal interpretations of such outstanding Carter tunes as "When Lights Are Low" (as on the disc with the AJO, the bridge is restored); "Lonely Woman," sung by Peggy Lee in 1947 and not to be confused with pieces of the same name by Ornette Coleman and Horace Silver; "Only Trust Your Heart," (a bossa nova introduced by Stan Getz and Astrud Gilberto in the 1964 TV film *The Hanging Man*); and "Doozy," a sinuous blues that lives up to its name, first recorded on *Further Definitions*, and performed twice on *Central City Sketches*.

Carter now records so frequently that it's become necessary to pick and choose among his albums. *All That Jazz at Princeton* (Musicmasters), his latest, recorded in concert last year at Princeton University, where he occasionally teaches, suffers from a humdrum selection of tunes—nothing new by Carter, who seems unfamiliar with the chord changes to Thelonious Monk's "Hackensack" and Clifford Brown's "Blues Walk"— and strained vocals by Carter, the trumpeter Clark Terry, and a glib singer named Billy Hill (once a member of the pop group the Essex, whose delightful "Easier Said Than Done" reached number one in 1963). Carter is the only reason for hearing *The Return of Mel Powell* (Chiaroscuro), which was recorded aboard the S.S. *Norway* in 1987. Powell, who once played piano in Benny Goodman's big band, and who last year won a Pulitzer for "serious" composition, sounds as though he's slumming here, or as though he thinks it's still 1938. His choppy, foursquare rhythm inhibits Carter, who generally seems more in his element when surrounded with relative modernists than he does in the company of musicians from his own era. (Practically his only shortcoming is as a blues player, and only because his style is so polished: when he growls a note, he tends to sound like a man in tails raising an eyebrow to indicate that he's perturbed.)

Along with *Central City Sketches*, the plums in Carter's recent discography are *My Man Benny—My Man Phil* (Musicmasters), from 1989, on which he piques the alto saxophonist Phil Woods into some beautifully animated playing, and *Over the Rainbow* (Musicmasters), from 1988, which rivals even *Further Definitions* in demonstrating Carter's unparalleled skill in writing for saxophones. The most irresistible of the eight performances on *Over the Rainbow* is of the standard "Out of Nowhere." After individual choruses by Carter and fellow saxophonists Frank Wess, Herb Geller, Jimmy Heath, and Joe Temperley (plus a brief spot by the pianist Richard Wyands), Carter leads the saxophones through a speedy series of harmonic variations so full of swagger that I at first assumed I was hearing an orchestration of the solo Coleman Hawkins played on this tune with Carter and Django Reinhardt in 1937.

Carter recorded for a variety of labels, large and small, in the 1930s, and this might explain why—with the exception of a no-longer-available boxed set in the Time-Life Giants of Jazz series—no comprehensive survey of his early recordings has ever been issued by an American company. But before berating domestic companies for depriving us of seminal Benny Carter in chronological order, it's good to remember that these performances are still protected by copyright in the United States, though they no longer are in Europe. Classics, a French label distributed here by Qualiton Imports, has come to the rescue with five volumes (so far) of *Benny Carter and His Orchestra 1929–1933*.

In addition to all of Carter's big band sides through 1940, these splendidly remastered compact discs include his work with the Chocolate Dandies, a small, studio-only group drawn from the ranks of the Fletcher Henderson Orchestra and other big bands, and the twelve ahead-of-their-time-and-then-some performances recorded in 1933 by the Ellington-smitten Irish composer Spike Hughes and "His Negro Orchestra," which was actually Carter's big band augmented by such star soloists as Coleman Hawkins and Red Allen. Carter isn't extensively featured on the material by Hughes, but his band distinguishes itself in interpreting the latter's ambitious scores, and both "Nocturne" and "Music at Midnight" offer striking examples of Carter's abilities as a clarinetist.

Reissues like these usually put elder musicians in the hopeless position of competing with their past accomplishments. But Carter actually seems to be gaining on himself as the years roll by. In baseball it's possible to chart the progress of a Darryl Strawberry or a Dwight Gooden by measuring his record against that of a Willie Mays or a Sandy Koufax at a similar stage in his career. In jazz, too, we can measure the accomplishments of Wynton Marsalis as he nears thirty by comparing them with the accomplishments of Louis Armstrong, Roy Eldridge, Dizzy Gillespie, or Miles Davis at the same point. We can compare Sonny Rollins at sixty to Coleman Hawkins at that age. But against what other jazz octogenarian can we measure Benny Carter? There's never been anyone else like him.

(SEPTEMBER 1991)

Old Man with a Horn

Though it's a touch grotesque, the artist Mark Diamond's hologram of Dizzy Gillespie is lifelike enough to halt you in your tracks as you hurry past the jazz club called Fat Tuesday's, on Third Avenue between 17th and 18th, in New York. Gillespie—white-haired even to the tuft under his lip and looking close to his present age of seventy-four—smiles and lifts his trumpet to his lips (it's that oddly designed horn of his, with the bell tilted up, away from the tubing and valves). Then he swells his cheeks into enormous pouches and blows, his neck expanding too, before the movements reverse and he smiles again, this time as though acknowledging applause.

Gillespie follows you into Fat Tuesday's, where there's a large poster of him to the far left of the bandstand. And on a wall opposite the bandstand at the Blue Note, a club a few blocks west and several blocks south, where I heard Gillespie perform with his quintet last year, there's a mural showing a much younger Gillespie in action with a handful of bebop's other originators, including Charlie Parker, on a similar bandstand in the 1940s.

At one point last year Gillespie seemed to be everywhere I looked. I saw him on TV with Johnny Carson, Joan Rivers, and Arsenio Hall (unlike most guests on their programs, he wasn't promoting new "product"—he was just being Dizzy Gillespie), and on the promos for *The Soul of American Music*, a black music awards show on which he appeared to be the token jazz musician. He even turned up last year in an issue of *Bon Appetit*, in which it was revealed that he once feasted on crocodile in Zaire and that the only thing he ever cooks at home is a breakfast of salmon and grits. In New York last June, I heard him at three different shows in one week, all presented as part of the JVC Jazz Festival. One of these was a tribute to Doc Cheatham, an indefatigable trumpeter twelve years Gillespie's elder. The others were memorials for Dexter Gordon and Sarah Vaughan, both of whom died in 1990, and both of whom made their first important records with Gillespie in the 1940s.

Gillespie, exercising a monarch's noblesse oblige, also appeared, unbilled, at "Bebop, Forty and Under," a JVC program I missed. The reviews indicated that Gillespie, the oldest man on stage by several decades, had set the pace for the trumpeters Jon Faddis, Roy Hargrove, and Wallace Roney on three numbers that climaxed the show, one of which was his own "A Night in Tunisia" (which he first recorded, under the title "Interlude," with Vaughan, in 1944).

At the three concerts I did see, Gillespie appeared to be struggling with his intonation and reluctant to test his upper register, although he compensated by delivering savory, low-pitched blues licks behind the singers Joe Williams and Billy Eckstine at the tribute to Vaughan. Both this show and the one honoring Gordon were somber affairs, at which the mortality of the senior musicians on stage supplied an unstated theme. In contrast, the evening for Cheatham, though overlong and indifferently paced, teemed with unruly virtuosity—most of it supplied by Faddis and the trumpeters Wynton Marsalis and Ruby Braff.

Even so, whenever Gillespie moseyed onstage, he instantly became the center of attention, and the other musicians seemed to huddle around him, as if awaiting their cues. In the sense that this concert and the others during the week amounted to opportunities to take measure of the small gains won and the enormous losses suffered by jazz in recent years, none of them would have been complete without Gillespie's participation. At this point, he symbolizes jazz to those who play it and those who listen to them.

Gillespie also symbolizes jazz to those outside of the music's circumscribed orbit. His name isn't included among the things that E. D. Hirsch Jr. thinks "literate Americans know," but then again, neither is Marlon Brando's. Lacking a hit record such as "Mack the Knife" or "Hello, Dolly," Gillespie isn't universally recognized and cherished as Louis Armstrong was, and the likelihood is that no jazz instrumentalist ever will be. Still, with the recent death of Miles Davis, Gillespie is probably the only living figure from jazz whose name—reminiscent of a time when both musicians and ball players were called things like "Dizzy," "Duke," and "Pee Wee"—rings a bell for most people. Gillespie is suddenly famous again, just as he was in the late 1940s, when bebop's virtues were being debated in the mainstream press and (as a glance at Richard O. Boyer's delightful 1948 *New Yorker* profile of Gillespie reminds us) the style was identified in the public imagination with such stereotypes as berets, goatees, dark glasses, meerschaum pipes, Islam, and flatted fifths—that day's equivalents of baseball caps turned backwards, "fade" haircuts, sneakers, hood-ornaments worn as medallions, Afrocentrism, and DJ mixes.

Bebop's image has changed over the decades, and so has Gillespie's. In his youth he was regarded first as a rebel without a cause, on account of his antics as a big-band sideman in the late thirties and early forties, and then as a rebel with one, after his musical experiments and those of Parker and a handful of others coalesced into jazz's first avant-garde movement. Today bebop is accepted on faith as classic even by people unsure of whether they've ever actually heard any, and Gillespie is venerated for having been one of its chief oracles, second in importance only to Parker, who died in 1955 and is therefore a phantom to us. Although the number of people able to name even one of Gillespie's tunes might be small, millions of newspaper readers and television viewers know that "bent" horn and those puffed-out cheeks. Wynton Marsalis and he have become this decade's young man with a horn and its old man, respectively.

What's missing from this public image of Gillespie, though, is what's unavoidably missing from that hologram of him in the window of Fat Tuesday's—the crackle of his music. Most accounts of Gillespie's career understandably dwell on his accomplishments in the 1940s, when every note he played was accepted as history in the making. But I happen to think that he reached his zenith in the early 1960s, a period in which he wasn't so much underrated (he's never been underrated) as taken for granted amid the clamor surrounding Ornette Coleman's free jazz, Miles Davis and John Coltrane's modes, and Horace Silver and Art Blakey's funk. This opinion is based, of necessity, on out-of-print records, such as *Something Old, Something New*, which featured what was arguably Gillespie's finest small band, with the then very young pianist Kenny Barron and the saxophonist and flutist James Moody, and *Gillespiana*, an album-length suite written by the pianist Lalo Schifrin, Barron's predecessor in Gillespie's group. (One of several orchestral works commissioned by Gillespie around that time, in a futile attempt to beat Miles Davis and Gil Evans at their own game, *Gillespiana* has aged surprisingly well, and Gillespie still frequently plays its "Blues" section with his quintet.) Records, of course, can be misleading. But a friend of mine, who heard Gillespie in nightclubs on numerous occasions during this period, confirms my impression that Gillespie was then topping himself nightly.

Gillespie was so much the compleat trumpeter that it was

difficult to say which was more impressive—his ease in unfurl-
ing lengthy and rhythmically compounded phrases or the
inflections he could squeeze out of one note. His high notes
whistled, and he tossed off entire choruses above the staff. His
low notes, when he held them, frequently sounded the way he
does when pronouncing the name of his birthplace: "Chee-*roh*,
South Carolina," spelled "Cheraw." (Though bebop was an
urban phenomenon, it's worth considering that Gillespie and
Parker, its pacemakers, grew up on or near farmland.) Filled
with passing chords and other harmonic brainteasers, Gillespie's
solos nonetheless had a rich sarcasm about them that immu-
nized them from excess abstraction.

In jazz as in classical music, there are two types of virtuosity: the utilitarian and the utopian. The utilitarian—that of an
Oscar Peterson or a Freddie Hubbard—leaves you feeling that
you've just heard a musician unsurpassed at what he does. The
utopian—that of Gillespie, Parker, Armstrong, Cecil Taylor,
Sonny Rollins, and Art Tatum—momentarily persuades you
that human knowledge has evolved to such an extent that
nothing is impossible. There was nothing that could be done
on a trumpet that Gillespie could not do, and nothing imaginable either rhythmically or harmonically that he hadn't seemingly already thought of.

Reviewers used to scold Gillespie for wasting so much of
his time onstage joking around or playing Latin percussion, in
an apparent effort to save his lip. "I went for Gillespie, but got
Dizzy," a disgruntled fan once put it, in a letter to a British jazz
magazine. But even though less effort is now expected of Gillespie (he is in his eighth decade, after all), he continues to circle
the globe as though campaigning for James Brown's title as
"The Hardest-Working Man in Show Business." Following
JVC, for example, he spent all but a few days of July playing
concerts and festivals in Europe, Asia, and the Middle East. He
practically lived on the road the rest of the year, appearing in
both Brazil and California in a single week in September, and

spending just a few days at home with his wife, Lorraine, in New Jersey during the Christmas holidays, between engagements in Tokyo and San Juan.

Gillespie spoke with me from a Monterey, California, hotel room in October. I asked him if he could envision a day in the near future when he would begin to take life easier. "You can't take it easy on trumpet," he replied. "You have to keep at it all the time." He told me that he thought his sound was now "brighter" and "better" than ever before, as a result of a new mouthpiece that he acquired early last year.

But the melancholy fact is that Gillespie's prowess has diminished to the point where hearing him attempt to swap high notes with his protégé, Jon Faddis, at the Doc Cheatham tribute was like seeing the picture of Dorian Gray in the same room with the still-unblemished Dorian. Virtuosity is as much mechanical as intellectual, and age delights in robbing virtuosos of the edge they once took for granted. Doc Cheatham remains a marvel at the age of eighty-six, but his style never depended on fireworks displays, even when he was younger. Gillespie's did, and he's no longer able to light up the skies with any regularity.

Gillespie still surrounds himself with excellent musicians, however, and he still has his moments. At the Blue Note, where his group included Ron Holloway, an unheralded tenor saxophonist from Baltimore whose solos achieved that remarkable combination of angularity and heft long associated with Sonny Rollins, I heard Gillespie play a blues full of wry shadings and comically deployed silences. It might have been lacking in the bravura that one used to expect from him, but it was a fine solo by any other conceivable measure.

Gillespie remains a prolific recording artist, and each of the three albums released by him last year has something to recommend it. On *Bebop and Beyond Plays Dizzy Gillespie* (Blue Moon), he joins a Bay Area group led by the saxophonist and flutist Mel Martin for a batch of tunes either written by or associated with him. He even sings a ballad: Gil Fuller's beautiful "I Waited for You," written for and recorded by Gillespie's big band in 1946. Although the trumpet solos that catch the ear with their imagination and clean execution tend to be those of Bebop and Beyond's Warren Gale, Gillespie is clearly the catalyst. The two tracks he sits out are run-of-the-mill, latter-day West Coast bebop.

In 1990 Gillespie starred in and wrote the music for Jose A. Zorilla's *The Winter in Lisbon*, a European-made film that only recently found an American distributor (which promptly shelved it). To judge from the synopsis that Gillespie gave me during our telephone conversation, Zorilla's movie reworks the same ground that Bertrand Tavernier's *'Round Midnight* did. Gillespie plays a black expatriate musician who forms a bond with a young white pianist who worships him. Apparently there's also a subplot involving the pianist's girlfriend, a gangster whose mistress she used to be, and a stolen painting.

The soundtrack was finally released last summer (Milan), and the problem with it is the problem with most soundtracks: motifs reworked ad infinitum in the interest of dramatic continuity just sound repetitive when extracted from their mise-en-scène. But this soundtrack is well worth hearing for the selections featuring Gillespie with the pianist Danilo Perez, the bassist George Mraz, and the drummer Grady Tate, who prod triumphant salvos from him on "San Sebastian," and elsewhere encourage from him an uncharacteristic lyricism so intimate in scale that even the notes he flubs seem fraught with meaning.

Perez, whose spacious chordal approach recalls that of the late Bill Evans, although his touch is more percussive, is also the pianist on *Live at the Royal Festival Hall* (Enja), a London concert recording demonstrating the many virtues of Gillespie's United Nation Orchestra, the fifteen-member ensemble he has led part-time since 1988. The United Nation Orchestra— so named because it includes musicians from Cuba, Brazil,

Panama, Puerto Rico, and the Dominican Republic—draws heavily on the classic tunes written (or co-written) by Gillespie employing South American or Caribbean rhythms (his and Frank Paparelli's "A Night in Tunisia," obviously, but also such durable items as his calypso "And Then She Stopped" and his and Chano Pozo's modified rhumba "Tin Tin Deo"). By so doing, this new orchestra begs comparison to the most fabled of Gillespie's big bands, the rough-and-ready outfit from the late 1940s that briefly included Pozo on congas and blended bebop with mambo and elements of Afro-Cuban ritualistic music. Although hardly as innovative as that band—or as talent-laden as the one that Gillespie assembled for a 1956 State Department tour and managed to keep afloat for a year or so afterward (Lee Morgan, Phil Woods, and Benny Golson all did stints in it)—this new outfit is likably volatile, thanks in large part to the gutsy arrangements by Slide Hampton, Bill Kirchner, and others.

Best of all, because the band is well stocked in animated soloists such as the trumpeters Claudio Roditi and Arturo Sandoval, the saxophonists James Moody, Mario Rivera, and Paquito D'Rivera, and the trombonist Steve Turre (who also plays conch shells), Gillespie doesn't have to carry the whole show by himself, as he sometimes does with his small band, if only to leave his audiences feeling that they've got their money's worth. What with showcases for Turre and D'Rivera, plus one shared by the singer Flora Purim and the percussionist Airto Moreira, Gillespie doesn't even solo on every number. Sandoval, the band's high-note specialist, does what amounts to Gillespie's stunt work, and Moody—whose association with Gillespie dates back to the 1940s—subs for Gillespie in speeding through the celebrated break in "A Night in Tunisia."

Sandoval, D'Rivera, and Moreira are one-trick ponies whose lack of subtlety works against them as leaders of their own small groups. But they sound terrific as featured attractions in Gillespie's genial musical variety show. It's a pity that economics prevent Gillespie from touring fulltime with the United Nation Orchestra. He's long displayed all of the attributes associated with successful big-band leaders, including the often-ignored one of showmanship. At several points in his career a big band seemed like the only format grand enough for him. At this point a big band serves the purpose of allowing him to take a well-deserved breather now and then.

(MARCH 1992)

Dizzy Gillespie died in 1993, at the age of seventy-five.

Pres and His Discontents

There are men who stir the imagination deeply and uncomfortably, around whom swirl unplaceable discontents, men self-damned to difference, and Edgar Pool was one of these," wrote John Clellon Holmes, the most conventionally "literary" of the postwar American beats, in *The Horn*, his jazz roman à clef:

> Once an obscure tenor in a brace of road bands, now only memories to those who had heard their crude, uptempo riffs . . . Edgar Pool had emerged from an undistinguished and uncertain musical background by word of mouth. He went his own way, and from the beginning (whenever it had been, and something in his face belied the murky facts) he was unaccountable.

Middling tall, sometimes even lanky then, the thin mustache of the city Negro accenting the droop of a mouth at once determined and mournful, he managed to cut an insolently jaunty figure, leaning toward prominent stripes, knit ties, soft shirts, and suede shoes . . . Edgar had been as stubbornly out of place [in the swing era], when everyone tried to ride the drums instead of elude them, as he was stubbornly unchanged when bop became an architecture on the foundation he had laid.

Pool holds his saxophone "almost horizontally extended from his mouth," with his head at a "childishly fey" angle. He addresses everyone, male as well as female, as "Lady," and has had an ambiguous relationship with a singer resembling Billie Holiday. Having already achieved immortality, he drifts through his days and nights in an alcoholic haze, as though the only thing left for him to do is to die. Though named for Edgar Allen Poe, a morbid ideal for all American artists driven to madness, Pool is a fictional double for Lester Young, the tenor saxophonist who died five months short of his fiftieth birthday in 1959, the same year that *The Horn* was published.

Young, the key figure in jazz evolution between Louis Armstrong and Charlie Parker, first appeared on the scene in the late 1930s as the most compelling soloist in the big band that Count Basie brought east from Kansas City—hardly "an undistinguished and uncertain musical environment," although Young's comings and goings to that point must have indeed seemed "murky" to jazz listeners of Holmes's generation. Born in Woodville, Mississippi, and on the road with his father and two younger siblings in their family vaudeville band for much of his childhood and adolescence, Young was twenty-seven and already in possession of his mature style when he made his first recordings with Basie, in 1936.

Jazz lore maintains that each of the leading soloists of the twenties and thirties gained an edge over his competition by developing an unmistakable "sound"—a tone that amounted to a personal signature it was impossible to forge. Black musicians may have felt especially challenged to do so. "Everybody knows that the ofay's playing is clean," the late trombonist Dicky Wells, a bandmate of Young's with Basie and a trailblazing soloist in his own right, observed in *The Night People*, his 1971 memoir, which has just been republished by the Smithsonian Institution Press. (It's an "as told to" book, to which Wells's collaborator, the critic Stanley Dance, selflessly refrained from adding "writerly" touches.) "No other way he knew. And deep down in, he's the master when it comes to cutting something, when you put the music up there. The Oxford Gray [a term for a black musician, coined by Young] was noted for his fuzz and just swinging."

Fuzz or no fuzz, by the time that Young arrived in New York from out of the blue—at what was then considered to be a ripe old age for a jazzman, with an almost imperceptible vibrato and an airy sonority influenced to some extent by Frankie Trumbauer's on C-melody saxophone—Coleman Hawkins's big, robust tone had been codified as a just and proper voice for the tenor saxophone. The story goes that in 1934, when Young briefly replaced Hawkins in Fletcher Henderson's orchestra, his arrival resulted in so much dissension that Mrs. Henderson sat him down at a record player for a crash course in Hawkins—luckily, to no avail.

What soon became clear was that in Young's case, no less than in Hawkins's, sound was determined by conception. Hawkins needed an ample, vigorous tone in order to accent two beats in each measure and meet each upcoming chord change head on (as did Herschel Evans, Young's opposite number in the Basie saxophone section). Young, whose approach was more elliptical, did not. The consternation over his light timbre initially deflected attention from the most innovative aspect of his style, gracefully described by Whitney Balliett as "Young's absolute mastery of broken-field rhythm and phrasing—the ability to emphasize the beat simply by eluding it." Balliett's comment occurs in one of the most perceptive of the thirty-seven pieces collected in *A Lester Young Reader*, the first in the Smithsonian Institution Press's planned series of anthologies devoted to major jazz musicians.

A case could be made for Young, who was nicknamed "Pres" (short for "The President"), as the first jazz modernist, based solely on his refusal to let bar lines dictate the length or destination of his phrases. If only in terms of their rhythmic flexibility, his earliest recorded solos with Basie anticipated bebop by a good ten years. And though he was essentially a "linear" (or melodic) improviser, his sophistication in implying, rather than spelling out, most of the notes in a chord (rhythm wasn't the only area in which he practiced sleight of hand) provided a model for developments after bop, including "cool" jazz, Lennie Tristano's harmonic extrapolations of popular standards, and Miles Davis's investigation of modes and scales.

Young set the stage for Charlie Parker in yet another way. He was probably the first black instrumentalist to be publicly recognized not as a happy-go-lucky entertainer, à la Armstrong, but as an artist of the *demimonde* whose discontents magnified those felt by his race in general.

Here's Holmes's Edgar Pool on the bandstand, alienated from his workplace in the manner of most laborers, but overcome by a disgust presumably unique to black performers resentful of their status as nightclub entertainers rather than concert artists:

> Almost gagging, he hated everything there—the smell
> of bad breath and dried saliva that filled his nose from
> the microphone, and the smell of melted Italian cheese
> and dishwater that came out of the kitchen each time
> the door swung, and the smell of his own liquored
> sweat and damp clothes, and most of all the *feel* of the
> impatient crowd out there who could see every stain
> down his tie, and every sleepless hour on his face, but

whom he could not see. He had never cared before that
a jazz musician was condemned to utter his truth in the
half-dark of dangerous, thronged rooms where everyone's breath tasted of alcohol and cigarettes, and everyone left something of the day behind him at the door.
But suddenly he saw that he had spent his life a moody
fugitive among sensation hunters, enunciating what
seemed to him just then . . . a rare and holy truth in the
pits of hell.

Race undoubtedly contributed to Young's alienation, as it
did, in a quite different way, to that of the very earliest white jazz
musicians, who had to be estranged from white bourgeois values even to *know* about jazz. (A number of them adopted what
they imagined to be Negro modes of behavior, Mezz Mezzrow
being the extreme example.) But the potential for alienation
can be found in the lives of most black musicians of Young's
era—certainly in the life of Dicky Wells, who was forced to go
to work as a Wall Street messenger (his first day job) at the age of
sixty, and whose memoir (among the most intimate and unselfconsciously lyrical reports we have of life on the road as a big-
band sideman in the 1930s) ends with an account of three mug-
gings at the hands of "soul brothers in action—no grays [slang
for white people], so I am still for the cat who treats me as I treat
him—black, green, white, or blue." Aside from complaints about
jazz having evolved into a different sort of music than what he
played in his youth ("It's a kind of imaginary thing when there
are no people dancing," he notes wistfully, at one point), Wells's
narrative is loquacious and engagingly lighthearted from start to
finish, like his best recorded solos.

The only possible criticism of *The Night People* in the present context is that it tells us little we don't already know about
Lester Young, who must have struck even fellow musicians as
strange. Young wasn't "part of the family, if that's what it was,"
writes the late Bobby Scott, in one of the remembrances

included in *A Lester Young Reader.* A pianist and singer who first hooked up with Young on a 1955 tour of Norman Granz's Jazz at the Philharmonic, Scott manages to draw a lifelike portrait of Young despite two dozen or so superfluous references to Nietzsche, Saint Augustine, and Padraic Pearse, among others. A friend of mine who attended many JATP concerts recalls Young standing aloof from the other horns and not playing exaggeratedly "hot," as they did, in an attempt to win the crowd. On tour with JATP, Young usually booked a room in a black hotel, rather than stay in integrated lodgings with the rest of Granz's troupe. Was he keeping his distance from whites, or just keeping his distance?

Although heterosexual, Young affected effeminate mannerisms, including what a "psychosomaticist" quoted in a 1959 *Down Beat* essay republished here describes as a "mincing" walk. (Others say he "sidled"—perhaps as a result of a degenerative case of syphilis diagnosed on his induction into the U.S. Army in 1943, suggests Frank Buchmann-Moller, in an addendum of sorts to *You Just Fight for Your Life,* his meticulous 1990 Young biography.) Young wore his hair unconventionally long in back and (we learn from Nat Hentoff) planned at one point to put ribbons in it. (He tells the aforementioned physician that photographs of Victorian-era women in their ribboned skimmers gave him the idea for his trademark wide-brimmed porkpie hat.) He imagined that people were looking at him in restaurants (they probably were) and, toward the end of his life, could only sleep with the lights on and the radio at full blast.

Despite his dissolute way of life (gin and marijuana, but nothing harder, perhaps due to his terror of needles), Young prided himself on always being on time for his engagements, often going to absurd lengths to avoid lateness. And as if to compound the enigma, many of the musicians quoted in the *Reader* insist that he was religious—or, as Scott puts it, that he at least believed that the existence of a Deity "was to be taken for granted." Calling on him in a New York residence hotel for a *Melody Maker* interview in 1950, Leonard Feather notices "soiled plates" and bottles of gin and sherry on a night table, and "innumerable figurines, many of them religious" on the mantelpiece.

Just as Young was measured against Coleman Hawkins and found wanting by some in the late 1930s, his unyielding rival after World War II was the memory of his former self. Critics usually trace his artistic decline to the ten months he spent in a Georgia detention compound following his 1945 court-martial for possession of marijuana and barbiturates. The problem with this "broken man" theory is that it makes no allowance for his innumerable total recoveries of form. Young's vibrato grew sluggish and his tone steadily darkened in the last fourteen years of his life, and, especially toward the end, some of his recorded solos were so wobbly that you can practically smell the whiskey on his breath. But sprinkled among his postwar discography are performances so graceful in execution and so powerful in their emotional range (his 1956 *Jazz Giants* session with Roy Eldridge and Teddy Wilson, for example) that they alone would guarantee him a ranking as one of the greatest of all jazz improvisers; they are at least as memorable as his early records with Basie and Billie Holiday.

Lewis Porter, the editor of *A Lester Young Reader* and the author of a previous book on Young that (for the most part) confined itself to musicology, has established himself as the leading defender of "late" Lester Young among American jazz academics. Given this advocacy, it's not surprising that many of the essays included in the *Reader's* third and final section (devoted to musical analysis) support his position. Graham Columbe is persuasive in extolling "the mature tragic awareness" of Young's 1950s recordings, and there are lucid points made along the same lines by Erik Wiedeman and Henry Woodfin, though (disappointingly) nothing from the editor himself.

Porter demonstrates evenhandedness by including both a 1953 *Melody Maker* review dismissive of Young at that point, as well as several appreciations of thirties Pres that adhere to conventional wisdom in assuming that postwar Pres is hardly worth mentioning. But in giving this cross-section of musings on Young something resembling a point of view, Porter's revisionist zeal also gives it value beyond its obvious handiness as a library time-saver. It's readable straight through, in a way that anthologies primarily intended for reference use seldom are. Combining old magazine clippings and previously unpublished oral history, Phil Schaap's opening essay traces Young's life more or less chronologically, the representation of so many different and often contradictory voices achieving a complexity in keeping with the book's enigmatic subject. The middle section is subtitled "Young in His Own Words," which is something of a misnomer in that it mostly consists of brief profiles whose authors bowed to 1950s jazz-magazine conventions in putting a happy spin on Young's malaise. But this section also includes the first complete transcription in English of the much-excerpted interview that François Postif conducted with Young in a Paris hotel room a month before Young's death—testimony so haunting that one American saxophonist is said to have obtained a dub of the original tape and to have memorized every word of it, as musicians have traditionally memorized recorded solos.

With so much of interest included, to chide Porter for what's missing smacks of ingratitude. Nevertheless, the lengthy passages quoted by Hentoff from Ross Russell's incisive 1949 *Record Changer* study of Young's work do raise the question of why Russell's essay isn't here in its entirety. I wish that Porter had included John McDonough's 1981 *Down Beat* article on Young's court-martial, or better still, Buchmann-Moller's chapter on it, which includes three full pages of Young under cross-examination. And at risk of seeming not to appreciate Porter's exemplary dedication in separating fact from fiction regarding his subject, I wish he had seen fit to include a chapter, or at least a few paragraphs, of Holmes's overwritten and factually suspect novel, which I think belongs here for the same reason that excerpts from Dorothy Baker's *Young Man with a Horn* would belong in a Bix Beiderbecke reader and posthumous supermarket sightings of Elvis Presley would belong in a biography of Presley. The ability to stir the imagination "deeply and uncomfortably" is, after all, a large part of what makes a major artist major.

(JUNE 1992)

Bebop and Nothingness

Charlie Parker looked like Buddha," Jack Kerouac declared in a poem about the alto saxophonist who was the single most important figure in the gestation of modern jazz. Kerouac wasn't indulging in fancy: some photos of Parker, showing him with a pot belly, round face, and eyes that Kerouac described (in *The Subterraneans*) as "separate and interested and humane," do suggest a likeness to one popular image of Buddha. But Kerouac's analogy depended less on Parker's physical appearance than on his vibe—on an awed perception of his music as god-like in its complexity.

Kerouac wasn't alone in ascribing divinity to Parker. There were hipsters in California who swore that Parker once walked on water. Soon after his death in 1955, at the age of thirty-four (from the cumulative effects of heroin and hard liquor, although lobar pneumonia was the official cause), the graffito "BIRD LIVES" began to appear on New York subway walls. If

27
■

interpreted to mean only that Parker's music was immortal, the message was indisputable. But who knows what else some of his more frenzied apostles had in mind?

Among fellow musicians, Parker was in the eye of the beholder: what he was like as a person depends on whom you ask. In the recently published *Miles: The Autobiography*, Miles Davis, who played with Parker as a neophyte trumpeter in the 1940s, portrays him as an id-driven monster willing to pawn a borrowed horn or pocket his sidemen's wages if that was what it took to stay high. According to Davis and others who knew him, Parker was a man of insatiable appetites and few inhibitions. In Davis's book, there's an amusing anecdote not meant to be amusing, about Parker in the back seat of a taxi, "smacking his lips all over [a piece of] fried chicken," while a white woman on bended knees on the floor of the car smacks her lips all over him (much to the embarrassment of an uncharacteristically prim Miles).

Yet what sticks in most musicians' minds about Parker was his erudition, not his self-indulgence. Even Davis marveled at him as "an intellectual [who] read novels, poetry, history, stuff like that." The alto saxophonist Frank Morgan, who was still in his teens when he chose Parker as a role model, remembers being as much impressed by Parker's elocution and vocabulary as by his mastery of his horn. John Lewis, a pianist sometimes accused of overrefinement in his role as music director for the Modern Jazz Quartet, defends himself by observing that he often used to run into Parker at classical concerts—the point being that no one would accuse Parker's jazz of being too refined. And Sheila Jordan, a talented singer who says she was "chasin' the Bird, just like everybody else," when she moved from Detroit to New York as a young woman in the 1950s, describes Parker as "a gentleman" who took her out for drinks and passed along musical knowledge but never exploited her worship of him to get her into bed.

On the subject of Parker and drugs, the only certainty is

that he used them flagrantly and in prodigious amounts. Everything else is open to conjecture. In jazz, no less than in the world of arts and letters, the early 1950s were a Scoundrel Time, but for a different reason. Heroin addiction was rampant, and you still hear rumors of how this or that well-known junkie kept his own butt out of jail by agreeing to name names. Some of Parker's contemporaries continue to wonder how he avoided arrest despite public knowledge of his habit.

What of Parker's role in turning others on? For many younger musicians, he was a walking advertisement for heroin; despite lectures from him to the contrary, they decided that the junk he was shooting into his veins must be the most vital of his creative juices. "You have to realize that [he] wasn't only a great musician," says the tenor saxophonist Sonny Rollins, one of several acolytes whom Parker tried in vain to discourage from following his path. "He was also a very sick man who was dying from self-abuse and felt guilty about the example he had set for others." But as the trumpeter (and nonuser) Art Farmer remarks, "Telling people to do as I say, not as I do, is never very effective advice."

Parker, who was born and started his career in Kansas City when it was a wide-open Nighttown, is such a creature of myth and supposition that it might be difficult for us to imagine that he ever really existed if not for the hard evidence of his recordings—and even these leave gaps. Parker, Dizzy Gillespie, and a handful of others planted the seeds of bebop (the name given their music, in onomatopoetic imitation of its quick, evenly accented quarter notes) in big bands during the waning days of the swing era. But due to a two-year musicians' union ban on studio recordings beginning in 1942, our knowledge of bebop's beginnings is largely based on hearsay. And most of the concert albums you'll find in front of Parker's name card in record stores give a misleading impression of what he must have sounded like in the flesh. The majority of these are from poorly recorded tapes made on the sly by Birdlorists who followed Parker from coast to coast, inadvertently removing him from his creative context by preserving only his solos, not those of his sidemen. Parker did the bulk of his official recording for three companies: Dial, Savoy, and what became Verve. His complete Savoys and Verves have been in general circulation, in one format or another, since his death. Not so the thirty-five numbers that he recorded for Dial beginning in February 1946, when Ross Russell, a writer and Hollywood record store owner, founded the label to take advantage of Parker's temporary residence in southern California.

Parker's Dials, including every surviving alternate take, were collected in a six-record series on a British collectors' label in the early '70s, and in a Warner Brothers limited-edition box set later in the decade. But if my experience is typical, most jazz fans now between the ages of thirty-five and fifty first discovered these classic performances in haphazard fashion on fly-by-night budget labels, or on the long-defunct label bearing Parker's name and operated by his legal widow in the early sixties.

The Legendary Dial Masters, Volume One and *Volume Two* (Stash) mark the first coherent reissue of this material on compact disc. All thirty-five "masters" are included, along with nine alternate takes and eight abbreviated performances recorded live at a L.A. jam session that bring the total playing time to just under two and a half hours. This music has never sounded better, thanks to the superb digital remastering. Parker's rhythm sections have been brought into sharper focus, and now you can actually hear—rather than merely sense—the sparks flying in both directions between him and his most tuned-in sidemen (the pianist Dodo Marmorosa and the drummer Max Roach, in particular). And as a thoughtful added touch, of special aid to novice listeners, the CD booklets identify Parker's raw material: his "originals," like those of many bebop musicians of the 1940s, tended to be derived from the twelve-bar blues ("Relaxin' at Camarillo," for example) or on the chord changes of a few familiar standards ("Bird of Paradise" from "All the Things You

Are," "Ornithology" from "How High the Moon," and "Moose the Mooch," from "I Got Rhythm," to cite just three).

Pop songs and the blues have served as launching pads for jazz improvisers almost from the beginning, but Parker and his confederates radicalized the procedure by disguising the material they appropriated almost beyond recognition, in an abstract of sleek harmonic lines and daredevil rhythms that gave the impression of blinding speed even at moderate tempos. Before beginning his affiliation with Dial, Parker had already recorded "Ko Ko," his most dazzling performance in this vein, at his first session as a leader, for Savoy in 1945. But the Dials represented his first sustained exposure on record and introduced (on the sessions recorded in New York in late 1946 and 1947, after Russell followed Parker back east) Parker's first truly compatible working group, with Roach, Miles Davis, the pianist Duke Jordan, the bassist Tommy Potter, and—on the last few titles—the trombonist J. J. Johnson. These were the recordings with which Parker virtually wrote the stylebook of modern jazz, originating phrases that would turn up again and again over the decades in solos by other musicians (for example: the ten-note "o-o-oh-baby, you-make-me-feel-so good" figure that Parker plays during "Moose the Mooch" served as the foundation of James Moody's "Moody's Mood for Love," itself an influential and much admired recording).

Once you hear Parker, he changes the way you hear what came before him and what came after. On "Don't Blame Me," for example (a ballad interpretation as elegant as the more celebrated "Embraceable You," which is also included here), the melodic surge of his uneven-length phrases confirms both his lineage from Lester Young and Young's importance as an oracle of bebop. And Parker's out-of-the-gate-and-running blues chorus in advance of the flatted theme on "The Hymn," though quintessential bebop, could be cited as a prototype of free-form.

In addition to a session on which Parker overcomes Erroll Garner's incongruous piano accompaniment and Earl Coleman's out-of-tune Billy Eckstine imitations, *Volume One* also includes the performance of his most likely to elicit a subjective reaction. Cut off from his drug suppliers due to a police crackdown, he was hours away from complete collapse when he recorded "Lover Man" and three other numbers on July 29, 1946. Yet the bassist and composer Charles Mingus, asked to name his favorite Parker performance, chose this version of "Lover Man," which the trumpeter Howard McGhee (who was on the date, playing over his head, as though in compensation) told the jazz critic Ira Gitler he preferred to a second, more self-assured version that Parker recorded five years later. "He didn't have the strength or the stamina to run through the horn," McGhee told the jazz critic Ira Gitler. "He was just barely getting the sound out, but I thought it was beautiful like a son-of-a-bitch." Heard now, this from-the-abyss solo sounds wild and uncertain. But it rivets you with its pain.

Some twenty years ago, the jazz critic Martin Williams complained that very little in the growing body of literature on Parker focused on his musical accomplishments. This was no longer true by the late 1970s, by when analysis of bebop in general and Parker's contributions to it in particular became the backbone of an emerging jazz pedagogy. But in the aftermath of *Bird*, Clint Eastwood's murky 1988 film biography, discourse has shifted back to Parker's legendary excess.

This extramusical line of inquiry isn't as irrelevant as some would argue, if only because it reminds us that bebop's original cult audience included the real-life models for the nomadic juicers and hopheads who hit the road in Kerouac's *Desolation Angels* and *Dharma Bums* and the blocked existentialists who wander from party to party, halfway between euphoria and despair, in Chandler Brossard's *Who Walk in Darkness* and John Clellon Holmes's *Go!*, post–World War II novels that could be retitled *Bebop and Nothingness*. In a period in which molds were being shattered, the beat poets, Abstract Expressionists, method actors, and scatological comedians who romanticized them-

selves as self-destructive enemies of society recognized a prototype in Parker's sex, drugs, and flatted fifths (jazz would never
again be in such close promixity to the other arts). And for
well-read mystics like Kerouac, Parker's genius was living proof
that excess really was the path to wisdom.

Like Parker, the late Art Pepper was both an alto saxophone
virtuoso and a junkie. Unlike Parker, he resorted to crime to
finance his habit and actually served time, including two
stretches in San Quentin. Pepper told of his exploits, in language as unflinching as that of William Burroughs and as eloquent as that of Jean Genet, in *Straight Life*, his 1979
autobiography (co-written with Laurie Pepper, his third wife,
and now available in a Da Capo paperback edition). Pepper
confessed that he had committed rape—and that he had wanted to commit a murder just to see if he had what it took. Like
Norman Mailer's White Negro or the characters in *Drugstore
Cowboy*, he got as potent a rush from the jobs he pulled to
finance his addiction as he got from shooting up. No jazz musician, including Parker, ever fulfilled the role of artist as outlaw
with such fierce compulsion.

How alienated was Pepper? He says in *Straight Life* that he
embarked on sexual escapades in order to have something to
picture when masturbating. He was a white jazz musician—an
outsider twice over—for whom black approval was crucial but
not always readily forthcoming. Bitter about this (and about
reverse racism in prison, where he watched Black Muslim
inmates chanting and performing calisthenics in the yard, in
preparation for a holy war of retribution), he voiced racial sentiments that many white jazz musicians share but would be reluctant to express for the record. His approach to improvisation
was confrontational, though not in the way of the jam-session
gladiator out to best all competitors. Pepper's "competition"
included anyone he felt had ever wronged him, and musicians
and audiences (present or not) unwilling to concede him a place
among the greats because of his race.

In another sense, of course, the competition was himself: in Don McGlynn's *Art Pepper: Notes from a Jazz Survivor,* a documentary film portrait released in 1982, the year of Pepper's death, Pepper stared into the camera, as though staring inward, and said that he wanted each performance to be the best he'd ever given, because he knew that each might be his last, in view of the physical punishment he'd put his body through. He was only fifty-six, but had already exceeded any reasonable life expectancy for a junkie.

Pepper was prolific. Along with hundreds of appearances as a sideman, he recorded more than three dozen albums under his own name. But this figure is misleading, because most of his output was recorded in two five- or six-year bursts (the rest of the time, he was high, in rehab, or in jail). The first period of intense activity was in the late 1950s, when he built a reputation as the hottest young alto player on the West Coast; the second was in the years just before his death—the period documented on *The Complete Galaxy Recordings* (Galaxy). This box set, which includes sixteen compact discs and roughly eighteen hours of music—about a third of it never before released—features Pepper in a variety of settings: unaccompanied solos, duets with the pianist George Cables, ballads with strings, live concerts, and studio dates with his own quartet or specially assembled rhythm sections.

Unlike Parker's Dial masters, which belong in every jazz library, the Pepper box is a luxury. It lists for $225 and contains a good deal of material already available on individual albums. For the collector, the previously unissued tracks are good to have, but in contrast to Parker's Dials, these sessions are of too recent a vintage for every scrap to seem of historical moment.

Still, there's no arguing with the music itself, which demands reevaluation now that its creator is no longer around to dwarf it with his will to prevail. The earliest tracks are from 1978, the tail end of a period during which Pepper grappled with the influence of John Coltrane. Pepper never imitated

Coltrane's sound, but in worrying his phrases to the point of obsession, as though more than music was at stake, he aimed for a similar emotional pitch. The difference was in the style of accompaniment best suited to each man. Coltrane's most intense solos tended to be shouting matches with the drummer Elvin Jones. Pepper required less aggression from his rhythm sections—something that took him and his sidemen a while to learn. He was most compelling on long, free, darkly lyrical near-blues pieces like his own "Patricia," from 1978, a track on which the pianist Stanley Cowell, the bassist Cecil McBee, and the drummer Roy Haynes all hung back, supplying a steady pulse but otherwise staying out of Pepper's way as he built to a slow boil.

Performances of this kind, although atypical of the earlier ones in the Galaxy box, became almost routine once Pepper formed the group heard on the almost four CDs' worth of material recorded in concert at a Los Angeles nightclub in 1981 with Cables, the bassist David Williams, and the drummer Carl Burnett. Pepper also played clarinet in a shy, pleasant manner reminiscent of Lester Young ("When You're Smiling" is a good example), and many of his alto solos were crisp, buoyant, and almost lighthearted (the three versions of "Straight Life," his signature tune, based on the chord changes of "After You've Gone"). But the tracks that catch his full measure tend to be rhythmically suspended soul-searchers like "Patricia" and the five versions of the rockish "Landscape."

Relaxation is supposed to be the secret of good jazz improvisation, but in these performances Pepper proves that tension can also do the trick. During this period he played as though possessed. He blew himself into his horn and was cleansed.

(APRIL 1990)

Cause of Death: Jazz

In 1967, when he was still a groundbreaking comedian and not yet himself a joke, Dick Gregory made his film debut in Herbert Danska's *Sweet Love, Bitter*, giving a remarkable performance in the role of Richie Stokes, a.k.a. "Eagle," an alto saxophonist and junkie loosely based on Charlie Parker. Also starring Don Murray (Marilyn Monroe's romantic interest in *Bus Stop*), Robert Hooks (Clay in the original production of Amiri Baraka's *Dutchman* and a founder of the Negro Ensemble Company), and Diane Varsi ("the female James Dean," best remembered for her roles in *Peyton Place* and *Wild in the Streets*), *Sweet Love, Bitter* is superior in every way to *Bird*, Clint Eastwood's dark (or maybe just underlit) 1988 Parker biopic. It should have been mentioned in the reviews of *Bird*, but few film critics knew of it. In fact, until *Sweet Love, Bitter*'s resurrection at New York's Film Forum as part of last summer's JVC Jazz Festival, and its release on videocassette earlier this year (Rhapsody Films), only independent film buffs and those vigilant enough to have caught one of its infrequent showings on late-night TV had ever seen it.

Shot mostly in Philadelphia (despite an implied New York setting) on a shoestring budget of $260,000, this black-and-white film is so brutally honest in its depiction of the jazz demimonde of the 1960s that more than one viewing is required to realize that there's very little jazz in it, apart from Mal Waldron's moody small-band score. Only one scene takes place on a bandstand and it's a doozy, dramatically as well as musically. After borrowing a horn and sitting in with a band in a nightclub, Eagle rudely dismisses his fellow musicians' request for an encore: "You jive niggers must be crazy to think I'm gonna stand up here all night and blow a freebie." While this is going on, the pragmatic club owner, instead of being pleased to have a living legend playing for free, frets that the presence in his dive of a convicted drug user might cost him his cabaret license. On his way out, Eagle bums $15 from a young white woman trying to put the make on him. He promises to meet her at the club the next night, but warns her, "I have to tell you in front: it ain't gonna rub off, baby."

Gregory inhabits his character so forcefully it hardly matters that the screenplay by Danska and Lewis Jacobs (also the movie's producer) takes even greater liberties with Parker's life than did the script for *Bird*. Sauntering but rocking slightly on his heels as he enters or leaves a room, and isolating every syllable in his bitter pronouncements on jazz or race (as if he's trying to give the impression that he's stoned even when he's not), Gregory captures his real-life model's arrogance and intellect— his talent for putting people on. For a nonactor, Gregory makes surprisingly efficient use of props, tilting his beret just so and wearing his sunglasses in such a manner that he looks not just bloodshot but somehow diminished when he takes them off. And there's a reminder of what a gifted comic he once was, in a scene in which he riffs at length about an imaginary biblical epic starring "the late J. C. Himself." But even when delivering lines lifted verbatim from John A. Williams's *Night Song*, the 1961 novel on which *Sweet Love, Bitter* was based, Gregory succeeds in making it seem as if he's making everything up as he goes along.

Thanks to Gregory's wit (Woody King Jr., a veteran actor featured in the nightclub scene, was his dialogue coach), we accept Eagle as a great improviser on faith, even before hearing him play his horn (Charles McPherson, the Parker-influenced alto saxophonist who ghosted for Gregory and taught him fingerings, would perform the same services for Forest Whitaker in *Bird* twenty-one years later). But *Sweet Love, Bitter* has more going for it than Gregory's powerful performance as part of a fine ensemble cast. In telling the story of an on-the-skids white college professor (Murray) and his ambivalent relationships with Eagle, a black coffeehouse owner named Keel (Hooks), and Keel's white lover (Varsi), Danska demonstrated an unerring eye for the claustrophobic jazz milieu of the 1960s.

Ironically, this faithfulness to its world helps to explain how *Sweet Love, Bitter* stayed "lost" for almost twenty-five years. A movie steeped in jazz ambience practically demanded a greater commitment to the music's nocturnal subculture than most moviegoers of its time were willing to make. Unless you count *Lady Sings the Blues* (1972), in which Diana Ross seemed to be playing Susan Hayward or Lana Turner instead of Billie Holiday, no jazz movie has generated much action at the box office. With their usual subtexts of drugs, black rage, and genius sociologically programmed to self-destruct, jazz movies tend to be downers. *Sweet Love, Bitter* was no exception. Finding Eagle dead of an overdose, Keel says, "Cause of death: resisting reality." (This isn't giving anything away, because Eagle's death occurs in a flash-forward precredit sequence, before we even know who he's supposed to be.) He might just as well have said, "Cause of death: jazz," an autopsy report that could have extended to the movie's commercial prospects.

In an era in which Sidney Poitier could create a fuss just by coming to dinner, and in which impotence was alluded to only in adaptations of Tennessee Williams, *Sweet Love, Bitter* further sealed its doom with scenes such as one of Varsi pleading with Hooks not to flee her bed after he's failed to become aroused. As in the novel on which it was based, the movie's climactic incident is one in which the professor betrays Eagle, after having earlier helped to save his life. Released at a time when black leaders were publicly questioning how far well-meaning whites were prepared to go in support of civil rights, Danska's movie delivered a message not even the liberal art-house audiences of its day were ready for.

But *Sweet Love, Bitter* was probably doomed from the start, on account of its low budget, its uncelebrated source material

(Williams later became much better known for *Click Song* and *The Man Who Cried I Am*), and an apparent lack of faith on the part of its executive producers. Although Danska's frequent use of hand-held camera and a mise-en-scène as murky as the dishwater in the sink of Keel's coffeehouse made a virtue out of penury, the point must have been lost on the movie's backers, who cut about twenty minutes worth of subplots, secondary characters, and what Danska calls "layering" from his and Jacobs's "final" edit. Streamlined into a more conventional narrative than Danska had intended, *Sweet Love, Bitter* bypassed a proper theatrical release and went straight to drive-ins and grindhouses under the salacious title *It Won't Rub Off, Baby*. Danska, who's based in New York and still active in television, says that no one knows what became of the discarded footage, which he'd like to find if only to rescue an outstanding performance by Carl Lee in a role based on Miles Davis ("Yards" in Williams's novel).

So in one sense, no one's ever seen *Sweet Love, Bitter*—at least not the version that Danska wanted seen. Even so, what's still there on the Rhapsody Films video shapes up as quite possibly the best feature-length film ever made about jazz.

(JUNE 1992)

Miles Agonistes

In *Miles: The Autobiography* (Simon & Schuster) the trumpeter Miles Davis remembers his excitement at hearing the Billy Eckstine Orchestra, with Charlie Parker and Dizzy Gillespie, in a St. Louis nightclub in 1944. "It was a motherfucker," Davis writes (notorious for his profanity, he hasn't toned himself down for publication) of his first in-person exposure to bebop, and also his baptism by fire as a musician—just eighteen at the time, he was pressed into service as an emergency fill-in. "The way that band was playing music—that was *all* I wanted to hear."

Davis's reaction was typical of that of most young musicians in the 1940s. What thrilled them about bebop was its impossible combination of the breakneck and the Byzantine. It was all they wanted to hear and all that they wanted to play. But an early mark of Davis's singularity was that soon after becoming Gillespie's protégé and Parker's sideman, he also became their loyal opposition. "Diz and Bird played a lot of real fast notes and chord changes because that's the way they heard everything; that's the way their voices were: fast, up in the upper register," Davis observes in *Miles*, which was written in collaboration with the poet and journalist Quincy Troupe. "Their concept of music was *more* rather than *less*. I personally wanted to cut the notes down."

Davis's entire career can be seen as an ongoing critique of bop: the origins of "cool" jazz (his collaborations with Gil Evans in the late 1940s), hard bop or "funky" (his 1954 recording of "Walkin'"), modal improvisation (the track "Milestones" in 1958 and the 1959 album *Kind of Blue*), and jazz-rock fusion (*In a Silent Way* and *Bitches Brew*, both recorded in 1969) can be traced to his efforts to pare bop to its essentials. His decision, in 1969, to court a younger audience by playing rock venues, adding amplified instruments to his ensemble, and cranking up both the volume and the beat, also amounted to a critique of modern jazz, which he felt had become tired and inbred. So, in effect, did his withdrawal from recording studios and public performance from 1975 to 1980, years in which "sex and drugs took the place that music had occupied in my life until then, and I did both of them around the clock." He barely touched his horn in these years, but he haunted jazz with his silence.

Two generations of listeners now feel that Davis has sold them out: jazz fans of a certain age who have never forgiven him for going electric, and the rock audience that discovered him with *Bitches Brew* and—try as it might—can't get with the slick techno-funk he's been recording since *The Man with the Horn*, in 1981. The audience he has his sights on now, though he's unlikely to reach it without a hit single, is the audience that grooves to Prince and Michael Jackson, and commercial survival doesn't seem to be his only motivation—ego, racial identity, and a desire for eternal youth (or continuing relevance) all seem to be mixed up in it.

For many of his more worshipful fans, of all ages and races, Davis's music has always been just one component of a mystique that also involves his beautiful women, his up-to-the-minute wardrobe, his expensive taste in sports cars, and his scowling black anger: his celebrity boils down to an insider's lifestyle and an outsider's stance. (Or as Ornette Coleman once put it, Miles is a black man who lives like a white man.) His magnetism is so powerful that fans who haven't liked anything he's done in years continue to buy his records and attend his concerts, irrationally hoping for a reversal of form.

On stage he remains an electrifying presence, though you wonder now (as you do with Dizzy Gillespie, but for a different reason) not how well he'll play, but how *much*. He's become a kind of roving conductor, walking from sideman to sideman, describing what he wants from them with a pump of his shoulders or a wiggle of his hips, blowing riffs into their faces and letting them pick it up from there. He still turns his back on the audience for much of a show, as he was infamous for doing in the fifties and sixties. The difference is that now he has a wireless microphone on his horn that allows him to be heard clearly with his back turned—and that audiences would be disappointed, at this point, if he failed to strike his iconic pose. Though his shows are never boring, you're not quite sure how you feel about them afterward. Is Davis admirable, as his apologists would have it, for refusing to rest on his laurels—for keeping up with the latest black musical and sartorial fashions? Or is there something pathetic about the sight of a sixty-three-year-old man in clogs, parachute pants, and jheri curls shaking his fanny to a younger generation's beat?

"When I hear jazz musicians today playing all those same licks we used to play so long ago, I feel sad for them," he writes.

> Most people my age like old, stuffy furniture. I like the new Memphis style of sleek high-tech stuff . . . Bold colors and long, sleek, spare lines. I don't like a lot of clutter or a lot of furniture either. I like the contemporary stuff. I have to always be on the cutting edge of things because that's just the way I am and have always been.

Anyone this vigilant about staying on "the cutting edge" is chasing trends—not starting them, as Davis did in jazz from the late forties to the early seventies (*Bitches Brew* and most of the double albums that followed it, though turbid in retrospect, were undeniably influential at the time).

Davis has two new releases in the stores, one of which is so shockingly good that you're slightly disappointed in it for not being perfect. *Aura* (Columbia), recorded in 1985, is a ten-part orchestral work by the Danish composer Palle Mikkelborg (who is also a Davis-influenced trumpeter, though he doesn't solo here); it bears the influence of certain pieces from the early seventies by George Russell, an American composer who was then living in Denmark. More boldly than Russell's works of that period, *Aura* attempts to reconcile electronically generated and acoustically produced sonorities, advanced harmonies, and a big crunching beat. The work sags in places: a duet between Davis and the bassist Niels-Henning Orsted Pedersen has too much New Age gloss surrounding it, as do the passages dominated by woodwinds. But a number of the ten sections cagily evoke Davis's landmark collaborations with Gil Evans, and three sections—subtitled "Red," "Blue," and "Electric Red"—are spectacular in their endless permutations of the work's initial ten-note theme and static but oddly compelling 7/8 rhythm. On these three sections in particular, Davis responds to the orchestra with ecstatic, sustained improvisations that give an idea of what he's still capable of when challenged.

Amandla (Warner Bros.) is more current and more typical of Davis's 1980s output. It has its virtues, not least among them its yeasty rhythms; Davis and his producer, the multi-instrumentalist Marcus Miller (who wrote most of the tunes), have obviously been listening to *zouk* and other African dance music. But too much of *Amandla* sounds like generic instrumental funk, with Davis playing sound stylist rather than improviser—in contrast to the alto saxophonist Kenny Garrett, whose brief solos inventively harmonize the signature attributes of two of his predecessors in Davis's group: Wayne Shorter's ascetic spatial sense and Cannonball Adderley's preacherly bonhomie. Davis, in a rare act of noblesse oblige, guest-stars on two tracks of Garrett's *Prisoner of Love* (Atlantic), a disappointing exercise in saxophone smooch-and-groove à la Kenny G. Even without consulting the personnel, you'd recognize Miles by that hornetlike middle-register buzz of his. He exudes presence, but puts so little of himself into his solos that he sounds like he's being sampled.

Aura notwithstanding, Davis's major accomplishment of recent years is *Miles*, which enjoys an obvious advantage over the Davis biographies by Ian Carr, Jack Chambers, Eric Nisenson, and Bill Cole. Without the full involvement of their subject, these were essentially turntable companions—critical guides to Davis's work within a biographical framework. But with *Miles*, Davis proves to be his own most perceptive critic (at least about his music before 1969), and the book is so successful in capturing Davis's voice (including his incessant, if tonally varied, use of profanity) that the odd line that sounds like the doing of Troupe (as when, for example, Davis supposedly resorts to quoting a jazz critic to describe the dramatic contrast between his style and that of his former sideman John Coltrane) calls for a double take.

"The challenge . . . is to see how melodically inventive you can become," Davis writes, giving the most succinct explanation I've ever read on the advantages of improvising on modes or scales rather than chord changes. "It's not like when you base stuff on chords, and you know at the end of thirty-two bars that the chords have run out and there's nothing to do but repeat what you've done with the variations." *Kind of Blue*, which popularized modal improvisation, was the most influential jazz album of its period, but it was a disappointment of sorts for Davis, he writes. The sound he wanted on *Kind of Blue*, and feels he didn't quite achieve, was that of the "finger piano" (probably an African thumb piano) that accompanied a performance he saw by an African ballet troupe. Though Davis himself doesn't make the connection, what an unexpected rationale this provides for the three electric pianos that phase in and out behind the horns on *In a Silent Way*!

He writes about fellow musicians with an eye for detail that brings them into photographlike focus. On Gil Evans, for example:

> When I first met him, he used to come to listen to Bird
> when I was in the band. He come in with a whole bag of
> "horseradishes"—that's what we used to call radishes—

that he'd be eating with salt. Here was this tall, thin, white guy from Canada who was hipper than hip ... But bringing "horseradishes" to nightclubs and eating them out of a bag with salt, and a white boy? Here was Gil on fast 52nd Street with all these super hip black musicians wearing peg legs and zoot suits, and here he was dressed in a cap. Man, he was something else.

Though acknowledging Charlie Parker's genius, Davis characterizes him as "a greedy motherfucker," who was "always trying to con or beat you out of something to support his drug habit."

Bird always said he hated the idea of being thought of as just an entertainer, but ... he was becoming a spectacle. I didn't like whites walking into the club where we were playing just to see Bird act a fool, thinking he might do something stupid.

Miles's considerable value as jazz history isn't what makes it such a page-turner. Autobiography is a problematical literary form, because it's never clear which is being submitted for the reader's approval, a book or its author. Davis writes that he loved Parker as a musician, but "maybe not as a person," and the Miles Davis who emerges from *Miles*—as complex as any character in recent fiction—elicits a similar ambivalence from the reader.

His treatment of women is contemptible: it seems like he's slugging another one every twenty pages or so. It isn't bad enough that he talks with unconvincing remorse of hitting his own women; a story intended to establish Billy Eckstine's tough-guy credentials has Eckstine slapping a would-be girlfriend while Davis looks on admiringly. He's spiteful toward the actress Cicely Tyson, the most recent of his ex-wives, whom he professes not to have felt "the sex thing" for after their marriage.

Cicely has done movie and TV roles where she played an activist or something like that, a person who cared a lot about black people. Well, she ain't nothing like that. She loves to sit up with white people, loves to listen to their advice about everything and believes everything they tell her.

Davis's fame and his relatively privileged upbringing (his father was a dentist and an unsuccessful candidate for the Illinois state legislature) haven't spared him from injustice, such as being clubbed over the head by a white policeman after he was ordered to move on from the entrance of a New York City nightclub in which he was performing in 1959. But much of what Davis interprets as racism is his own hubris, as when he speculates that white jazz critics of the 1960s wrote as much as they did about such black avant-gardists as Ornette Coleman, Cecil Taylor, and Archie Shepp in an effort to deflect attention from *him*. (Never mind that the critics most identified with what was then called "The New Thing" were Amiri Baraka and A. B. Spellman, both of whom are black.) He's peacock vain. He tells of admiring himself in a mirror in 1956, when his star was on the rise. He wasn't yet making as much money as he thought he should be, but he was looking "clean" in Brooks Brothers and custom-made Italian suits. "I felt so good that I walked to the door and forgot my trumpet."

He writes of getting together every so often with the late James Baldwin in France and "lying our asses off." You have to wonder, as you do with all autobiographies, how much lying is being done here. Probably not a lot, because for a man this caught up in his own mystique—a man fully aware that his art and life are already the stuff of legend—just telling the truth about himself as he sees it amounts to a form of self-aggrandizement.

(JANUARY 1990)

Miles Davis died in 1991, at the age of sixty-five.

Philly Guy

It was an odd hour for a concert (10:30 A.M.), but no odder than the audience (average age, seven and a half) or the venue (the Abington Friends School, in the Philadelphia suburb of Jenkintown) or the fact that the Josephine Muller Auditorium was under construction as the show went on.

The performer was Grover Washington, Jr. The following night Washington would officially inaugurate the 400-seat auditorium, donating his services for a $75-a-ticket concert to benefit the private Quaker school's minority scholarship endowment. The following week he would take his seven-member band (including his younger brother, Darryl, on drums) and his eight-man road crew (including Grover 3d, twenty-one) to New York for two sold-out shows at the Beacon Theater, on Broadway—the first stop on an eight-city tour to promote "Sacred Kind of Love," his new single with the singer Phyllis Hyman, taken from the album *Time Out of Mind*, which was already number one on *Billboard*'s contemporary jazz chart.

But on this Friday morning, as laborers trimmed the landscape, painted the lobby, and waited to carpet the aisles, Washington had come to play for Abington Friends' student body, beginning with the elementary and preschoolers (the auditorium smelled of milk). Grover Washington, Jr., age forty-six, was simply a father putting in some time at his daughter's school (Shana, fourteen, is an Abington "lifer," as the kids who go through school there call themselves). Still, it's not every father who brings with him, at his own expense, six musicians, instruments (including two drum sets), speakers, sound and lighting technicians, and a road crew.

Even before the musicians assembled on stage, the kids were

47

visibly excited to see the guitars and monitors and amps; the drums on risers; the stacked electronic keyboards; and the four gold-plated saxophones (soprano, alto, tenor, and baritone), each in its own rack.

Washington—dressed as though setting out on a comfortable morning jog, in rubber soles, black jeans, and a red T-shirt from a recent charity bowling tournament organized by Gary Maddox, the former Phillies centerfielder, for the Philadelphia Child Guidance Center—reached for the soprano first. He led the band through a slow, cresting, stoptime blues: the kind of piece he would play for an audience of adults. Though the volume remained quite reasonable, one little girl, apparently unaccustomed to live music, covered her ears on the crescendos.

The kids were restless, but Washington didn't talk down to them. He got their attention with his second number—a stomper called "Jamaica," halfway between reggae and Motown. He played both tenor and baritone on this one, honking through the bigger, deeper horn at well-timed intervals and clapping his hands above his head to encourage the youngsters to do likewise.

"This is a tune for six friends of mine who, as we speak, are transversing Antarctica—the South Pole," Washington told the kids, his offstage stutter gone. "They started in June and they have to be finished before the end of March, when the Antarctic winter begins. They don't want to be around for that, because it's unbearably cold! These six gentlemen are crossing Antarctica by dogsled and skis, not by snowmobile. They're going thirty-five miles a day—the equivalent of a marathon every single day! So see if you can imagine in your mind's eye, as we start to play, the South Pole, the dogsleds running, the wind blowing, and the snow falling down."

Who knows what the children thought? To adult ears, as Washington's alto vibrated on a soft cushion of keyboards and guitar, the tune ("Protect the Dream") evoked images of seduction in front of the fireplace. It's Washington's trademark sound, one that's sold millions of records and become generic in the hands of his imitators, the soul-kiss school of saxophonists: George Howard, Najee, Gerald Albright, Kirk Whallum, and Kenny G.

If sales were the only test, Grover Washington, Jr. would loom larger in jazz than Charlie Parker, John Coltrane, and Wynton Marsalis combined. Consider *Winelight*, Washington's Grammy-winning 1981 album, which featured the hit single "Just the Two of Us" with singer Bill Withers. It went double platinum (selling in excess of two million units) and spent a full year on *Billboard*'s pop album chart and an unprecedented *three and a half* years on the jazz chart. ("We used to throw it birthday parties," quips the attorney Lloyd Zane Remick, Washington's longtime personal manager.)

But it's virtually impossible to find a nationally recognized jazz critic who's written anything good about Washington. Or anything bad about him, for that matter. The jazz press seldom bothers to review him (the most negative criticism of all, as Washington himself points out). *The Rolling Stone Jazz Record Guide*, a reliable index of received opinion, says, "Washington has little to offer . . . beyond the fact that he's a popularizer of jazz."

Harsh, but accurate. Washington is no innovator, and according to Bob Porter, a former critic record producer now best known as a disc jockey on WBGO-FM in Newark, New Jersey, that's why the jazz intelligentsia ignores him. "Critics are always on the lookout for something that no one's heard before, something brand spanking new, and probably rightly so," says Porter, who gave Washington his first opportunity to record (as a sideman on Charles Earland's *Living Black*, in 1970). "Grover is already a known quantity, and his music isn't aimed at critics, anyway."

Maybe not, but others give Washington the cold shoulder as well. No performer receiving fewer than forty votes was listed in *Down Beat*'s most recent readers' poll. Washington failed to make the cut on any of his instruments.

So who's buying all those copies of *Time Out of Mind*? A recent TV spot for the Philadelphia adult-contemporary radio station WMGK-FM provides a clue. "In a given hour," notes an "average listener," a black businessman in his late thirties, "you might hear a little Grover Washington, Jr., along with some Stevie Wonder or Carly Simon. You won't hear head-banging music you can't work to, or elevator music that puts you to sleep."

Like most of what's optimistically termed "crossover," Washington's latest album is tailored to that sort of listener. It's Gold Card Soul—a plush, creature-comfort sound for an affluent, stressed-out audience that shies away from deep jazz, just as it does from rap, hardcore, metal, or anything else too aurally strenuous.

Regardless of his disputed rank in jazz, everyone who knows him agrees that Grover Washington, Jr. is a class act. In his adopted hometown of Philadelphia, he's as well known for his charitable and community work as for his music. And in contrast to such southern California transplants as Bill Cosby and Sylvester Stallone, Washington actually lives in Philadelphia's West Mount Airy section, with Christine, his wife of twenty-two years, and their three children (including Loran, twenty-five, Christine's son from a previous marriage).

"I might drive up to New York for a recording session, or fly out to the coast," says Washington, who even does most of his recording locally. "But I always want to come back right away, because Philly is my home."

"Grover is a family man and a hometown kind of guy," explains Lloyd Remick, whose Zane Management also represents the basketball player Hersey Hawkins and the junior welterweight champion, Meldrick Taylor, among others. "Of all the superstars I've ever had contact with, he's the one who's stayed most real."

W. L. Gore & Associates, manufacturers of Gore-Tex outerwear, and one of the corporate sponsors of the Antarctica expedition that Washington spoke about at Abington Friends, also sponsored one of Washington's tours, in return for his endorsement. But the rest of Washington's social activitism—including his efforts on behalf of the Variety Club, the United Negro College Fund, and the Settlement Music School—is done gratis. For him, charity really does begin at home. "As parents, Chris and I are part of the Abington Friends community," he says of his benefit concert. "I just happen to be in a more visible profession than most parents, so that becomes another way of contributing."

An involvement with the Special Olympics (he appears on the organization's public service spots, and both he and his wife have co-chaired fund-raisers) also grew out of his commitment to his own family. "Loran, who is severely retarded, is so cool," Washington says with pride. "He's competed in the wheelchair race and the ball-throwing event and things like that. In the middle of running all around the world playing music, he helps me to remember what's really important."

Washington is a guy who shamelessly roots, roots, roots for the home team. He plays the national anthem before Philadelphia 76ers games, "as often as they let me. Sure, I'm a frustrated athlete. But most athletes are frustrated musicians, so go figure that out."

The son of a beautician and a steel-plant foreman who moonlighted as a club saxophonist, Washington envisioned a career in classical music, before realizing that blacks—let alone saxophonists—seldon get such opportunities. He left his hometown of Buffalo at age sixteen—"after graduating from high school, my folks insisted on that"—to travel with the 4 Clefs, a rhythm and blues instumental group that played record hops and such throughout the Midwest. "I was shocked by the lack of professionalism on the part of some promoters," he says, "who would give us a sad story or try to pay us in pizza or hamburgers."

In 1965, Washington was drafted into the army and stationed at Fort Dix in New Jersey, within driving distance of Philadelphia's jazz clubs. While sitting in one of them, he met his wife and decided to settle there for good. After his discharge in 1967, he worked by day for a one-stop record distributor or as a supermarket security guard. At night he made the rounds of the neighborhood lounges with groups led by the organists Charles Earland, Johnny Hammond, and Don Patterson, and Trudy Pitts. "Trudy and Bill [her husband, the drummer Bill Carney, also known locally as Mr. C] were especially helpful to me," Washington recalls. "Trudy even used to write out exercises for me to study."

Then Washington got two lucky breaks. In 1970, Earland recommended him to Bob Porter as a last-minute replacement for an errant tenor saxophonist who was supposed to cut a live album with Earland at a club in Newark. A year later in New York, Washington was supposed to back the alto saxophonist Hank Crawford on a session for Kudu Records. But Crawford had been detained on a drunk-driving charge in Memphis. Creed Taylor, the date's producer, intended Kudu to be a label that would offer jazz cover versions of the latest hits (in this case, Marvin Gaye's "Inner City Blues"), which meant that postponements weren't written into his budget. He asked Washington to step in for Crawford, and Washington took care of business.

Twenty albums later he's still taking care of business—literally as well as figuratively. Incorporated several times over, he "conducts his career in a very organized, very professional manner, with a very tight organization around him," says Remick, who adds ruefully that not many of the musicians he's come into contact with have been as adept as Washington at planning ahead.

Washington's business acumen is an outgrowth of his practicality in all matters. When asked if he and his wife splurged after receiving the first royalty check for *Inner City Blues*, he looked incredulous.

"We put it in the bank," he said,

Washington's supporters include Sonny Rollins, universally regarded as the greatest living jazz saxophonist, who invited

Washington to play a concert with him in New York in 1981.
"He's a good saxophonist who plays with a lot of feeling,"
Rollins says, "and he deserves everything that's come his way."

"I look at Grover as an extension of King Curtis," Bob
Porter says. "It looked as though the sound of the blues saxophone was going to disappear when Curtis died in 1971. But it
reappeared with Grover. The thing I most respect about him is
that no matter how far he goes into pop, he always has one
track on his albums for the jazz people."

And sometimes more than just one: at Washington's insistence, his current contract with Columbia Records gives him
the option to alternate straight-ahead jazz albums (like *Then and
Now*, with pianist Tommy Flanagan, from 1988) with his
crossover releases. This was unexpected from Washington,
because—as Remick points out—he doesn't have to alter what
he does, and his record company probably wishes he wouldn't.
"Grover might favor pure jazz, but he knows that pure jazz
albums aren't going to reach as many people," Remick says.

Isn't it good for jazz if, with his crossover albums, Washington reaches audiences who otherwise resist jazz as too obtuse?
Possibly. As Washington puts it, "Jazz isn't all avant-garde." But
such albums—full of languorous, even cloying music—may also
reinforce the notion among the young that jazz is safe and pre-
dictible, for the chronically out-of-it.

Therein lies Washington's dilemma. Despite Creed Taylor's
sanitized production, Washington's early albums had the bite of
the blues—the legacy of grooving with organists in tiny
Philadelphia bars. And along with his superior technique, Washington's intimacy with that tradition is what gives him the edge
over his clones. You can tell he's listened to Charlie Parker and
Cannonball Adderley. Najee and the others sound like they've
listened only to *him*.

But Washington tends to come across like a muscle-bound
studio musician when playing bop. And when playing pretty
for the people, as he has on most of his albums since *Winelight*,

he can sound as bland as any of his imitators—like a smile button with the blues.

At Abington Friends, asked by a student if he always plays his numbers the same way, Washington reflexively answered as any jazz musician might. "The arrangement would be the same, because we've already worked that out, but not my solo," he claimed. "I couldn't play it the same if I tried, but that's okay, because that's what this music is all about."

In New York a week later, however, Washington's solos pretty much followed the same route as at Abington Friends. This in itself was no disgrace: the men in Duke Ellington's band, once they had recorded their solos, used to repeat them verbatim night after night. But Washington's answer revealed a man treading a fine line between jazz (which values spontaneity, even in the recording studio) and pop (in which performers are expected to "do" their records live on stage).

What was surprising in New York was the manner in which Washington and his band stretched out on even his most pop-oriented tunes. The music wasn't state-of-the-art jazz, but it did what it was supposed to do—it grooved.

The show demonstrated why Washington's audience adores him. He gives them more than he has to, and he's a genuinely nice guy. The grating Phyllis Hyman, who opened the show, had made her entrance behind a puff of smoke that lingered far longer than it should have (as did she—giving a textbook illustration, on a few Duke Ellington tunes, of why jazz singing isn't simply a matter of repertoire). Midway through Washington's set, the musicians were ordered from the stage and the exit doors flung open to the cold till the smoke cleared. If Washington was flustered, he didn't let on. "Strange night, huh?" he asked the audience when the show resumed.

"We'll see you again in the NBA playoffs, New York," he said after his encore, local hero to the last. "From Philadelphia, with love."

(MAY 1990)

Silver Minus One

In Bernard Malamud's *A New Life*, S. Levin—a typical Malamud hero, a Jew shouldering a cross—pays a high price for the woman he loves. Levin is a nontenured instructor at a small northwestern college, and the woman in question is his department head's wife. The vengeful husband grants her custody of their children on one condition: that Levin promise never to set foot inside a college classroom again. "An older woman than yourself and not dependable, plus two adopted kids, no choice of yours, no job or promise of one, and other assorted headaches. Why take that load on yourself?" the husband asks Levin, once the bargain's been struck.

"Because I can, you son of a bitch," Levin replies.

That was the drummer Mel Lewis's attitude toward leading a big band. Lewis, who died earlier this month of melanoma, at the age of sixty, kept the big band he co-founded with the cornetist Thad Jones in 1966 afloat for almost a quarter of a century. This was a remarkable achievement for a man who wasn't a Swing Era name brand (like Count Basie or Woody Herman), a famous songwriter who could subsidize an orchestra band with his ASCAP earnings (like Duke Ellington), or an exhibitionist who could draw paying customers with nothing but his flying sticks (like Buddy Rich).

"I'm not losing money on the band now, but I lost so much from before that I'll probably never catch up," Lewis told me when I dropped in on him in his West End apartment about a month before his death. "But I don't care about money," he said, before adding in a near-whisper, "Doris [his wife] doesn't like to hear me talk that way."

Lewis's survivors include his band. For twenty-three years, beginning in February 1966, the Vanguard Jazz Orchestra (as

Lewis renamed the Thad Jones–Mel Lewis Orchestra after Jones's defection in 1979) has been the regular Monday night attraction at the Village Vanguard—as unique a part of the venerable cellar's decor as the tubas on both side walls and the red arrow leading to the men's room. February also happens to be the month that the late Max Gordon, the Jazz Orchestra's friend and benefactor, opened the Vanguard at its present location in 1935. So once a year, sometime during the month, the club celebrates the double birthday by bringing the band in for a full week.

Lewis didn't live to hear his band's silver-minus-one anniversary gig, with his appointed deputy, Dennis Mackrel, manning the drums. Bald as a result of radiation therapy (the cancer had spread to his brain) and still wearing his long nightgown late into the afternoon, he looked both infantlike and sepulchral when I called on him. He explained that he'd spent the day in bed, recovering from an accident the day before: returning from the doctor's, he'd grown weak and fallen from the higher of the two low steps outside his apartment building, landing on his back and hitting his head on the pavement. By that point, he was playing drums with the band for just one or two numbers every Monday.

He was diagnosed with melanoma—the most fatal form of skin cancer—in 1985. "Cute, huh?" he asked, holding up his left arm to show me the ugly scar tissue near the inside of his elbow, where the initial growth was removed. "Then, in 1988, at one of my periodic checkups, they detected another one on my chest, then another one on my arm. 'If it's reached one of your organs, we're in trouble,' the doctor told me. Well, it did— it reached my lung. It's still there. It's in remission. It doesn't hurt. It's nothing. You don't even know you have it. The only problem is energy—I run out of it. Otherwise I feel fine. My lungs are in good shape, and so is my heart. Being a drummer has made me strong inside. I heal fast."

I remember thinking: *He either doesn't know he's going to die or won't admit it.* The unspoken question was what would happen to his band. He probably would've told me that if the Jazz Orchestra could survive the loss of Jones, its star soloist and resident composer, it surely could survive the loss of its drummer.

Lewis cried twice as we spoke, but not when talking about his illness. The first time he wept was when he called my attention to a self-portrait by the eldest of his four daughters, a disturbed young woman who took her own life in 1988, at the age of thirty-four. (Another daughter died when she was ten months old.) The second time he cried, he was reminiscing about his father, the late Sam Sokoloff, a drummer who was unknown outside of his hometown of Buffalo. (Lewis acquired his stage name while with Ray Anthony's band in the late forties.) "My father used to work at a club called McMahon's, and he always took me along with him. One night, when I was about fourteen, the last show was about to start, and my dad was nowhere to be found. My Uncle Mo Balsam—not my real uncle, but a friend of the family, and a good pianist—motioned to me, 'Come on, Moischele, you gotta play drums,' calling me by my Hebrew name, which [the valve trombonist Bob] Brookmeyer still calls me to this day. I played the first number for the chorus line, and then I looked over and saw my father sitting at a table with the drummer Cozy Cole, both of them laughing. He was leaving with my mother the next day to visit my aunt in Florida—the first vacation he ever took in his life. I was wondering who was going to replace him. Me, that was who. But he first wanted to see if I could cut it. That was my dad for you, a professional in every way."

By 1966, Lewis enjoyed a reputation as one of the most capable big-band drummers, on the strength of his work with Stan Kenton, Benny Goodman, Terry Gibbs, Gerry Mulligan, and Maynard Ferguson. His own band evolved out of what he perceived as a crying need for one at a moment when players with big-band experience were still plentiful but bands becoming increasingly scarce. The other factor was Lewis's admiration for Thad Jones's writing, dating to the day a few years earlier when Jones brought an unfinished arrangement of his own "Little Pixie" to a Mulligan band rehearsal.

But there was conflict between the co-leaders right from the start. "Thad didn't give a damn, especially when he was drinking," Lewis told me, with a rancor that shocked me. "He wouldn't write unless someone paid him to write. Half of our book was vocal arrangements he had done for various singers, fixed up a little bit for a big band. That wasn't right. He should've been writing new stuff for us."

When Jones bolted for Denmark in 1979, it was "for a chick, a woman over there who had some money and wanted him because she was pregnant with his baby," Lewis said. "He left his wife in New Jersey with nothing, to raise a couple of very good kids on her own." According to Lewis, Jones also left the Jazz Orchestra thousands of dollars in debt. "I'm no quitter," Lewis said, when I asked if he'd considered disbanding. Instead he regrouped. "There were a number of guys who were in the band because they were friends of Thad's, who I didn't think were good enough and who didn't particularly want to be there with him gone, either. Plus there was a lot of racial bullshit I was tired of: trying to keep the band evenly mixed, like it was in the beginning, which had always been a point of pride with us, because there weren't many bands like that. I finally called a meeting of the section leaders [the trumpeter Earl Gardner, the trombonist John Mosca, and the saxophonist Dick Oatts, all of whom remain in the band today], and told each of them to put together a dream section. If that meant firing somebody, I would. And if it meant becoming a whiter band, so be it.

"We still had Thad's charts, but I wanted to broaden our horizons. So I went after Brookmeyer." The trombonist, a life-long friend of Lewis's and an original member of the Jones-Lewis Orchestra, assumed the post of music director, and thanks to what another musician once saluted as Brookmeyer's "thirteenth-chord thinking," the band took on a more adventurous profile. Jones returned to the states in 1984, to assume leadership of the Count Basie Orchestra. He died two years later. Though Brookmeyer is no longer associated with the Jazz Orchestra in an official capacity, his influence lingers in the writing of a number of past and present bandmembers, including the pianists Jim McNeely and Kenny Werner, graduates of Brookmeyer's BMI composition class.

Lewis's renown as a big-band drummer sometimes caused his assets as a fine drummer, *period*, to go overlooked. For my money, the best recording he ever made is the recent *The Lost Art*, a Musicmasters release featuring him with a small group drawn from the Jazz Orchestra, on a program of exploratory tunes written by Werner, Oatts, and the baritone saxophonist Gary Smulyan (all of whom also play on the date). The disk begins and ends with Lewis's freestanding drum solos; the title track, another drums-only performance so melodic it doesn't sound out of place coming after a ballad medley, demonstrates his sensitivity with brushes. Even so, the truest measures of his musicianship might be the guidance he lends Werner's outward-bound "Voyager" and the broken march cadence with which he sets up Oatts's rustic "Native American." He was the rare drummer who relished the role of accompanist.

For an example of Lewis's ability to drive a big band with a minimum of flash, look no further than *The Definitive Thad Jones*, also on Musicmasters, a companion release to *The Lost Art* recorded during the Jazz Orchestra's anniversary at the Vanguard two years ago. Hearing the delicious sax voicings on "Three in One," you know why Lewis put up with Jones for thirteen years, and the rightness of Lewis's tempos substantiates his boast that he was Jones's ideal interpreter. The finale is a romp on Jones's "Little Pixie," sort of an orchestral enlargement of Charlie Parker's "Moose the Mooch," based on the same "I Got Rhythm" chord changes. It's a rousing performance that brought the Jazz Orchestra and its leader full circle.

A week or so after I visited with Lewis, he flew with his band to New Orleans to be feted at the National Association of Jazz Educators convention. I don't know how he made it, but he did. Because the trip wore him out, he didn't make it to the Vanguard the following Monday. I called him later that week to fact-check some of what he'd told me, but mostly just to inquire how he was. His speech was slurred from the medication, and he had difficulty understanding me. But he perked up when I told him that I'd been to the Vanguard a few nights earlier.

"You heard my band?" he said. "That's a great band, isn't it. I'd stack my reed section up against anybody's past or present, including Ellington's."

(FEBRUARY 1990)

Apple Pie

I was sick, but I'm getting better," Art Blakey told me without naming a specific ailment when I visited him in his Greenwich Village penthouse apartment this summer. In 1964, when Blakey was still in his mid-forties but already regarded as a hard bop father figure, Blue Note titled one of his albums *Indestructible*. For decades, the word fit the man known in jazz circles as the world's healthiest (and most discreet) junkie. But now, at the age of seventy—white-haired, stooped, and with a weak handshake—Blakey no longer seems impervious to time.

In his right ear he wore the hearing aid he was fitted with a few years ago, but which he eschews onstage. "I feel the vibra-

60
■

tions through the floor, just like Beethoven," he said, gingerly lowering himself into a stuffed chair in his spacious living room. "That's all music is, anyway. Vibrations."

He spoke in a phlegmy rumble that made me recall Dan Morgenstern's description of a Blakey press roll as "the sound of a giant clearing his throat."

Blakey's physical deterioration shocked me into asking formulaic questions, most of which I was forced to repeat several times, and several of which I finally had to yell. He laughed frequently—not by making a sound, but by throwing back his head and showing his teeth—as though self-amused by the disingenuous ring of some of his answers, as when I asked him why drummers make such good bandleaders (think not only of him, but of Chick Webb, Gene Krupa, Max Roach, Mel Lewis, Ronald Shannon Jackson, Jack DeJohnette).

"I just play and try to make a showcase for the youngsters, so they can hone their art."

Asked if he considers himself a teacher (he's usually spoken of that way), he protested, "Hell, no. How can I be, if I don't tell them what to play." On the other hand, he answered a question about whether, for the sake of camaraderie, he ever wished that his sidemen were closer to his own age, "Can't teach old dogs new tricks."

And when I pointed out to him that so many of the musicians who have joined his band in the last two decades have been graduates of college music programs (in contrast to their predecessors, who, like Blakey himself, were self-taught), he joked, "When I came along, you couldn't mention jazz in colleges. So there's been progress. Youngsters today go, learn theory, learn harmony. Then they graduate, join the Messengers, and start their real education." But he pointed with an autodidact's vindication to his own honorary degrees from the New England Conservatory of Music and the Berklee School of Music. "They're over there, bound in leather, on top of the piano, if you want to look at them."

Blakey's relationship with his young sidemen has been one of tough love, though—the painful truth—for the last few years, they've been carrying *him*. "I tell them what *not* to play. They're not youngsters. They're young men, old enough to make babies. I treat 'em that way." He admits to nudging them out of the Messengers when he feels they're overdue to start their own bands.

The position of music director (held over the years by Horace Silver, Benny Golson, Wayne Shorter, and Bobby Watson, among others) is strictly titular, Blakey told me when I asked him what the qualifications for the job were.

"I'm the real music director back there. I'm the one directing the traffic," he said, suddenly adamant. "But I like to give each of my men some responsibility, and the ones you named were good composers."

How come Blakey himself hasn't composed more?

"I compose," he protested. "Don't you think I don't. I'm composing on drums up there."

But composition in the formal sense?

"Give them the chance to do it," he shrugged.

"Want some apple pie?" Blakey asked me, putting our conversation on a different footing. "Best in New York! From Balducci's!" he said temptingly, naming a well-known Village gourmet shop. "You know what they say about Balducci's. Spend a hundred dollars there and you can fit what you buy in the glove compartment of your car. Daniel, bring him some pie. And bring me a cigarette."

What the hell, the interview wasn't going anywhere anyway.

The strapping German fellow who handles Blakey's bookings from an office just off of the kitchen brought pie for me and an ashtray with a Marlboro Light already burning in it for Blakey. In the background, the radio was tuned to WBGO-FM. The disc jockey gave details of a public memorial service for pianist Walter Davis Jr., a two-term Messenger who'd died of liver and kidney failure three days earlier, at the age of fifty-seven.

Taking shallow drags on the cigarette, Blakey started bitch-
ing about his most recent ex-wife, who had left him two years
earlier, fleeing to her native Canada with their two adopted
children and (Blakey says) a large sum of money that was supposed to have been set aside for his taxes.

"I've had four wives, all jealous of me," he rasped conspira-
torially, balling his fingers into a fist and adding, "they weren't
interested in Art Blakey *as a man.* The last one told me, 'You
make more money in one night then my father made in a year.'
Well, whose fault was that? He could have been Prime Minister of Canada, couldn't he? Wasn't nothing stopping him. He
was Caucasian.

"I miss Buddy Rich," he suddenly exclaimed, apropos of
nothing in particular, as the radio played something by Freddie
Hubbard. "The year before he died, I saw him at a festival in
Europe. I asked him, 'Why don't you go somewhere and retire,
old man. All those heart bypass operations you had.' You know
what he said to me? He pointed to that stage and said, 'There's
no place else I want to be.' "

Taking advantage of his reflective mood, I asked Blakey
about his days as a teenage singer and pianist in Pittsburgh (the
story goes that he switched to drums after being intimidated by
the young Erroll Garner).

"Hell, I wasn't no piano player," he protested. "I just sat at
the piano and knocked off a few chords. It was a means of
escape. There was child labor in my day. I started work in the
coal mines when I was eleven. I was by myself, no brothers or
sisters. It was tough, but I had to be tougher. My mother died
when I was five months old. I never even saw a picture of her.
Her best friend took care of me. They got married in the
church, my mother and my father. He sat my mother in a car-
riage, said wait here while I go to the drugstore and buy a cig-
ar. They told me she sat there for nine hours waiting for him
to come back. He ran off to Chicago with some other chick,
because my mother was too dark for him. He was a mulatto.

Lived to be a hundred and three. Must have been a hell of a man. He loved me but couldn't accept me as his own, because of the times. When I met him later on, I wouldn't even talk with him, because he wouldn't act like a man.

"My first child was born when I was thirteen. I never abandoned my kids. I love children. I fathered seven. I adopted seven more. That makes fourteen. I don't remember how many grandchildren I have. I haven't met them all yet. But I'm a great, great grandfather," he said, coughing between the "great"s. "So that's my life. I have no regrets. I've had a ball. I've outlived some of my children. I've outlived some of my grandchildren. I've outlived most of my contemporaries. And I've been fortunate to be an American. This is the greatest country in the world. Nobody's going to tell me that it's not! You got the freedom to do anything you want.

"Somebody dies—crocodile tears! Liars!" he fairly seethed, perhaps thinking of the upcoming services for Walter Davis Jr. "I didn't go to Monk's funeral. I loved him. He and I were like brothers, birthdays one day apart in October. But I didn't go to his funeral. People asked me why. I said the day somebody comes back from the dead and says to me, 'Oh, what a beautiful funeral they gave me,' that's the day I'll start going to them. Nature takes its course. Slowing up, retiring. You're born, you die. It's what you do in between."

In parting I asked Blakey if he'd read Miles Davis's autobiography (in which Miles accuses Blakey of once having fingered him to narcotics agents, back when both of them were using).

"I ain't got time to read that. That's garbage. I read books I can get knowledge from, the Koran, the Torah, the Bible from Genesis to Exodus," he said, sweeping his arms toward a shelf full of what appeared to be books on World War II.

I told him what Miles had said about him.

"Did he spell my name right? Then, good."

Downstairs in the lobby, the security guard was listening to a vibrant uptempo tune on the radio. It could have passed for something by the Messengers, circa 1978, except for an element that was missing. Call it the crust. It turned out to be the Harper Brothers, the band co-led by drummer Winard and trumpeter Philip Harper (a recent Messenger).

Thanks to the many successive generations he's sired, there will always be bands that sound like Blakey's. But will there ever be anybody else like him?

(NOVEMBER 1990)

Art Blakey died on October 16, 1990—about four months after my visit, and five days after his seventy-first birthday.

Jazz Rep, Continued

Mingus Mingus Mingus

Thirty musicians—including Wynton Marsalis, no less—crowded onstage for the premiere of *Epitaph*, a newly discovered work by the late Charles Mingus, at Alice Tully Hall on June 3. The advance word on *Epitaph* was that the full score, pieced together by the Canadian jazz historian Andrew Homzy from scattered fragments he found among Mingus's personal effects, ran some five hundred pages (or roughly 5,000 measures), weighed "fifteen pounds on the bathroom scale" (according to Susan Graham Mingus, the composer's widow), and would take over two hours to perform. The conductor would be the estimable Gunther Schuller, who had conducted recordings of Mingus's earlier extended works (and whose new book on the swing era, coincidentally, is a hefty 919 pages).

The staggering raw figures, however, weren't what made this concert more of a must than anything else in jazz this summer, including the JVC Festival. Ten years after his death, Mingus is widely recognized as the only postbop composer to produce a body of work comparable in breadth to Duke Ellington's. Schuller described *Epitaph* (once characterized by Mingus as "a whole symphony that has never been played") as "unprecedented in Jazz . . . not just a bunch of strung-together pieces, like most jazz suites" (presumably including Ellington's). Mingus is due for a major resurgence: Fantasy will soon bring out a twelve-CD box of the sessions he produced for his own Debut label in the early fifties, and later this year he gets the Hal Wilner treatment, with various rockers, jazz musicians, and unclassifiable downtown types reinterpreting his music. And the evening at Alice Tully promised posthumous vindication for Mingus's most humiliating debacle: a 1962 Town Hall open recording session at which an ill-prepared big band debuted several ambitious pieces that resurface in *Epitaph*—although at the time no one, perhaps not even Mingus, suspected that these were excerpts from a large-scale work.

Within the jazz community, attendance at *Epitaph* was mandatory. Would this be Mingus's equivalent of Ellington's *Black, Brown, and Beige*? The giveaway that we were building up to an awful letdown came in the *Stagebill* insert, which announced changes in the order in which *Epitaph*'s nineteen movements would be played. If the sequence was that arbitrary, what hope was there for the "sense of inevitability" that Schuller finds lacking in Ellington's suites and the "overall continuity" he promised for *Epitaph*? None, as it turned out. As performed at Alice Tully, *Epitaph* wasn't a suite, much less a symphony. The individual movements contained such Mingus fingerprints as bass strings slapping wood, wah-wah brass counterpoint, and escalating tempos even on ballads. But these hardly amounted to recurring motifs.

Separating composition from performance is always the difficult task in appraising a work that is both ambitious and unfamiliar. But *Epitaph* wasn't, in fact, *that* unfamiliar—I have in my collection, on bootlegs or legitimate releases, at least eight of the detachable movements, including Mingus's elegant and harmonically advanced variations on Vernon Duke's "I Can't Get Started" and the main theme, which expands on the opening unison sax riff of "Pithecanthropus Erectus," and which Mingus performed as "Epitaph" at Town Hall in 1962. So the pertinent question becomes whether the concert succeeded as a program of old and "new" Mingus, not whether it unveiled a major new work.

The negative answer raises, in turn, the more fundamental question of whether jazz repertory can do Mingus justice, as it has other pantheon composers, including Ellington. In the liner notes to a 1964 album featuring a few tracks with Mingus on piano instead of bass, Schuller wrote, "Like Ellington at the piano, Mingus 'feeds' the orchestra with his impelling beat, his personal magnetism, and the intensity of his on-the-spur-of-the-moment exhortations." A pianist friend was saying pretty much the same thing, I think, when he conjectured that Mingus, in light of his orchestral inclinations and his habit of second-guessing the pianists he hired for his bands, probably would have been happy to park himself at the piano full-time, "but his music depended on him standing up and staring down his sidemen and the audience from behind his bass." What Mingus wrote on scorepaper usually bore slight resemblance to what we expected to hear onstage. And he was willing to use all manner of intimidation to get his sidemen to make up the difference. His music required bodily participation, which is why so few of his pieces were played by other musicians during his lifetime ("Goodbye Pork Pie Hat," I'm afraid, owes its second life to the weightless versions by Joni Mitchell and John

McLaughlin) and why his records lost something vital when he was confined to a wheelchair toward the end of his life.

Everything about Mingus, including his potential for failure, was Brobdingnagian, and what was disappointing about Schuller's interpretations was that they seemed smaller than they should have been: their failure was as much the result of cautious good taste as of inadequate rehearsal time. A fellow jazz critic who enjoyed the concert much more than I did conceded, during a brief conversation we had going out the door, that "there wasn't enough gris-gris at the bottom of the bowl." What was lacking was the fever pitch that was frequently all that sustained Mingus's most successfully realized works, most notably the album-length *The Black Saint and the Sinner Lady*.

Mingus's spirit strutted the hall only once all evening, when the trombonist Britt Woodman, the alto saxophonist John Handy, the tenor saxophonist George Adams, and the trumpeter Jack Walrath—all Mingus alumni from various epochs—came down front to jam on "Better Git Hit in Your Soul." They tore into the piece with such abandon that you imagined they were heeding Mingus handclaps and mock Holy Roller moans and shouts that only they could hear. But there was no bite to the brass interjections on the pieces involving the entire ensemble; and there wasn't enough whiplash in the intersecting bop lines on "OP," a piece dedicated to the late Oscar Pettiford, Mingus's fellow bass virtuoso. The rubato ballad sections were more convincing, even though Schuller brought out their voluptuousness at the expense of their volatility, rather as though he thought he was conducting Gil Evans, not Mingus. His approach at least emphasized the danceband existentialism that Evans and Mingus ballads have in common.

The solos were the evening's saving grace. On "Noon Night" (a variation on "Nuroog" and not on *Tonight at Noon*, as might have been expected), Adams's scooping, Ben Webster-goes-modern choruses swung the whole band. Marsalis turned in two bravura solos, one on open horn, the other wah-wah muted and devilishly comic. Walrath, the trumpeter Randy Becker, and the alto saxophonist Bobby Watson also played their hearts out, and I only wished that Schuller had permitted them to go on at greater length, as I suspect Mingus would have.

The concert ended on an unresolved note. Explaining that the performance was being recorded and apologizing for having "screwed up" two sections, Schuller had the ensemble perform those sections again, as an encore. Midway through the second, at exactly 11 P.M., a union stagehand gave the signal to cut it off, and that was that. Would the concert have been smoother if Schuller and his musicians had been allowed more than a week's rehearsal? I don't doubt it, but smoothness wasn't something Mingus aimed for. I suspect that Mingus without Mingus isn't going to sound like Mingus no matter how much you rehearse.

(JUNE 1989)

Wynton's Ellington Jones

Duke Ellington's "Portrait of Louis Armstrong," from his *New Orleans Suite* and the last in what was actually a series of concertos for Cootie Williams, becomes a veritable hall of mirrors on the Lincoln Center Jazz Orchestra's *Portraits by Ellington* (Columbia): Wynton reflecting Cootie reflecting Pops. On the lips of another trumpeter his age or younger, Marsalis's whole notes and squeezed exclamations might amount to nothing more than a soundcheck of brass techniques, or a modernist's condescending attempt to go old-timey. What enlivens Marsalis's choruses here (and on "Second Line," another of the album's selections from *New Orleans Suite*) is the orchestral sophistication he's acquired as a result of his immersion in Ellingtonia: his configuration of Duke's countermelodies (themselves buoyantly Armstronglike) even during his stoptime diminuendo over just bass and drums.

Such thematic ingenuity would have been unimaginable from Marsalis a decade ago, during his recapitulating-Miles phase, or even five years ago, when he first discovered his horn could growl. No longer sharing much in common with his tad-bop progeny, he's evolved in surprising directions, beginning with his embrace of New Orleans polyphony on *The Majesty of the Blues,* in 1989. He might be uninterested in, even hostile to, innovation, but he's helped to widen this era's bebop status quo by lending his name to jazz rep. And though his Ellington jones has yet to result in a major composition (this year's *Blue Interlude,* modeled on Duke's "Pretty and the Wolf," showed him trying to display a sense of whimsy without first developing a sense of humor), it's stimulated his growth as a soloist. Whatever impropriety might be involved in Lincoln Center awarding its first jazz commission to its own artistic director, Marsalis can hardly be accused of monopolizing the spotlight on the LCJO's first album, or at its Ellington tribute at Avery Fisher Hall last week (a homecoming for the band after a month touring the hinterlands). Marsalis seems to relish submerging himself in ensemble tasks, much the way that Kenneth Branagh and Emma Thompson do while returning to the Royal Shakespeare Company.

Reinterpreting Ellington can be tricky, not just because his pieces seldom suggest a specific era, but also because of his unusual covenant with his soloists (whose contributions were so integral to his scores that a repertory bandleader can't afford to allow *his* musicians much elbow room), and finally because we're talking about an impressionist whose music was seldom "pure." To do justice to Ellington requires doing justice to his imspiration, whether that be Bert Williams, Bill Robinson, a happy-go-lucky local, or a daybreak express. The beauty of the LCJO's conductor David Berger's transcriptions of late and/or seldom done Duke on *Portraits* (including the complete *The*

Liberian Suite) lies in capturing more than just Ellington's textures and inflections; something approaching the Ellington Orchestra's irresistible surge takes over, thanks in no small part to Kenny Washington's authoritative rim shots and willingness to let the tempos occasionally race ahead of themselves. Along with Washington and Marsalis, the album's heroes are Sir Roland Hanna, cast in the most difficult role of all, as the band's pianist; and Todd Williams, its youngest saxophonist, who—though unable to convey Coleman Hawkins's elder statesmanship (as opposed to just his harmonic buzz) on "Self Portrait of the Bean"—thrives in the near-modal climate of "Thanks for the Beautiful Land on the Delta" and amid the mock pandemonium of "Total Jazz." On *The Liberian Suite*, the guest violinist Andy Stein strings as whimsically as Ray Nance on the 1947 Carnegie Hall premiere, even if Milt Grayson's proper, Eckstinelike enunciation is no substitute for Al Hibbler's relaxed and delightfully unaccountable cockney.

Herlin Riley, only slightly less dynamic than Washington, was the drummer at Avery Fisher, where the band was robbed of some of its sensuality by the hall's colorless acoustics and management's (or somebody's) decision to keep the houselights up, as though this were an evening with the Philharmonic. Still, the LCJO showed the benefits of its road work on a snarling "Ko-Ko" and a "Jack the Bear" properly assembled from the bottom up, with telling contributions by the bassist Reginald Veal, the baritone saxophonist Joe Temperley, and the plunger-trombone specialist Art Baron (a regular Son of Tricky Sam).

People used to wonder when jazz would finally be welcomed in bastions of high culture and if big bands stood a chance of surviving, little realizing that the answer to both questions would turn out to be the same—that the future of big bands would one day rest with monied institutions such as Lincoln Center, whose sponsorship would dictate a curatorial approach similar to that in highbrow music. Like it or not, concerts such as last week's now generate as much controversy as the taken-for-granted avant-garde once did. That's one of the many ironies attending this curious period in jazz evolution, and although the ultimate outcome of this retrospective trend is anybody's guess, mine is that jazz as a side effect of its official sanction as "art" will splinter (or arguably already has) into two camps resembling those in classical music, with its own entrenched rebel elite as well as its own preservationist establishment. My other hunch is that Marsalis will continue to surprise us, though never leaving any doubt about which camp he's in.

(OCTOBER 1992)

Fringes

Cat Clubbing

It's been ages since Americans danced to jazz as part of their normal social routines. With bebop in the late 1940s and free a decade or so later, jazz completed its evolution into an art music understood to be for sedentary pleasure only. In 1990 jazz and dance on the same bill usually signifies a creative collaboration between a composer and a choreographer (avant-gardists on equal footing, like John Cage and Merce Cunningham), with audience participation limited to applause at the end. This tends to make divided souls of those jazz fans who like to party: they derive their identity from listening to Miles and Coltrane but wind up dancing to Motown and Paula Abdul, just like everybody else.

Except at the Cat Club, the grungy downtown basement that plays host to the New York Swing Dance Society every Sunday night (the rest of the week the club's walls shake to bands with names like Skin & Bones, Snatches of Pink, and Every Mother's Nightmare). They do the Lindy Hop there, but not the way your Uncle Oscar and Aunt Edith do it after a few drinks at weddings and bar mitzvahs.

Named by its originators, the airborne dancers at Harlem's Savoy Ballroom, in honor of Charles Lindbergh, shortly after his transatlantic flight in 1927 (or so the legend goes), the Lindy isn't a cobwebbed, Swing Era relic—it's the modern dance from which countless others have evolved. Teenagers did it to rock and roll in the 1950s, long before the twist, the mashed potato, or the frug; and eighties breakdancers inherited at least a few of their airsteps from the daredevil Lindy Hoppers you see in old movies and big band "soundies."

I'd like to pretend that I knew as much all along, but the truth of the matter is that I'd never much thought about it until watching the dancers at the Cat Club on my visit there to hear the Loren Schoenberg Orchestra on a Sunday in May that (strictly by coincidence) turned out to be the anniversary of Lindbergh's takeoff. The NYSDS, which has been in action downtown since 1985—and whose members first got together informally at Small's Paradise, in Harlem, a year earlier—brings in a different band every week. But the eager and knowledge-able dancers go on twirling straight through the intermissions, to the recorded sounds of Glenn Miller and early R&B instru-mentals, like Lee Allen's "Walkin' with Mr. Lee."

Dancers once did their part for jazz by keeping musicians on their toes, encouraging a supple beat and discouraging lengthy, involuted solos. But the relationship went deeper than that, according to Loren Schoenberg: "I never fully understood [Duke Ellington's] 'Ko Ko' until I saw dancers respond to that minor key, that baritone saxophone, that bass drum," Schoen-berg told me between sets. "It's like the difference between hearing a concert performance of arias and seeing a fully staged opera."

The man to keep your eyes on at the Cat Club (the musi-cians and the other dancers do) is Freddie Manning, a limber seventy-six-year-old who perfected his moves at the Savoy Ballroom in the 1930s, as a member of Whitey's Lindy Hop-pers, the professional dance troupe featured in many of those above-mentioned films, and who last year won a Tony for the two numbers he choreographed in *Black and Blue*. Every Sun-day, at the top of the third set, the featured band kicks off "Stompin' at the Savoy" (what else?), and Manning—one of a handful of elders who are treated like royalty here—leads a line of young disciples in the shim sham, a fluid variation on the shimmy, with a bit of the Charleston thrown in.

Flanking Manning during the shim sham are the members of the NYSDS's Big Apple Lindy Hoppers, practiced dancers—dance instructors, some of them—who are cheerfully tolerant of beginners, but scornful of showoffs (they shook their heads in dismay when I told them how much I enjoyed watching a black man in his fifties who occasionally broke free from his partner and did the electric boogaloo, fluidly wiggling his shoulders and neck while otherwise standing perfectly still.) The crowd dresses every which way, with no period drag in evidence, and fewer layers of character armor than the habitués of most Manhattan clubs. Before checking out this scene for myself, I'd read that this was the best-integrated gathering in New York, both racially and generationally. This turned out to be wishful thinking: young means thirtysomething and black means eligible for Medicare. But in New York these days any little bit of civility between the races goes a long way.

With its reinterpretation of classic performances from the late twenties through the early forties, Schoenberg's band typifies a recent trend in jazz. In an odd turnabout, controversy now surrounds old music, not new. Because jazz has been romanticized as ad-lib music hellbent on innovation, the very notion of reinterpretation strikes some observers as a contradiction. And race complicates the issue, as it usually does in jazz, because so few black musicians of Schoenberg's postwar generation play anything earlier than bebop.

But an evening with the NYSDS serves as a reminder that jazz used to appeal to audiences as both dance music and intellectual stimulation, and Schoenberg's band adds a third level of appreciation: respect for the experimental thrust of so much of what we've been conditioned to think of as "premodern" jazz.

Schoenberg and his bandmate and fellow tenor saxophonist Mark Lopeman, who transcribes much of the band's material from records, accomplish this by avoiding generic swing tunes in favor of neglected material by such visionary composers and arrangers as Ellington, Billy Strayhorn, Benny Carter, Eddie Sauter, and Fletcher and Horace Henderson. Schoenberg formed the band after dropping out of the Manhattan School of Music in 1980; it was then a repertory outfit pure and simple, led by a man who desired nothing more than to hear live performances of his favorite older records, complete with the original improvised solos. Since then both Schoenberg and the band have broadened their horizons. The band's book now includes band-generated arrangements and performances of older numbers for which no "definitive" interpretation already exists—either because they were never recorded (for example, the Bob Brookmeyer and Gary McFarland arrangements that Benny Goodman commissioned for a 1958 USSR tour, to which Schoenberg has access from having served Goodman in various capacities in the years just before his death), or because a single recorded version fell short in one way or another (Sauter's "The Maid with the Flaccid Air," for example, a through-composed piece with no improvisation recorded by Artie Shaw in 1942, but reinterpreted with more panache by Schoenberg's band on last year's *Solid Ground*).

Sauter, one of Schoenberg's favorites, is represented twice on *Just A-Settin' and A-Rockin'* (Musicmasters), Schoenberg's fourth release. Both charts are faithful transcriptions (the album's only two), and it's difficult to imagine two numbers more dissimilar in tempo and dynamics than the jumping "Superman" (Sauter's 1940 exercise for Goodman and Cootie Williams, whose roles are here ably filled by Ken Peplowski and John Eckert) and the dreamlike "Remember" (reharmonized Irving Berlin, with Peplowski and the pianist Dick Katz recalling Red Norvo and Hank D'Amico's ghostlike counterpoint on the Norvo band's 1937 recording). It's also difficult to imagine another band, including those Sauter wrote for, doing justice to both arrangements. You don't need to be familiar with the originals to enjoy these new versions: they possess a timeless vitality.

Just A-Settin' and A-Rockin' demonstrates that Schoenberg's band is no longer just a model jazz repertory orchestra, but a wide-ranging big band that has to be counted among the most accomplished in contemporary jazz. In addition to the two Sauters, the other highlights include a moody Lopeman original called "Forlorn," his arrangements of "The Lady's in Love with You" (featuring the classy singer Barbara Lea) and "Smoke Gets in Your Eyes" (with a songlike solo by Schoenberg and sensitive brush work by the late Mel Lewis, who was without peer as a modern big-band drummer), Brookmeyer's surging treatment of "I Gotta Right to Sing the Blues" (from the Goodman archives), and no fewer than six Ellington numbers, ranging in scale from McFarland's imaginative, if somewhat overextended, fantasia on "C-Jam Blues" to the footloose blowing on Lopeman's skeletal arrangement of "Stompy Jones."

At the Cat Club, Schoenberg's repertoire was a little more predictable, not so much in deference to the dancers, Schoenberg said, as on account of the unusually large number of subs in his band that night. Even so, along with "Stompin' at the Savoy" and "Jumpin' at the Woodside," he sprung such surprises as Ellington's "Starcrossed Lovers" (from *Such Suite Thunder*) and Fletcher Henderson's arrangement for Goodman of "You're a Heavenly Thing."

It wasn't the Savoy Ballroom, circa 1936, by a long shot: what was missing—along with what Otis Ferguson poetically described as "a hopeless intricate mass of flying ankles, swirls, stomps"—was the sensation the original Lindy Hoppers must have had of being at the epicenter of *where it's at* (and of where it's at being only a dancestep away from "a sidestreet of gray poor doorways, empty stores, pinched tenements . . . the rags and tatters of Harlem, an American community bled dry"). Still, I can't imagine anyone showing up here and not having a good time. And, no, I don't dance. But thank you for asking.

(JUNE 1990)

Old and New Gospel

Say Amen, Gracie

Among the pious I am a scoffer: among the musical I am religious," wrote George Bernard Shaw, presumably in his guise as music critic. I can't cite chapter and verse because I didn't read it in Shaw. I happened upon it in the liner notes to an old Ray Charles album—only fitting, I suppose, in that a song like "What'd I Say," with its sacred vocal cadences in the service of profane injunctions to "shake that thing," is a more forceful illustration than any work in the European canon of what I assume Shaw was driving at. There was, of course, a sense in which Shaw was being coy in making such a distinction: as a critic with a flair for invective, he obviously prided himself on being a scoffer among the musical, too. And though I share his sentiments, Shaw's distinction is becoming increasingly useless in jazz, where the pious and the musical often turn out to be the same people.

True believers liken jazz to religion, but what initially lured many of them into the fold was jazz's irreverence and the sinful excesses associated with so many of its greatest performers—titillating evidence that jazz isn't on the side of the angels. But jazz is as much the offspring of black church music as of the blues. Probe deeply enough into the background of any black instrumentalist said to be self-taught and you'll generally discover that he learned the rudiments of harmony from a mother or aunt who was a church pianist or choir leader. Jazz got funky in the late 1950s not by imitating rhythm and blues, but by instrumentalizing the moans of the Sanctified Church, in such numbers as Horace Silver's "Sister Sadie" and Bobby Timmons's "Dat Dere." What makes gospel palatable even to atheists and agnostics is that its lyrics can be interpreted as coded protest or sublimated lust. Even devoid of lyrics, however, pious conviction combined with smug musicianship can be deadly. Jazz has acquired such a thick air of religiosity over the last two decades (though the spiritual hectoring has more typically been in the name of Islam than Christianity—or in the case of the Wynton Marsalis axis, in the name of jazz itself) that we scoffers in the audience sometimes have to wonder what we're doing there.

All of this is an admittedly roundabout way of confessing that I wasn't prepared to be as delighted as I am with *Go Tell It on the Mountain* (Silkheart), an album of traditional hymns and originals with heaven-gazing titles by Booker T. Williams Jr., a New York-based tenor saxophonist originally from Seattle who performs as Booker T. The obsessive soul-searching implicit in the programming suggests an affinity with John Coltrane. But unlike too many of the saxophonists who aim for Coltrane's spiritual elevation, Booker T has a devilish sense of humor— best illustrated by his "Say amen, Gracie" drollery on "What a Friend We Have in Jesus," a homey little melody he elongates and fragments with the comic élan of a Sonny Rollins.

In fact, the classic album that *Go Tell It on the Mountain* most recalls is *Way Out West*, Rollins's 1958 album of cowboy tunes—and not just because Booker T, like Rollins before him, finds inspiration in unlikely places. It's also because Booker T's interaction with the bassist Saheb Sarbib and the drummer Andrew Cyrille is as carefree and almost as electrifying as Rollins's with Ray Brown and Shelly Manne thirty years ago (or better yet, with Wilbur Ware and Elvin Jones on *A Night at the Village Vanguard*, from around the same time).

Despite the sarcasm implicit in Booker T's low-register bleats, his performances of "What a Friend We Have in Jesus" and "Jesus Loves Me" exude sincerity, much the way Rollins's interpretations of oddball pop tunes do. For Booker T, as for Rollins, satire is a sign of respect, not condescension. Booker T is ecumenical: one of the album's most infectious cuts is "Halle Kalle Mazeltov," a hora whose modality he cagily exploits. The Spartan trio format means that Sarbib and Cyrille have to function as soloists as well as rhythm stalwarts, and both men shoulder the added burden gracefully, maintaining melodic continuity in a manner that bassists and drummers seldom do when they solo.

Despite the length of some of the tracks (the title tune, which is just over sixteen minutes, is a Booker T original, not the folk song of the same name), Booker T's solos never deteriorate into self-indulgent braying. His sense of thematic exposition is too well developed for that—another cue he takes from Rollins. (And as if to underscore his lineage, the CD-only bonus track is Rollins's calypso "St. Thomas.") He switches to alto on his own "When Mama Cries I Cry," and his phrasing is impressively speechlike on this lighter horn. To the best of my knowledge, Booker T's only other recording has been as a sideman on *Cold Sweat*, a recent album of James Brown tunes (also featuring Craig Harris and David Murray) that illustrates the sloppiness jazz musicians are capable of when trying to show they can be Regular Guys. But *Go Tell It on the Mountain* is stunning enough to make me a believer in Booker T's potential.

I tend to listen to it along with two other recent albums of what might be called (to borrow a title from Ornette Coleman) Old and New Gospel. According to the producer Michael Cuscuna's liner notes, *Nightingale* (Blue Note), the first release by the tenor saxophonist George Adams since the breakup of the band he co-led with the pianist Don Pullen, was originally conceived as an album of spirituals, but the song selection eventually "became broader and included many popular songs . . . rooted musically or in feeling to the spiritual." So, in addition to "Precious Lord, Take My Hand," *Nightingale* includes "Ol' Man River," "Moon River," "Bridge Over Troubled Water," "Going Home," and "What a Wonderful World"—all the tearjerkers you never wanted to hear again.

Yet Adams and a superb rhythm section captained by the pianist Hugh Lawson interpret these threadbare melodies with easygoing mastery, and the album is pleasantly reminiscent of the similar ones that Gene Ammons made for Prestige in the 1960s, minus the congas. Adams does his lustiest blowing on "Ol' Man River": before surging into a rocking 4/4, he plays a wrenching, out-of-tempo intro that conjures Paul Robeson's emblematic performance of the Jerome Kern song in James Whale's 1936 film version of *Show Boat*.

Anyone smitten with Adams's "Ol' Man River" or Booker T's "What a Friend We Have in Jesus" should also hear the gospel alto saxophonist Dr. Vernard Johnson—or "Brother" Vernard Johnson, as he's perhaps strategically billed on *Rocking the Gospel* (ROIR), his first release for a secular label. Though he's been likened to Junior Walker, King Curtis, and Clarence Clemons, to jazz ears, Johnson's lunging vibrato and screaming glossolalia recall no one so much as the late Albert Ayler (who, it should be remembered, gave his pieces such titles as "Spirits Rejoice" and "Holy Ghost"). Johnson has what an ENT doctor might call a "productive" tone—there's a lot of lung in it. Though his musical framework owes something to the lighter-than-air pop-gospel approach of Andrae Crouch (represented here as a songwriter), Johnson's music is gritty and heart-poundingly visceral—unmistakably carnal, as perhaps befits the work a man playing what is still considered to be the most profane of musical instruments.

Johnson also sings wonderfully, in a soft, lispy, affectless voice that seems almost too intimate for worship. It's a shame that this cassette-only release of a 1985 Fresno, California, revival meeting is so dimly recorded; it doesn't hit with as much force as Johnson's albums for Savoy (which, unfortunately, tend to be found only in stores where the help speaks in tongues). Still, this ROIR cassette could serve the worthwhile purpose of introducing this unique performer to secular audiences. I like to believe that Johnson could appeal to a mass audience if given enough exposure. Of course, I also believe that about George Adams and Booker T and all of the out-of-the-pop-mainstream performers that I like, though the masses have done nothing to substantiate that conviction. I guess that's what people mean by faith.

(OCTOBER 1989)

Callin' 'em

A pastor's son and himself an ordained minister in the Church of God in Christ, Dr. Vernard Johnson has dedicated himself to spreading the gospel on a horn regarded as blasphemous by many, on account of its nightclub associations.

"Many times, I was denied by people who were ashamed to have a saxophone in church," Johnson said earlier this week, during a hurried phone interview from a Dallas airport. "They said, 'Vernard Johnson is just a novelty.' But when the people heard me blow, they realized that Vernard Johnson was sincere. They realized that God had made a difference in my life, and that I was here to stay."

Subtract the choir that appears on most of *I'm Alive* (Nonesuch Explorer), Johnson's first major-label release, and you're left with saxophone plus piano, organ, guitar, bass, and drums—a rhythm section similar to those that backed Otis Redding on his classic sides for Stax and Al Green on his early hits for Hi. Johnson justifies the comparison with his gritty vocals (*I'm Alive*, produced by the New Jersey-based retro rocker Ben Vaughan with Elektra's Danny Kahn, is the first of Johnson's albums on which he's sung more than halfheartedly), but also with saxophone solos as naked in their appeal to the senses as the vocals of any of the great soul shouters.

Like Bach's liturgical music, Johnson's sanctified soul appeals to disbelievers for whom music amounts to a form of religion.

But for Johnson, whose admirers include Don Cherry, Ornette Coleman, and Yusef Lateef, music is simply a means of delivering a message. "I'm not just blowing licks," he told me. "I'm trying to *say* something on my horn."

Johnson spoke from an airport pay phone because a delayed flight prevented him from doing the interview from his Fort Worth ministry as planned. (He was due in Philadelphia later that week for a Sunday night service at the B. M. Oakley Memorial Temple—famous in gospel circles as Marion Williams's church.) Frequently referring to himself in the third person, he delivered many of his thoughts in preacherly metaphors at odds with his conversational tone. The first African-American to receive a master's degree and a doctorate from Southwestern Baptist Theological Seminary in Fort Worth, he resorted to street argot to describe the friendship shown to him by fellow members of the college's men's choir on a road trip through segregated Mississippi in the late 1960s.

"We all walked into that restaurant, two of my friends on either side of me, two in front of me and two behind—these white dudes actin' real hostile-like, like they was *brothas*—you understand, man? Anybody who wanted to mess with 'Nard was gonna have to mess with *them*."

Originally from Kansas City, Kansas (also the birthplace of Charlie Parker, whose music Johnson says he knows only by reputation), Johnson is coy about his age, but his school record and recollections of his early days on the gospel circuit would seem to put him in his early to mid-forties. He broke into gospel in the mid-1960s, barnstorming the Midwest with the Reverend Hubert Lambert, an itinerant preacher who went on to become the pastor of a church in Kansas. "Reverend Lambert, who died just last year, wasn't a polished speaker, but he had charisma," Johnson recalled. "He didn't advertise or nothing. Just drove into a town and put up a tent. Then he'd tell me, 'Call 'em, Ber*nard!*'—long as I knew him, he thought my name was Bernard.

"I would blow for maybe forty-five minutes, with my eyes closed," Johnson said, bursting into a full-throated, melismatic scat that must have drawn stares from others in the Dallas airport. "And when I opened my eyes, the tent would be filled. That's how I learned to improvise: being placed in a situation where I needed the Lord's inspiration."

I'm Alive, although a studio album (only Johnson's second), gives some idea of the pandemonium he must have stirred up in those small midwestern towns. But Johnson at his most inspired is also Johnson at his most subtle, as on "I Love to Praise His Holy Name," a traditional "praise" song resembling the familiar "This Little Light of Mine." Johnson, accompanied by just two percussionists and a female vocal quintet, recasts the tune in a dark minor key, ad-libbing serpentine lines of remarkable length and complexity for someone whose record-company bio mentions chronic childhood asthma.

"I used to have asthma attacks so bad my folks thought I must be dying," Johnson said, loudly demonstrating over the phone how he used to gasp for breath. Nobody believed that he could summon enough lung power to master alto saxophone, an instrument that appealed to him as a grade schooler because "I saw one somewhere and it just looked so *cool*. But I kept pleading, and my folks remembered that even if I didn't have enough wind, there was someone who sits high and looks low who did."

Johnson played alto with teenage "cover" bands around Kansas City. Then came a "spiritual awakening" on a K.C. street corner, after which he briefly considered giving up his horn. "But God spoke to my heart and said, 'Don't put your horn down, Vernard. Just change your song.'"

One day soon after, while practicing, he felt "a powerful surge that passed through my feet, my legs, my belly, and then into my lungs. I took a deep breath and that asthma was gone ...."

On the subject of contemporary pop, Johnson voiced objection to "artists who cut music that promulgates sexual immorality," though acknowledging that his eleven-year-old daughter, Lynitra Janese, listens, with his blessing, not just to gospel but to such pop and rap acts as the Boys, the Perfect Gentlemen, M. C. Hammer, and Kool Moe Dee.

Although *I'm Alive* stands a chance of winning Johnson a mainstream following, he said that he wasn't sure he wanted to walk through all of the doors that might be opening for him. But despite his reluctance to perform in venues where liquor is served, he isn't ruling out club work.

"Jesus went everywhere, man, with people we would call sinners. But He went with a message. If I do it, that's what I will do."

(AUGUST 1991)

Johnson's reluctance to play clubs ultimately stymied his label's and his secular manager's efforts to expose him to a wider audience. There was no follow-up album.

Johnson, who's played before audiences in the thousands on tour with Billy Graham, drew only two dozen or so churchmembers (mostly older women with their small grandchildren) to his Sunday night service I attended at the B. M. Oakley Memorial Temple, next door to a drug rehabilitation center on a crumbling block in North Philadelphia. He gave a spirited performance despite the poor turnout, and despite having to rely on a prerecorded tape for accompaniment for much of the night. He still knows how to call 'em, too—verbally as well as musically. At one point during his sermon, he invited anyone who wished to pray for a loved one with a drug problem to join him on the altar. Sobs filled the church, and there was hardly anybody left in the pews.

Groovy

Ruby Braff can be a pip, a jazz festival press agent warned before giving me Braff's New York phone number. And whatever you do, don't call him before 2 P.M.!

Actually, the cocky little cornetist was irresistible—a goodnatured grouch for whom complaining is a way of letting the world know he's full of sass. When Braff answered his phone, he was watching live TV coverage of Jim Wright's resignation as Speaker of the House. "He's been talking for about half an hour now, and all he's had to say is that he's innocent," Braff cheerfully grumbled. "They all say the same thing, and they're all no good. We have no statesmen anymore, just politicians. The last one who had any intellect was John Kennedy—and look at what they did to him."

Much of what Braff hears in contemporary jazz irks him, too. Asked if he had a theory on why so few younger musicians bother to learn the classic pop songs of the twenties, thirties, and forties that served as springboards for Louis Armstrong, Coleman Hawkins, and Lester Young, Braff replied. "Because they don't respect melody. How can you embellish something that you don't think is beautiful to begin with?

"And some of these guys have the effrontery to call themselves composers. How can both Duke Ellington and one of these little shits be composers? One of them's not a composer, and it's not Ellington. They're just looking for shortcuts so they can stand up there and masturbate with their horns."

These are fighting words to committed modernists, some of whom foolishly let their disagreement with Braff deafen them to his virtues as a soloist.

Braff, who was born in Boston in 1927, is a decade younger

than Dizzy Gillespie, and a year younger than Miles Davis. Having rejected bebop for swing, however, he's stylistically a generation their senior.

"It doesn't matter what style or era it is. Something's either music or it's not," Braff said, and he's living proof of his own adage. The hallmarks of his style—melodic incandescence, harmonic acumen, rhythmic individualism, tonal savoir faire—are hallmarks of all great jazz, regardless of stylistic label. "Ruby will often play a note like he's blowing up a balloon: it swells up," writes John Snyder in the liner notes to *This Is My Lucky Day* (RCA Bluebird), a recent CD reissue of Braff's sessions from 1957. Snyder's notes amount to the best published technical analysis of Braff's style, and what's surprising about them is that they were written by a man who's produced albums by Ornette Coleman—a musician whose approach to jazz would seem to be antithetical to Braff's.

But maybe not. With his pianoless quartets, Coleman rid modern jazz of its harmonic clutter. Despite his differences in rhythmic values and emotional pitch, Braff has much the same agenda—that of letting the melody shine forth and of getting the musicians to concentrate on one another, not just the chord changes or the beat. This is evident on *Me, Myself, and I* (Concord Jazz), an album that introduces Braff's new working trio, with Jack Lesberg on bass and Howard Alden on guitar—no piano and no drums.

"I don't want drums just to have drums, and the toughest thing in the world is finding a piano player who knows how to let you breathe," Braff said, in explaining the trio's streamlined instrumentation (and that of an earlier group he co-led with the guitarist George Barnes). "Talk about chamber music. When you're down to three pieces, you're close to the bone."

His interpretation of "You've Changed" is so melodic that it's difficult—and ultimately unnecessary—to detect where embellishment ends and improvisation begins. This is a romantic performance that, paradoxically, gains much of its tenderness from the ribald glee of Braff's low notes and the imperiousness of his upper-register rasp.

Braff's unclichéd repertoire is one of the album's constant delights. The title tune is a Billie Holiday favorite, and several of the numbers, including "That's My Home," "Jubilee," and "You're a Lucky Guy," are associated with Louis Armstrong, though hardly anybody does them anymore. "Let Me Sing and I'll Be Happy" is from the Al Jolson songbook, and Richard Whiting's "Honey"—not to be confused with the Bobby Goldsboro weeper from the late sixties—is, as Braff puts it, "an old barroom song that was always requested right after 'Peg o' My Heart.'"

"My father's side of the family was from Philadelphia, and they were all classical musicians who didn't approve of the direction I was heading in," Braff told me, bringing up my hometown. "Because back then, you know, there was no such thing as swing or jazz, or at least nobody called it that. If you were a musician, you played symphony or you played popular. And if you played popular, you were a bum."

More wit and wisdom from Ruby Braff:

On America's jazz and pop heritage: "All of the great popular songs are jazz songs. It's all in how you play them. We once lived in a time when the popular songs were written by masters of melody, with the lyrics by great poets like Lorenz Hart. And masterful performers sang and played those songs. Most of the pop singers were jazz oriented. Even Al Jolson, believe it or not, had a very good beat. Oh, sure, there were some corny songwriters and performers, but the corniest of them was a genius compared to the people responsible for the crap you hear on the radio today."

On today's jazz audiences: "Playing for the jazz audience of today—so-called—isn't much fun, because the younger people in the audience are ignorant. They don't know what to like unless a critic tells them it's new, it's old, it's modern, it's swing, it's bop, it's avant-garde, or whatever. They have no reference point. They have to look in books: 'Oh, it says this guy's great, OK.' Jazz audiences once were the most knowledgeable audience in the world, because they participated in the music. They heard everything as it came out, danced to it, romanced to it, went to all the joints. You couldn't fool them. They knew whether the tune was good, whether the band was good, whether the soloists were good. They knew everything."

On European jazz festivals, at which as many as half a dozen bands might be featured on the same bill: "It's like going to Barney's [a New York men's store] and looking at suits. You see so many, in so many different fabrics and colors, that you forget what you were looking for in the first place. Stravinsky once said there's too much good music too readily available. He said that in order to appreciate music, you should have to walk a few miles to a concert once or twice a month. He was right."

On invitation-only jazz "parties," like those in Denver and Minnesota, where elder swing musicians are said to be paid handsomely and treated like royalty: "I've given up on them, because I always wind up with six or seven horn players on the front line. Man, there is no musician on earth who can play anything meaningful when that many guys are lining up to solo. If they miss me, maybe they'll ask me back to play with the guys I *choose* to play with. Otherwise just leave me alone."

In response to a question about whether the great musicians he admired as a kid turned out to be the way he thought they would be: "You mean as people? Oh, I'm afraid not. It used to drive me crazy, because when you hear someone play very deliciously, you like to imagine that they're nice people. But they went to the bathroom just like you and I do. They were disappointed, they were frustrated, they were crazy. Certain guys, like Buck Clayton, were very nice. Lester [Young] was very nice. But not to mention any names, a lot of those cats were human beings with scars, some of whom had experienced horrors and didn't really like anybody.

"These days, if I hear someone I think is a good musician and he also turns out to be a groovy person—hey, it's a pleasant surprise."

(JUNE 1989)

Tristanoitis

In 1978 when I agreed to host a once-a-week radio program of out-of-print jazz, I resolved never to mention matrix numbers or mint prices, for fear of sounding like your typical white collector broadcasting from his musty basement. Instead, as though to prove that some of us store books down there, too, I equated recorded music with "the audible past" (apologies to Henry James), and promised nothing less than a parallel history of jazz restricted to what was on the auction lists and in the cut-out bins.

For my pilot broadcast, I chose the pianist Lennie Tristano as an example of how a musician could be peripheral but major (this was a few months before his death, when nothing by him was in print). Tristano was the first jazz performer to owe his reputation to cult propaganda. As late as 1959—the year of *Kind of Blue*, *Giant Steps*, and Ornette Coleman at the Five Spot—Tristano's advocates, including the editors of *Metronome*, continued to point to his work of the late forties as the next step for jazz after Charlie Parker. (They had very little new Tristano to point to, because he rarely recorded or accepted night-club engagements after 1950 or so.) Even now some hail

Tristano as the father of free jazz on the flimsy evidence of his "Intuition," a from-scratch improvisation recorded at the end of his session for Capitol, in 1949. But with the saxophonists Warne Marsh and Lee Konitz forgoing vibrato and the drummer Denzil Best sitting out at Tristano's request, "Intuition" sounds like chamber bop, not free.

By the same token, Tristano was odd man out among the boppers, even though he shared their predilection for the higher intervals of standard chord progressions. Try to imagine how bop might have evolved if its rhythms and dynamics had failed to keep pace with its harmony (or, maybe another way of putting it, if all of its leading figures had been white), and you've pretty much described the music on *Live at Birdland 1949* (Jazz), a posthumous release finally available on CD, featuring Tristano with the guitarist Billy Bauer and Marsh (but not Konitz).

But historical linkage is just one way to approach *Birdland*, and not necessarily the most astute. Wiser to savor this music for its undated virtues, which include restless melodic invention, a healthy disregard for bar lines, rigorous and frequently surprising piano-sax-and-guitar counterpoint (in lieu of the expected fours after the solos on "Lennie's Pennies," for example), and the unlikely but seductive combination of rectitude and abandon that made Tristano a genre unto himself. As a bonus, the disc offers what I believe were Tristano's earliest recordings: four rifling piano solos from 1945, as tightly packed with chords and (one suspects) as tactile in orientation as those of that other blind pianist, Art Tatum.

Tristano's legacy amounts to more than his recordings. Insofar as he was the first to teach improvisation rather than harmonic theory or instrumental mechanics, he practically invented jazz pedagogy. To jazz as Stanislavsky was to theater, he insisted that his pupils be able to sing—not just play—recorded solos by Parker, Lester Young, Roy Eldridge, Charlie Christian, and other canonical figures. Advanced students were urged to read *War and Peace* and enter psychoanalysis, preferably with Tristano's brother, a practicing Freudian.

Bud Freeman, Phil Woods, Bill Russo, Sheila Jordan, Bob Wilber, and Marian McPartland were among those who regarded Tristano as a teacher, not as a guru. But most of his students became devout Tristanoites and, in so doing, contacted Tristanoitis, a chronic ailment whose symptoms include burrowing introspection, a seeming preference for practice over performance, and a disinclination to mix with musicians outside the fold. Only Konitz ever successfully licked it; only he refused to swallow the Kool Aid. You have to be well versed in the Tristano aesthetic to have even heard of Sal Mosca, which might explain why the shouts and whistles that follow each of his piano solos on *A Concert* (Jazz)—recorded in 1979 at an undisclosed location, but just now released—sound more like those of a support group than of a typical jazz audience. Nearly Tristano's equal at conducting rounds of Name That Chord Change (a basic tenet of Tristanoism is that a few tunes are all you need to know, so long as you know them well enough to realize that their harmonic possibilities are endless), Mosca frequently gives the game away with his titles: "All of It" is "Body and Soul," for example, though don't ask me to explain the logic behind "Murph" ("I Cover the Waterfront") and "Fantacid" ("Over the Rainbow"). What finally matters is that Mosca, much like Tristano, manages to keep you in suspense with his right-hand spin and his left-hand rumble long after you've unraveled his sources. He's the sort of self-reliant, two-handed pianist who might win adulation at a club like Bradley's or on NPR with Marian McPartland, if not for his dogged, partly self-imposed obscurity.

Though few black musicians studied with Tristano, his last wave of initiates included a good number of women, the most visible of whom have been the pianists Connie Crothers and Liz Gorrill. On *A Jazz Duet* (New Artists), Gorrill teams up with tenor saxophonist Charley Krachy (another Tristanoite, to judge from his clear, thin, Marshlike intonation) for four brief free improvisations and six lengthier interpretations of Tristano-favored standards, including a slowed-down, partially eclipsed "How High the Moon." Whereas Mosca's album sounds as though it could have been recorded anytime between 1949 and yesterday (that's part of its charm), Gorrill slamdances between registers with such aplomb that her duets with Krachy occasionally remind you not only of Tristano and Marsh, but of Cecil Taylor and Jimmy Lyons. In other words, *A Jazz Duet* summons up memories of piano-and-saxophone duets you only *think* you've heard—testimony to its power, if not to its originality. The only drawback is the fuzzy recording quality.

Crother's *Concert at Cooper Union* (New Artists), a CD reissue of a 1984 LP on which she drags tempos and pounds too hard on her bass notes, fails to showcase her properly. The album that does is *New York Night* on the same label. Recorded at the Blue Note in 1989, it features the quartet that Crothers co-leads with Lennie Popkin, another Marsh-out-of-Lester Young tenorist who sounds like he's also paid close attention to Charlie Rouse's sides with Thelonious Monk. The bassist is Cameron Brown, the unsung hero of the George Adams-Don Pullen Quartet, whose percussive attack on "Lennie Bird" ("How High the Moon" again) spares Carol Tristano, the drummer, from having to keep strict time. Given Lennie's phobia of assertive percussionists, it's quite a jolt to hear his own daughter booming accents so freely behind Crothers—though not so freely as to compete with the pianist's thick clusters, resounding bottom notes, and artful, drummerlike (which is to say, Tristanolike) comp.

The Tristanoites have ruled their own little turf uncontested for so long now that it's anybody's guess whether they'll be flattered or irritated by *Eight (+3) Tristano Compositions* (Hat Musics) by Anthony Braxton, the only black avant-gardist (at least to my knowledge) to claim Tristano as a direct influence. (The "+3" is for two undisguised standards and "Sax of a Kind" by Marsh, to whom the album is dedicated.) Braxton's Tristano resembles stuntwork, much like his Monk album of a few years ago, or his bop albums on Magenta and SteepleChase. Though he obviously enjoys playing changes every once in a while, he just isn't very good at it. He also fails to recognize that the Tristano legacy has less to do with a body of tunes than with an *approach* to whatever tune is at hand. Hearing Braxton, Tristano might have advised him not to be so notey, not to arpeggiate so much, and to just *relax*, for Christsakes.

The tracks that succeed do so in direct proportion to the liberties they take: most notably, Braxton's pointillistic reflection on "Sax of a Kind," which carries Tristano's obsession with counterpoint to lovely extremes. (The piece is based on "Fine and Dandy," though you'd never guess it from this interpretation.) Cecil McBee and Andrew Cyrille move things along with characteristic alacrity, despite being miscast in this setting, and the pianist Dred Scott (not a pseudonym, but the actual name of a former Braxton student) and the baritone saxophonist Jon Raskin (anchorman in the Braxton-inspired ROVA Saxophone Quartet) turn in idiomatically confident, tick-free solos.

Immune to Tristanoitis by lack of direct contact with the germ, Braxton is prolific. This means not to worry if his latest album fails to please: another two or three will be in the stores in a few months. Two other current releases feature duets and are more typical of his work. On *Kol Nidre* (Sound Aspects), he and ROVA dropout Andrew Voight spend too much time playing Pete and Repeat on their high reeds. But on Voight's title composition, they create an effectively eerie Walpurgis-night mood, switching to bass and tenor saxophones, respectively.

On *Duets: Vancouver 1989* (Music & Arts), Braxton and the pianist Marilyn Crispell make improvised Webern out of four of Braxton's diagrammatic compositions. In the process Crispell demonstrates her ability to animate even Braxton's most static lines, and Braxton himself exhibits reed techniques that are remarkable for their harmonic complexity, if deficient in what's usually called swing. Despite his AACM credentials and his influence on ROVA, Crispell, George Lewis, and Anthony Davis, Braxton seems as at odds with his contemporaries as Tristano did with his. Like Tristano, he's both peripheral and major, but *Eight (+3) Tristano Compositions* suggests they have absolutely nothing else in common.

(JUNE 1991)

Anthony Braxton, All American

Wait until I turn this down," Anthony Braxton said from his home in New Haven, explaining that he almost hadn't heard the phone. Wide awake despite the early hour, the saxophonist and composer was auditioning tapes made by his quartet during a European tour that had ended just the day before. For the next hour or so there were no distractions, except for once when Braxton's cordless phone went dead, necessitating a call back, and once when he excused himself to scold his barking dog.

The only interview subject more frustrating than one who says nothing is one who talks at length but says nothing you can comprehend. Braxton—an American maverick in the tradition of Charles Ives, Sun Ra, Ornette Coleman, John Cage, Harry Partch, Moondog, Lennie Tristano, and Thelonious Monk—speaks his own language verbally as well as musically.

"At this point in time, when I now talk of the work that I

have been involved in for the last twenty-five years, I no longer talk about solos or compositions as much as my attempts to build a tripartial perceptual platform that will seek to demonstrate the restructural implications of postnuclear architecture, philosophy, and ritual and ceremonial particulars . . . ," he began in response to a question about his teaching activities at Wesleyan University (more specifically, how his pedagogical methods compared to those of Tristano, a Braxton favorite, who also emphasized a holistic approach to music, though teaching privately rather than at a university).

Later Braxton expanded on "high-register formings," "target-register logics," and "repetitive sound stages," among other things. In other words, his conversation is as obfuscatory as his composition titles, which typically consist of mathematical equations, geometric drawings, numerological symbols, chess moves, and friends' initials (as opposed to impressionistic titles like "Lonely Woman" or winking musicological titles like "Take Five").

Viewed sympathetically, though, the shapes and squiggles in Braxton's titles really do mirror the oblique attack and rhythmic angularity of his music, which blurs composition and improvisation with results as emotionally riveting as they are intellectually stimulating. As for his pidgin academese . . . well, like *The Tri-axium Writings*, his three self-published journals, it reflects his position as "a professional student of music" for whom the crucial step is codifying what he learns.

Fortunately, in talking about the nuts and bolts of everyday life, Braxton was not only lucid but witty. "My eldest son, Tyondai, is twelve now," he said as though it was clear what trouble might be in store for him and his wife, Nickie. "Our daughter, Keayra, is ten, and Donari, our other son, is eight. We're going to have at least one teenager in the house for the next twelve years. We should be stocking up on tranquilizers, huh?"

Born and raised on Chicago's South Side, in what even then

was one of the nation's most hopeless ghettos, Braxton is what used to be called "self-made," back when the phrase signified intellectual attainment, not merely the accumulation of wealth. Despite what you might assume, he wasn't a high school brainiac. "I cut class and read a lot on my own," Braxton explained. "I became a Dostoevsky man. *Notes from the Underground.* There was somebody I felt I could trust."

As a teenager, he also found the music of Ornette Coleman and John Coltrane on his own, along with that of John Cage and twentieth-century European composers such as Karlheinz Stockhausen. But his first musical idol was the late Paul Desmond, the alto saxophonist in the Dave Brubeck Quartet, whom he emulated to the point of wearing "rims just like Paul's" before he actually needed glasses.

In 1967, after three years in the Army and a brief stay at Roosevelt University in Chicago, Braxton joined the Association for the Advancement of Creative Musicians, a Chicago-based collective whose rallying cry ultimately became "Great Black Music, Ancient to the Future," a phrase that created false expectations in Braxton's case.

As different as Braxton's music is from Wynton Marsalis's, they have at least one thing in common: opposition to the common perception of black music as strictly intuitive, never intellectual—what Braxton has called "the mystique of the sweating brow." "It's been difficult for me from the very beginning," he said. "Here I was, an African-American man, saying 'I love Coltrane and Ornette, but I also love Stockhausen and Arnold Schoenberg,' whose music was assumed to be alien to my experience as a human being. I was a black saxophonist who acknowledged the influence of white saxophonists like Paul Desmond and Warne Marsh, which was difficult for black and even some white musicians to accept."

Under contract to Arista Records from 1974 to 1981, Braxton was, for much of that time, the only "jazz" avant-gardist to enjoy major-label backing, a situation that failed to win him a larger audience but resulted in the sort of critical backlash directed against musicians who achieve high commercial visibility. Since then, as before, he has recorded prolifically for a variety of game but financially restricted European labels. For the most part, these European releases have documented his works for unaccompanied saxophone, his duos and quartets, and his reinterpretations of Monk, Tristano, and jazz standards—not his music for large ensembles.

"When I look back on it now," he said about his Arista years, "I'm grateful that I was able to document a good cross-section of my music, even including a piece for four orchestras and another for two pianos, each of which the company probably pressed only five hundred copies of. I've had enough success that I can't complain as much as I might like to complain."

To use his own terminology, Braxton is a "restructuralist" (an explorer like Monk or Sun Ra) rather than a "stylist" (like his beloved Paul Desmond, for example) or a "traditionalist" (like the New Orleans revivalists of the late 1940s or the young neoboppers currently being pushed by the major labels). "You remember in the 1960s when everybody in jazz was talking about freedom? I was never into that. I was never interested in improvisation with no forethought. But now, ninety percent of those guys are playing bebop again, because of the marketplace, and a guy like myself is thought of as maybe irrelevant."

Braxton's involvement in academia—at Wesleyan since last fall, and before that at Mills College in northern California, where he was appointed to the faculty in 1985—has enabled him to survive without compromising his ideals. "Around ten years ago, I found myself on the edge of an abyss, with my family sinking into deep poverty," he recalled. "Now I have health insurance for my children and for myself for the first time in my life. Life is changing for Nickie and me. It feels like we've reached the end of a long tunnel.

"It's been beautiful in the sense that it isn't too different from what I would be doing anyway," he said of the scholastic life. "I've reached a point in my life where I want to go back and study the Bible, Plato, and Aristotle, the early writings of the Egyptians. I need to better understand science to properly integrate my musical system. There's just so much to learn."

One final question: Is Braxton, as rumored, a Trekie?

Braxton, who last fall was spotted marching with the band between halves of Wesleyan's football games, laughed heartily before answering. "Anyone who's serious about creativity has to follow the adventures of Captain Kirk on the starship Enterprise," he said. "I love science fiction, and in the case of *Star Trek* ... well, I did grow up in America, after all."

(JUNE 1991)

Color, Rhythm, Design

The composer and pianist Muhal Richard Abrams on the current proliferation of young jazz musicians reworking old swing and bebop grooves: "If you're not oriented toward innovation, then by all means keep the flame! That's important work. But the tradition also calls for change, for renewal, for innovation. In the beginning, jazz was an abstract process. It wasn't any particular style yet. It sounded like whatever the musicians wanted it to sound like. It stood for the freedom to experiment, the excitement of things never quite coming out the same."

Despite a few such eloquent outbursts, Abrams was for the most part unforthcoming during our interview. Not that

I hadn't been warned. "In the years I've known Muhal, I've heard him talk what for him amounted to a blue streak only once," a poet friend of his had told me. "And that was about what he called 'cosmic matters,' not about his music or about himself personally." For years, Abrams turned down most interview requests, distrustful of jazz critics as a breed (as many musicians tend to be), but perhaps also uncomfortable with the idea of talking about music, instead of making it. Sitting on the sofa in his apartment in Manhattan Plaza, a complex a few blocks west of Times Square, he impressed me as someone used to spending most of his waking hours in musicland, in the company of others similarly preoccupied with isorhythms and augmented ninths.

I asked him if, like some musicians, he composed only when a concert was near, or if—as I guessed—he found himself constantly jotting down music. "The fact is I'm always *studying*," he said, fingering his tidy gray-flecked chin whiskers and pointing to the sheet music neatly stacked in piles atop the coffee table and piano. "Practice, you play. Study, you write. Fragments of things, all of the time."

"That's the delightful thing about Muhal," Marty Ehrlich, a saxophonist in the eighteen-piece orchestra on *The Hearinga Suite* (Black Saint), Abrams's thrilling new release. "He probably knows as much as it's possible for one man to know about music, but he thinks of himself as the perpetual student."

At sixty, Abrams isn't very well known to casual jazz fans, much less to the general public. But among the cognoscenti, he is as venerated as any living composer. In 1989, for example, an international jury selected him as the first recipient of the Jazzpaar Prize, a lifetime achievement award likened to the Nobel in literature by its sponsor, a Danish jazz federation. (In addition to the prestige, the prize, which will be given annually to a musician in the prime of his career, brought Abrams $30,000 and a commission.)

There used to be a simple way to determine who the most

important jazz composers were: those whose tunes caught on with fellow musicians. But that was before "tunes" were supplanted, in the more abstract realms of jazz, by compositions reckoned to be too idiosyncratic for easy transfer to other bands. Says Ehrlich about Abrams's scores, "[They're] very difficult to play, because he doesn't use the harmonic and rhythmic patterns that have become standard for jazz. His music demands of you a broad knowledge not only of jazz practically from its beginnings, but also of European classical music."

To my knowledge, no other bandleader has ever rerecorded one of Abrams's pieces. For that matter, Abrams told me that he doesn't like to perform his own pieces more than once if he can possibly avoid it; he'd rather move on to something else. "Maybe if I have a concert with a large ensemble and no time to prepare music," he said. "But I try to organize my time so that doesn't happen."

As a consequence, none of Abrams's compositions has achieved the status of a jazz standard. (By contrast, Duke Ellington, although continuing to write new material even on his deathbed, reprised two dozen or so songs over several decades.) But Abrams's influence has manifested itself in other ways, beginning, in 1965, with his role as a founding member of, guru to, and first among equals in the Association for the Advancement of Creative Musicians (AACM), in his hometown of Chicago. Still active there although most of its charter members have scattered far and wide, the AACM fostered Anthony Braxton and Henry Threadgill, and spawned the Art Ensemble of Chicago. It set the agenda for the international jazz avant-garde throughout the 1970s and eighties by embracing the influence of Africa on the one hand and Stockhausen and Cage on the other. Even now its membership consists largely of musicians who have come under Abrams's tutelage, either privately or in the AACM's South Side music school.

Abrams balks at the notion that he himself represents a "school" of jazz. "A lot has been written about me as a kind of teacher," he complained. "But I've always been a musician first, and a teacher only incidentally. It just so happened that I met some musicians younger than myself, who I may have been an example for—*set* an example for some of them—in terms of showing them the importance of proceeding in your own direction."

After years of backing such musicians as Dexter Gordon, Max Roach, and Sonny Stitt during their Chicago engagements, Abrams made his recording debut in 1957, playing piano and writing most of the material on an Argo LP called *Daddy-o Presents the MJT+3* (good luck trying to find it). But the early music that everyone agrees forecast most accurately the shape of things to come happened out of public earshot: the Experimental Band, a rehearsal group that Abrams led in the early 1960s, and that planted the seeds for the AACM, not only never recorded, but never actually played a gig.

Abrams remained somewhat phantasmagoric even after his recording career gained momentum in the AACM's wake. A working knowledge of ragtime, stride, and boogie woogie underlay even his most pointillistic piano solos, and his efforts with small groups ranged from post–Schoenberg chill to lava-hot free improvisations and hard bop. But this wide compass didn't necessarily make him sound protean—sometimes just diffuse. He was assumed to be a major figure because his disciples said he was, and you had to wonder if they were confusing genius with inspired pedagogy.

It wasn't until Abrams began to record with larger ensembles, in 1981, that he was able to integrate all of his separate parts. The breakthrough album was *Blues Forever* (Black Saint), whose wailing title track amounted to a virtual panorama of blues and big band history. *The Hearinga Suite* (Black Saint) also includes a blues, though one designed not to jump out at you, but to rope you in. "Oldfotalk" (try saying it aloud, with a Southern accent) opens with a unaccompanied, speech-inflected, Louis Armstronglike (but with modern rhythmic values)

trumpet blast by Jack Walrath and fades on a dreamy, contrapuntal soprano saxophone and cello duet by John Purcell and
Deidre Murray. The piece succeeds in inducing nostalgia for a
mythic rural past without trying to imitate the exact rhythms
of the rocking chair on the front porch; Cecil Bridgewater's
speedy trumpet solo, which occurs midway through and is
backed by roaring trombones and saxophones, reveals the
piece's tough-minded core.

"Oldfotalk" is a breathtaking piece of music, interpreted
with such a command of nuance that you know what's coming
over your speakers is what Abrams heard in his head. It's just
one of the album's treasures. An African-style painting by
Abrams graces the album jacket. "I go to museums and look at
paintings and read what the artists had to say about color,
rhythm, design," he told me. "When I'm composing music, and
especially when I'm orchestrating a piece, I fasten on colors."
"Hearinga," the suite's opening movement, demonstrates
Abrams's genius for tone coloration, with a looping, circuslike
theme voiced first by synthesizer, drums, and glockenspiel (talk
about unusual instrumental combinations), then recapitulated
by trumpet and alto saxophone. "Finditnow" rivals Charles
Mingus's compositions for wild mood swings, typified by the
contrast between Murray's poised cello coda and the bolting
exchanges among Ehrlich, the saxophonists Charles Davis and
Patience Higgins, and the trombonists Dick Griffin and Clifton
Anderson. And "Bermix," a sumptuous if angular ballad given
emotional pitch by Courtnay Wynter's dark tenor saxophone
ruminations and Purcell's keening lead alto saxophone lines,
recalls DeFalla, Ellington, and Gil Evans, and stays with you
long after it's over.

The Hearinga Suite isn't *The Compleat Muhal Richard Abrams.*
The shapely chorus he plays on "Seesall" hardly satisfies the
craving for his piano, nor does "Conversations with the Three
of Me," a solo piano-and-synthesizer exercise that, whatever its
other virtues, sounds out of place amid the works for full

orchestra. (Abrams's best showcases as a pianist are two albums of duets with bassists: *Sightsong*, from 1976, with Malachi Favors, on Black Saint; and *Roots of Blue*, from 1986, with Cecil McBee, on RPR Records.) Despite a pleasing, swarming finish, a track called "Aura of Thought—Things" fails to show what Abrams is capable of in the area of "scored" improvisation. And the album offers no example of his demystifying use of classically trained voices (listen to "The Heart Is Love and 'I Am'" with the soprano Janette Moody, on the 1983 Black Saint album *Rejoicing with the Light*). But as the result of three decades of relentless experimentation, *The Hearinga Suite* is a superlative introduction to the work of an American master dedicated to making it new.

(FEBRUARY 1991)

Well-Tempered

Dave Burrell is doing fine, thank you. As pianist and music director for several of the tenor saxophonist David Murray's small bands, Burrell is busier now, at the age of fifty, than at any other time in his career, which dates back to the stormy era of free jazz, in the 1960s. Things are fine on the home front, too, as he and his wife, the poet Monika Larsson, put the finishing touches on *Windward Passages*, the jazz opera they began soon after their marriage in 1978. The couple moved to Philadelphia in September 1985, after two years in Larsson's native Sweden workshopping the opera at the University of Gothenburg. Pre-

viously they had lived in New York. While they were away, the
Philadelphia-based saxophonist Byard Lancaster, a classmate of
Burrell's at the Berklee School of Music in Boston in the early
sixties, wrote in a letter that rents in Manhattan had at least
doubled during their absence. They probably wouldn't be able
to continue living there on their return to the U.S., Lancaster
warned. So why not try Philadelphia? Burrell and Larsson initially rented a coach house in an integrated neighborhood in
West Philadelphia, moving in on the afternoon of Hurricane
Gloria. The weather proved to be an omen. The block was
crack infested, says Larsson, who found the talk of "guns and
blood and murder" that she overheard from teenagers on the
street showing up in her poetry. "Dave took one look at what I
was writing and said, 'Monika, I think it's time for us to move.'"
They eventually settled into their current apartment not far
from the University of Pennsylvania, where they like the used-
bookstores and ethnic restaurants, and where Larsson feels safe
when Burrell is on tour in Europe, as he has been much of the
time since joining Murray in 1987.

Just back from Paris, Burrell is sitting in the spacious living
room, having coffee with me and Monika, and explaining how
he and Murray hooked up.

"In the late seventies, when I still lived in New York, I used
to spend a lot of time in Soho, at a loft owned by Roberta Garrison, the dancer, who was Jimmy Garrison's widow. This
became the place for the new guys in town to meet the relative
oldtimers, like myself. David and James Newton were just in
from California, and there were articles in all the papers about
how they and the guys from Chicago, like Chico Freeman and
the three guys in Air, had the right approach, as opposed to
people like us who had been in New York since the sixties."

The crowd from Slug's, in other words, many of whom had
lived at 77 East Third, before the building became the unofficial East Coast headquarters of the Hell's Angels, who, with
the super's cooperation, turned the basement into a Quaalude

factory and pushed Burrell's piano through the eighth-floor window while he was on the road with Archie Shepp.

Ah, the sixties. But that's another story. Back to the Murray connection.

"Well, you see, many of us weren't too happy about being invaded by these new guys who we felt were stealing work from us. So there was usually a little bit of hostility in the air at Roberta's dinners. But there was also this other, friendlier vibe: of feeling that we were all in this together and wondering what people from other parts of the country had been up to. One night, after dinner, David said to everybody, 'Let's do 'Naima,' and we did—me, him, Chico, Grachan Moncur, Eddie Jefferson, and I don't remember who else.

"I was busy with Archie Shepp back then, but the experience of playing with David stuck with me. And Sunny Murray used to bring both him and me to Philly whenever he had a job there. So we got used to playing together, although I didn't begin to work with him steadily until 1987, when I called him up and suggested doing something together and for a minute, I think, he had me mixed up with Stanley Cowell.

"David's very lucky in business. He works more than anybody I know. Just being in some of his groups, I'm working more now than I ever did being with Archie Shepp full-time. I'm music director for David's octet, and the piano player in one of his quartets, the one with Wilber Morris on bass and Tani Tabal on drums. Plus the cooperative groups, like the Lucky Four and the Last of the Hip Men, when he's offered a record date as a leader that he can't do under his own name because of contractual obligations.

Plus the duets, as documented on 1989's *Daybreak* (Gazell), whose title ballad, written by Burrell, is as beautiful a piece of music based on a series of minor-to-major chords as you're ever likely to hear, saved from mere prettiness by Burrell's bass-clef hammering and Murray's falsetto decimation of the theme toward the end. Remarkably, *Daybreak* was just Burrell's second album as a leader for a U.S. label (eleven others have been released in Europe and Japan). But he was back in the studio in May to record an album of Jelly Roll Morton compositions at the suggestion of Gazell's Sam Charters, the noted jazz and blues historian whose books include a fictional biography of Morton.

The exposure with Murray hasn't made Burrell a "star" (are there jazz stars anymore?), but it's focused attention on him as an overlooked veteran of an era in which pianists were easy to overlook.

In the early seventies a friend of mine heard Shepp's band at a club in Philadelphia and told me that Burrell sounded great. Then, after giving it some thought, he qualified his statement: "He *looked* like he sounded great, if you know what I mean."

I did. Volume was just part of the problem, though. When Burrell arrived in New York after his graduation from Berklee in 1965, piano was becoming identified as the enemy—European hegemony in a pop-up box. Unless played by Cecil Taylor (McCoy Tyner was by then laying out much of the time behind Coltrane), the instrument was considered too well tempered to hold its own against the era's smashing drums and screaming horns.

Against such odds, Burrell quietly went about the business of forging a personal style from the demands made on him by the different leaders he played for. "Pharoah [Sanders] wanted a drone," recalls Burrell, who gives the impression of being pretty well tempered himself. Bald on top but still lanky at fifty, he wears glasses, speaks in an inflectionless baritone, and fits the stereotype of the university professor, though his formal teaching experience has been limited to residencies here and there and two years at Queens College in New York under an antipoverty program in the '70s. "That prayerlike, harp kind of thing that Alice Coltrane did behind him and Trane in Trane's band after McCoy left. But Marion Brown favored more of an Ornette Coleman approach. He didn't want the piano to play the chords. He wanted it to play a one-note unison with the horns on the heads of his tunes, and the heads were complicated and tricky."

More than a decade before Henry Threadgill made it hip to dig Scott Joplin, Burrell wrote a rag for his 1968 debut album, which also included a medley of tunes from *West Side Story*. A year later, for BYG, in the aftermath of the Pan-African Festival no less, he reworked material from Puccini's *La Boheme*. Given such evidence, Burrell has long enjoyed a reputation as a "song" man within the jazz avant-garde. So it was surprising to hear him say that he didn't know very many jazz or pop standards before joining Shepp in 1969, at the tail end of what Burrell describes as the tenor saxophonist's "angry period, when he was glaring at the front row of the audience, which stared back at him in wonder at his Charlie Parker-inspired wardrobe, and playing so hard and fast and long that there would be a pool of sweat in front of him and his fingers would sometimes bleed.

"But he was also playing a lot of Ellington, and he told me I had to master the standard repertoire. That area of my development had been stunted, because I had never been in a band where the pianist was expected to know how to make a nice intro to a ballad. Archie was a very good pianist himself, and he would show me the chord movements. He and [the trombonist] Roswell Rudd would tell me that if I was going to play with them, I had to know 'Sophisticated Lady' and 'Prelude to a Kiss,' and so on. I said 'OK, I want to play those songs, but I also want to play those Ornetteish, postbop one-note unisons. I want to play the vamps that Pharoah and Coltrane used.' Coltrane was my idol, and I wanted to scream on piano like the horns were doing, but I wanted structure and beauty along with the scream."

Another surprise: before accepting Charters's invitation, Burrell had no working knowledge of Jelly Roll Morton, even though his own pieces tend, like Morton's, to be multithematic, with what sound like conscious allusions to earlier styles of jazz.

(His solos likewise bracket frolicsome ragtime or stride episodes with pinging dissonance and blood-on-the-keys assaults.)

"It's been an education," Burrell says, offering for inspection a book of Morton transcriptions by James Dapgony. "When I bought this in New York, the music looked difficult and probably boring. Well, it *is* difficult, but not at all boring. I just told Sam that if I'm going to do this right, I have to learn all of Jelly Roll Morton's work, not just the pieces I'm going to record. That's the essence of jazz piano right there, in the work of that one composer.

"I remember a time in the early seventies when I was booked in advance every weekend, usually just playing for transportation money and a share of the door, but glad to be working. But now I don't have time to take most of the jobs I'm offered, what with being on the road with David, learning Jelly Roll Morton, and working on the opera with Monika."

The opera. In talking about it, Burrell and Larsson tend to finish each other's sentences. *Windward Passages* is set in Hawaii, where Burrell, who was born in Middletown, Ohio, grew up, moving there with his parents when he was five (Burrell's father, an early race man, who still lives in Kailua, taught sociology at the University of Hawaii, in Honolulu).

At a loss for words after admitting that the opera is "semiautobiographical," Burrell asks his wife, who wrote both the book and the libretto, if she can explain it.

"It's about the coming of age of a young black man at the same time that Hawaii matured into statehood, in 1959," explained Larsson, who was living in Honolulu with her first husband, a scientist at the University of Hawaii, when she met Burrell in 1974. "It was a very traumatic experience for Dave and his friends. They had a little musical group at that time, which played at the statehood celebration, although their hearts were not in it, because the land developers who moved in [in anticipation of statehood] had changed their way of life. In Hawaii today, when there's a hurricane, the homes of the indigenous people, who were forced out of the valleys and the plateaus and are very, very poor, are the only homes that get hit. Meanwhile, Waikiki is one of the biggest tourist traps in the world."

An opera co-written by an African-American and a naturalized Swede about the plight of Polynesians and Samoans, *Windward Passages* has multicultural written all over it, which should mean that somebody will eventually stage it. Thus far portions of it have been sung by choirs in Philadelphia and Europe, and Burrell has recorded instrumental versions of most of its movements on his own albums and those with Murray. But Murray has been talking it up to potential backers on his travels, and there have even been feelers from the Metropolitan Opera.

"Hilda Harris, the great mezzo-soprano, was one of the first people to encourage us," Larsson explains. "We wrote the role of Sarah, the boy's mother, for her. Not just her voice, but her looks, her entire manner. When we had only the first act written, she and her husband, who is a concert promoter, put us in touch with Maestro [James] Levine of the Met, whose only concern was 'Is it a grand opera? Will it fill up the stage?' So Dave and I went home and wrote the second act, and it's so big that . . . "

"We put elephants in there," Burrell interrupts.

"Just about," Larsson says. "Damn near."

"A company in Atlanta said they could do it, because they could get the Atlanta Symphony for free," Burrell says. "I told them we didn't need a symphony. We needed a choir, eight principal singers, and a twenty-piece, Ellington-type orchestra with no violins. They said, 'Who's going to pay for all that? And besides, how can it be an opera without violins?' I said, 'Well, it *is* an opera . . . .'"

"It's a *grand* opera," Larsson interjects.

(OCTOBER 1991)

Burrell's Jelly Roll Morton interpretations were released as Jelly Roll Joys *(Gazell). The opera still hasn't been staged.*

"This Is Not Jazz!"

"Sitting on the beach all day," Sonny Sharrock scolded Abe Speller, one of his two drummers. "You're going to be blacker than Art Blakey if you're not more careful. On account of you, I'll have to play surf guitar tonight."

Sharrock started humming "Pipeline," as Speller laughed. This was at Tramps, a New York club. Sharrock had finished his soundcheck and was sitting in the window soundlessly strumming his Les Paul Standard when I arrived. The plan was to taxi downtown for dinner with his manager and a few friends. But first we retired to a basement dressing room to gab about the good old days.

For guys our age (Sharrock was then fifty, five years older than me), that inevitably means the 1960s. More specifically, when the guys in question are a critic and the first free-jazz guitarist, it means Slug's, the fabled (and long-defunct) Lower East Side dive that had a Robert Thompson mural and an out-of-tune upright on the bandstand, and was unofficial headquarters for what used to be called the New Black Music.

"Slug's used to be jumpin' every night, and we didn't have to pay to get in," Sharrock recalled. Less chunky than he used to be following angioplasty earlier this year, he was wearing red sneakers, jeans, a Last Exit T-shirt, and a Sonny Sharrock Band satin tour jacket—rock and roll togs. Though his sideburns had turned gray, his mustache was still black. "There was another place called the Annex, on Avenue B or C, that we used to go to first, because they had peanuts on the bar. You'd go there, look around for somebody to buy you a beer, stuff yourself with peanuts, and that would be your dinner, because none of us were making any money.

"I remember standing at the bar once, eating peanuts with

Sunny Murray. As usual a bunch of musicians were there, looking for work, looking for chicks, whatever. We heard a fire engine, so we went to the door to watch. Running behind the fire truck blowing his saxophone for all he was worth was Frank Wright. What had happened, the truck had raced by Frank's apartment while he was stoned or practicing, and he must have thought the siren was the wildest thing he ever heard. Sunny and I died laughing. But there was always something like that going on back then.

"How did it end? A lot of things happened. To begin with, Trane died, and he had been the center of what we were about. That was the first blow. Then the Lower East Side started to change, including Slug's. It got too rough for us there. A couple of guys got beat up, Lee Morgan got shot, and it was all over. Plus, guys started getting a little success and moving away. Including me. I went with Herbie [Mann], and all of a sudden I was making $250 a night after doing gigs with Pharoah [Sanders] for the door at Slug's and maybe having to split $25 five ways."

Sharrock elaborated on his days as the token howitzer—a combination Coltrane and Jimi Hendrix—with Mann, who was still playing standards, movie themes, and tepid bossa novas when Sharrock joined his band. "But I gotta tell you about Herbie Mann," Sharrock said of the bearded flutist. "He never once tried to tone my shit down, even though he maybe should have, because I was turning his music inside out and making it impossible for him to develop what he was trying to develop. I realize that now, as a bandleader myself. But Herbie's got big ears, and he's a nervy cat. He'll try anything. The audiences, though, sometimes we had a little trouble. The worst reaction we ever had was in Oshkosh, Wisconsin."

Oshkosh, Wisconsin? I thought he was going to describe the night the band played at a Florida marina and all the yachts turned sail the split second Sharrock opened fire (or so the legend goes). But I didn't interrupt.

"The promoters were a group of ladies, very nice and obviously very well off, who had rented a hall with the proceeds from the concert going to local charities. I didn't expect them to enjoy what I was doing, but they didn't seem to be enjoying Herbie's flute solos, either, like audiences usually did. After the show, they came backstage and said, 'Well, that was very nice but we wish you had played some of your Tijuana numbers.' They thought Herbie was Herb Alpert!

"The best reaction I ever got? It might not sound like the best, but the first time I went to Europe with Herbie, a guy in Berlin rushed down the aisle during my solo and started pounding on the stage, screaming 'THIS IS NOT JAZZ! THIS IS NOT JAZZ! THIS IS NOT JAZZ!' At least I reached him. What bugged me a little bit, though, was, you know, who was he to say if it was jazz or not?"

Eruptions circle around mountaintops like storm clouds, nanoseconds of echo trailing every note, notes hunching together like orgiastic sardines."

As you see, Sharrock's champions do some serious pounding, too, but on their word processors, and in ecstasy rather than rage. "The most seismic axmonster on earth," Chuck Eddy calls him in *Stairway to Hell*, a metal consumer guide, also the source of the above quote. Counting Sharrock's four albums with Bill Laswell's skronk-jam band Last Exit and his unbilled echoplex cameo on side two of Miles Davis's *Jack Johnson*, Sharrock appears no fewer than seven times on Eddy's honor roll—as many as Metallica and Guns 'N Roses combined. "This is 'jazz,' by the way," Eddy ends his capsule on Last Exit's *Iron Path*. And irony, like my twelfth-grade English teacher used to lecture us, is the difference between what is said and what is meant.

Asked if he himself considers his music to be jazz, Sharrock answers affirmatively and unequivocally—my answer, too (it sure as hell isn't fusion). But he's namechecked on a recent Sonic Youth twelve-inch, and his cult following probably includes more metalheads (cerebral metalheads like Eddy, to be sure) than Village Vanguarders, who tend either to shrink in horror from him or ignore him altogether. Like most over-the-edge guitarists, Sharrock is often stereotyped as one of Jimi Hendrix's progeny. But I recall hearing him playing more or less the way he does now as a member of the alto saxophonist Byard Lancaster's group in Philadelphia in 1966, a full year before Hendrix's *Are You Experienced?*

Circumstances conspired to make Sharrock an original. With the exceptions of England's Derek Bailey and Canada's Sonny Greenwich, neither of whom received much U.S. recognition, Sharrock was the only guitarist to play "out" in the 1960s. Independent of Hendrix, Pete Townshend, or Jimmy Page, he discovered the joys of speed, distortion, and volume on his own. Luckily for him, he hit the scene in the sixties, when anything was permissible—even a duet between a tripping tenor saxophonist and a speeding hook and ladder. Emulating saxophonists who were themselves emulating snake-pit screams, he heated up his own metal alloy. "The first thing I remember working to develop was a sound like Albert Ayler's buzz," he says. "I heard Albert and thought, 'Wait a minute. That sound can be done on guitar by playing a fast trill real loud and sustaining it.' That was the first evidence that I had my own thing—that buzzsaw trill."

Sharrock's bio reads more like an autodidactic art-rocker's than that of one of today's Berklee and Messenger-certified studious young Cosby kids with horns. The son of a grocer, he was born and raised in Ossining, New York, about thirty miles north of Manhattan (it's the site of Sing Sing state prison, but also "a typical small town with beautiful, ivy-covered houses, like Carvel in the Andy Hardy movies," according to civic booster and film buff Sharrock). He started guitar at the rather advanced age of twenty, after awakening to "the beauty of art," but dis-covering that he had no talent for painting, sculpture, or writing. Although he'd sung baritone as an adolescent with a doo-wop group called the Echoes ("Teenage Lovers' Lullaby," their only single, which was produced by Johnny Brantley, an Alan Freed associate, was shelved in the aftermath of the payola investigations), Sharrock never considered singing jazz. "Vocalists were superfluous in jazz." And guitar wasn't his ax of choice, either (he had no desire to copy Wes Montgomery, Jim Hall, or Kenny Burrell. "I liked tenor players and drummers, Coltrane and Elvin [Jones]." But his asthma ruled out a wind instrument, and he couldn't afford a trap set. "Guitar was just available."

To get started he enrolled with a local teacher who tried his patience by attempting to guide him through the Mel Bay instruction booklets page by page. "But when we were on maybe book three, still playing 'Mary Had a Little Lamb' in open position and not getting anywhere, I snuck a look at book seven, the last in the series. It said, at the very end, 'Now you are ready to begin to learn to improvise.' And I thought, 'Oh, shit, that's what I want to do now.'"

Despite his disinclination to do things by the book, he somehow wound up with the nerds at the Berklee School of Music in Boston, "twenty-sixth in a class of twenty-seven guitarists, and the only guy behind me had sense enough to drop out." After a year and a half, Sharrock followed his lead, eventually braving New York, where he ran into Sun Ra in the street one day and asked to study with him. Ra did better than give him lessons: he indirectly landed him a paying gig. Arkestra members Marshall Allen and Pat Patrick were moonlighting with Babatunde [then Michael] Olatunji, who happened to be looking for a guitarist. That gig, combined with Sharrock's friendship with former Berklee classmates Byard Lancaster and Dave Burrell, gained him entrée into the Lower East Side inner circle.

"Are you a movie-trivia buff?" Sharrock asked me in the taxi, pointing to a doorway on East 13th Street that I immediately recognized as the one from which Harvey Keitel pimps for Jodie Foster in *Taxi Driver*. I guess what most pleased me about Sharrock, as we chatted over salads and sweetrolls, was what a next-door-neighbor sort of guy he was, as opposed to the human torch his music had led me to expect.

So I was surprised by his stubborn self-confidence when he asked me, "Do any of the people you write about ever ask you what you think after you've heard them play? I can't see that. You ought to know if what you just did was any good or not without asking someone else." He's been known to tongue-lash crowds he doesn't feel are responding viscerally enough to his band. "The worst audiences, in my experience, are in Europe, where they tend to analyze every note you play. France, in particular. You look out and see hundreds of people just sitting there with their hands on their chins like Jean-Paul Sartre. My music is very hard-hitting and emotional, straight from the heart and aimed at the heart. It's nothing you should need to think about."

Twenty years ago Sharrock's youthful arrogance led him to decline an offer to audition for Miles Davis's band. "He'd heard me play on his record [*Jack Johnson*], so why did he need me to audition?" With the avant-garde in retreat, turning down Davis—a starmaker, after all—wasn't a smart career move. Sharrock drifted into obscurity following three albums featuring his first wife, Linda's, moaning blaxploitation vocals (*Black Woman*, the first and best of these, introduced the stark "Blind Willie," still Sharrock's most requested composition, based on Blind Willie Johnson's "Dark Was the Night, Cold Was the Ground"). Although he continued to gig around New York, he wasn't being recorded, "so it was as though nothing I did counted for anything." At various times, he supported himself as a record store salesman, a chauffeur, and a teacher of emotionally disturbed children. He eventually moved back to Ossining, where he lives now with his second wife, Nettie, a bank employee, and their daughter, Jasmyn, thirteen.

Enter Bill Laswell, bassist, record producer, mastermind of

the studio-only art-rockers Material, and a Sharrock fan since his teens. Laswell engineered Sharrock's "comeback" by getting him on the bill as James "Blood" Ulmer's opening act at the Public Theater in 1979, including him on Material's *Memory Serves* that same year, and inviting him to join Last Exit (with himself, Peter Brotzman, and Ronald Shannon Jackson) in 1986. Laswell has produced (or co-produced) half a dozen albums by Sharrock since then, beginning with the solo *Guitar* (a lovely bouquet of cankers and thorns) and culminating with this year's *Faith Moves* (CMP) and *Ask the Ages* (Axiom).

Faith Moves is a series of duets with fellow plectrist Nicky Skopelitis, who doubles on saz, baglama, tar, and "coral" sitar (a guitar/sitar hybrid left over from the George Harrison era). Perhaps due to Skopelitis's exotic instruments, *Faith Moves* occasionally drifts into scenic territory uncomfortably reminiscent of John Fahey and more recent New Age avatars. But Sharrock's "Uncle Herbie's Dance," reprised from his 1988 *Live in New York*, rolls vigorously along, with Skopelitis laying down a hellacious fuzztone counterpoint to Sharrock's driven lead.

Ask the Ages, which reunites Sharrock with Pharoah Sanders, with whom he made his recording debut on *Tahuid* in 1967, burns from beginning to end in a way that conjures up a sixties chitlin circuit combo despite the deliberate echoes of that era's avant-garde. The drummer is Elvin Jones, one of Sharrock's early idols, whose thunderous rolls lend authenticity to "As We Used to Sing," a seesawing modal waltz à la Coltrane. Sharrock's swollen reverb and exquisite slide-bar vibrato on "Who Does She Hope to Be?" result in balladry with sting, and although he doesn't comp behind Sanders, their unison heads and overlapping freakouts on "Promises Kept" illustrate that they share the same rapport they did twenty-five years ago, but with one important difference—Sharrock no longer sounds at a disadvantage for not playing an actual horn.

Ask the Ages is jazz, by the way (no quotation marks needed), right down to Charnett Moffett's fleet but ultimately superfluous bass solos. By contrast *Highlife* (Enemy), Sharrock's self-produced album from earlier this year featuring his working band (Dave Snider, keyboards; Charles Baldwin, bass; Abe Speller and Lance Carter, drums) is "pop" so vivacious that somebody ought to create a radio format for it. As things stand its shapely rhythms and synth-reinforced melodies might erode the small following Sharrock already claims among metalists, whose distrust of hummability gives them more in common with the typical jazz lug than they might care to admit. Generally speaking, the problem with primitives (John Lydon, for example, or even David Byrne) is that they gradually acquire just enough expertise to confirm that a little bit of knowledge really is a dangerous thing. Sharrock's technique now far surpasses just enough, but it isn't what seizes the ear upon hearing his whizzing feedback and fast-fingered sheets of sound on his hacienda ballad "No More Tears" or his lyrical-as-Aaron Copland 6/4 conversion of the folk tune "All My Trials." What does is his simplicity and directness, qualities you'd never have expected from him twenty-five years ago, but which seem in keeping with his current self-identity as an aging ex-doo-wopper who answers most questions about his current direction by saying, "I'm in my fifties now," as though that were sufficient explanation.

If *Highlife* is a persuasive argument for the advantages of maturity, so was Sharrock's set at Tramps, which was indulgence-free and included almost everything from *Highlife* (though not his swinging demystification of Sanders's "Venus/Upper Egypt," unfortunately). His hands almost touching on the neck of his guitar as he clubfooted to the just out-of-sync beat of his two drummers and sang silently with his lips and audibly on his strings, Sharrock pulled off the illusion that the electricity was within him, not in his amp.

The gig was part of a New Music Seminar showcase of mostly unsigned "baby" bands—irritating proof that music bizzers continue to stigmatize Sharrock as a career minor leaguer because of his jazz background. You wanted to bang their heads together and shout "THIS IS NOT JAZZ" even though you'd be lying.

(SEPTEMBER 1991)

Sonny Sharrock died of a heart attack while exercising in 1994, at the age of fifty-three. He had just signed with (but not yet recorded for) RCA.

White Anglo-Saxon Pythagorean

Roswell Rudd, a trombonist now in his late fifties, will, regardless of what he accomplishes or fails to in his remaining years, always be identified with the jazz avant-garde of the 1960s, so indelible was his mark on it and its on him. Last summer I heard him sing "The Beer-Barrel Polka" as a member of a show band in a Borscht Belt resort and sound as though he was having a good time doing it. It would heighten the incongruity if I could say that I walked in on this by chance. But I didn't. I was looking for Rudd, and I knew exactly where to find him, thanks to an item in *Down Beat*.

Toward the back of each issue that magazine runs a feature called "Pro Session," in which a recorded improvisation is transcribed and analyzed for the edification of those readers who are themselves musicians. The subject of "Pro Session" in December 1990 was the pianist Herbie Nichols's 1955 recording of his own "Furthermore." The transcription and analysis were supplied by Rudd, who was identified as "a trombonist currently working in the Catskill Mountains at the Granit Hotel [in] Kerhonkson, N.Y.":

> He has recorded with Archie Shepp, Carla Bley, Gato Barbieri, Charlie Haden, and John Tchicai, and his recording, *Regeneration* (Soul Note)[,] with Steve Lacy and Han Bennink, included a number of Nichols' compositions.

No mention of Rudd's having thrice been voted best trombonist in the magazine's own International Jazz Critics Poll (in 1975, 1978, and 1979), or of his having finished no worse than seventh as recently as 1987, strictly on reputation (his last New York concert had been in 1983, and he hadn't been featured on a new jazz release since his appearance on one track of *That's the Way I Feel Now*, the auteur record producer Hal Wilner's 1984 double album of novel Thelonious Monk interpretations). Nor was there any hint of how long Rudd had been in the Catskills—the last I'd heard, he was teaching in Augusta, Maine, at a branch of the state university—or of what on earth he was doing there.

Much of the romance of jazz improvisation is in its evanescence, and as if in keeping with this quality, jazz musicians themselves tend to disappear. Years ago when a musician vanished from the scene, it was usually for one of two reasons: drugs, or steady work either making TV-ad soundtracks ("jingles") in the recording studio or playing in the orchestras for films or Broadway shows, depending on which coast the person in question called home. Today when someone goes a few years between records or concerts, it's assumed that he's grown weary of improvising an income for himself and his dependents and has accepted a university teaching position or taken a day job. Or that he's become homeless.

But few musicians ever disappear completely or put away their horns for good, even after learning the hard way that there's very little chance for a big payoff in jazz. Pop musicians and their fans are often puzzled by this, for the same reason that screenwriters—even unproduced screenwriters—are puzzled by novelists, and even more so by poets (at least a novel is of some potential value as a "property"). Publication is almost anticlimactic for most poets. They just *write*. It's the same with most jazz musicians. Jazz isn't just a craft; it's a calling, and one that they can never completely stop heeding.

What about those of us who merely listen to jazz? Like serial monogamists, most of us find ourselves drawn to a certain type. Mine seems to be the Missing Person—the great player who drops out of sight. Browsing in record stores these days, or listening to many of the bland new releases sent to me to review, I feel as many voters say they do when forced to choose between equally unqualified candidates: there must be something better than this. That's when I begin to think of musicians like Roswell Rudd, unforgettable but apparently forgotten, and wonder what on earth has become of them.

It was sticky even in the mountains on the Saturday afternoon last summer that my girlfriend and I drove to Kerhonkson, about twenty miles south of Woodstock. When we pulled into the parking lot of the Granit Hotel and Country Club, at around three o'clock in the afternoon, a band we later found out was the Sherri Orchestra—*not* the band with Rudd—was playing "Tea for Two" as a cha-cha next to the outdoor swimming pool. This was my first time in the Catskills, and I felt terribly out of place, despite having been briefed on Borscht Belt dos and don'ts by my companion, a Brooklyn native who had summered here with her parents when the Catskills were really something (what she meant was, before her parents and a massive number of Jews of their generation retired to Florida, for summer all year round). My alienation wasn't entirely due to my not being Jewish (the activities sheet we picked up in the lobby on checking in listed bocci, and where there's bocci there must be Italians), nor to my companion and I being among a

distinct minority of guests under retirement age. The problem
was my aversion to group activities and my bewilderment at
other people's enthusiasm for them. Fortunately for me, participation in the Granit's daily shuffleboard tournament was
optional, as it was in the basketball free throw contest, the iso-
metric exercises with Sam, the financial seminar with George
Kimmel, the class in skin care and "hi" fashion with Miss Jeri of
Estelle Durant Cosmetics, and the open discussion (presumably
on the day's burning issues) with Trudy Berlin. By virtue of our
late arrival we'd missed all of these events anyway. But if we
hurried, we could still compete in the daily Ping-Pong tournament, take a lesson in ballroom dancing from the Tiktins, and
mingle at the happy hour in the Mystic Lounge (to the music
of somebody calling himself Ralph Mellow).

Such an industrious approach to leisure struck me as Protes-
tant, not Jewish. But my companion said that the old adage
about the devil finding work for idle hands had nothing to do
with it. Keeping yourself occupied from morning on was a way
of ensuring that you were getting your money's worth, since
most of the activities were *included*, as they say in the Catskills.
So were meals and anything in between, she added, which
meant never saying no to that second helping or dessert, regardless of what restrictive diet your doctor might have you on back
home. To hear her tell it, food was to the Catskills as slots were
to Atlantic City, the difference being that here you gambled
with your cholesterol, instead of with quarters. Shuffleboard
and the rest of it were just something to do between feedings.

The day's most looked-forward-to activity was dinner,
which she said was going to remind me of one of her family's
catered affairs without the bar mitzvah boy or the bride and
groom. Were we staying at the Granit for a month or the entire
season, the maitre d' would call on his knowledge of human
nature to seat us at a table with couples just like ourselves, with
whom we would make friends for life, perhaps even planning
to meet here again in coming summers. As things stood, how-

ever, we'd probably be put wherever there were two empty seats. Even so, she warned, small talk would be expected of me.

As we rounded the lobby into the Golden Tiara Nite Club for predinner cocktails (another excuse for *noshing*, because everybody knows it isn't wise to drink on an empty stomach), we heard an innocuous bossa nova above the chatter of those already helping themselves to hors d'oeuvres. It was Burt Bacharach's "The Look of Love," being played (we surmised) by David Winograd and the Granit Orchestra, the seven-piece combo that would be backing the comedian Nipsey Russell and the singer Karen Saunders at the Tiara's "Broadway Show-time" in just a few hours. Before we could spot the musicians, a trombonist broke free of the ensemble just long enough to let loose three staccato blats. He then smeared Bacharach's melody into a lopsided glissando before blending into the other horns.

I think I would have recognized that sound anywhere, and the absurdity of the setting only intensified my delight. I jokingly asked my friend what she thought our chances were of being seated for dinner with others like us who were here just to listen to the band. It should have bothered me that nobody else was paying Rudd much attention. But sometimes it's better that way—anybody who loves jazz so much that he's become somewhat possessive about it (and somewhat resigned to other people's hearing it as background music) will know what I mean. I didn't even mind it when, during the band's version of Kool and the Gang's "Celebration," an *alter kocker* doing an arthritic lindy hop in front of the tuxedoed musicians admonished "No, no, *rock-and-roll*," clapping his hands on the wrong beat as Rudd stretched the funk rhythm deliriously out of shape. More important, Rudd didn't seem to mind either.

Thirty years ago when Rudd was a new face in jazz, the critic Martin Williams praised him for combining "the robust earthiness of a Kid Ory plus all the refinements jazz trombone has been through since, including some of the latest developments in [jazz] as a whole."The comparison to Ory—the trombonist in Louis Armstrong's Hot Five and Jelly Roll Morton's Red Hot Peppers, and a rallied-around figure in the Dixieland revival of the 1940s—was no idle hyperbole. Rudd, while still an undergraduate at Yale, had recorded two albums of Dixieland as a member of a ragtag collegiate outfit called Eli's Chosen Six. This was before he obtained citizenship in the New York avant-garde through his association with Steve Lacy, Archie Shepp, Bill Dixon, and Cecil Taylor. An ironic consequence of Rudd's apprenticeship as an Ivy Leaguer playing Dixieland, a style that demands a vocalized approach from its horn players, was that he became the first (and, until the emergence of George Lewis, Ray Anderson, Craig Harris, and several Europeans in the seventies and eighties, the only) trombonist capable of matching split tones and glossal outbursts with saxophonists who were bidding their horns to speak in tongues.

This is how innovation usually spreads in jazz: one or two or as many as three or four players make breakthroughs on their horns, and the rank and file play catch-up. In that fashion J. J. Johnson became the ne plus ultra of bebop trombonists by negotiating Charlie Parker's and Dizzy Gillespie's harmonic abstractions and fleet eighth-note runs with his slide. (His West Coast counterpart was the sadly overlooked Frank Rosolino.) In the case of many of Johnson's followers, though, as in the case of those who sought to emulate Tommy Dorsey's unperturbed lyricism, this meant ignoring the trombone's potential for mirth. Zipping around on their horn as though the instrument were a darker-toned and only slightly unwieldy trumpet, they sounded like fat men running up stairs with huge bundles. They were ill suited to free improvisation, though many of them tried their hand at it.

Rudd achieved his primacy among free trombonists without emulating Ornette Coleman, John Coltrane, Albert Ayler, Archie Shepp, or any of the other pacesetting saxophonists of the 1960s. He simply reversed the process begun by Johnson, reacquainting the horn with the whoops and hollers, the slow-motion horse laughs and elephant snorts, that had been part of its jocular vocabulary before bop.

Thanks to his sprung time and his knack for locating dissonances between positions on his slide, he was able to do this without sounding like an old-timer who had wandered into the wrong gig. Even on dirges (his forte, as such composers as Michael Mantler and Carla Bley quickly realized), he often sounded as if he were shouting or laughing or cursing into his mouthpiece, with or without a plunger stuck in the bell of his horn to facilitate such vocal effects.

The other keepsake of his Dixieland experience that made Rudd such a valuable asset in free jazz was his commitment to collective improvisation. The problem with much bebop is that the musicians playing it are simply blowing on chord changes rather than taking full advantage of the melody and rhythm. The problem with free jazz is that even though the chord changes have been dispensed with, the musicians are frequently still just blowing. The New York Art Quartet, the band that Rudd co-led with the alto saxophonist John Tchicai for a short time in the 1960s, was notable for many virtues, not the least of them the contrapuntal chatter that Rudd and Tchicai kept up behind each other's solos. Rudd's presence in a band of more than four or five pieces virtually guaranteed attention to color and dynamics. It also guaranteed levity. He brought a touch of John Philip Sousa to one of Archie Shepp's best small groups of the late 1960s, and, a decade or so later, gleefully played the ham in the midsize ensemble led by Carla Bley, a composer who doesn't so much select sidemen as cast them to type.

Rudd's sense of himself as first and foremost an ensemble member was so unshakable that when an Italian label invited him to make a solo album, he chose instead to overdub himself singing and playing piano, bass, drums, and even extra trombone parts. That was in 1979, on *The Definitive Roswell Rudd* (Horo), an eccentric tour de force that proved to be his last opportunity to date to record an album of his own compositions. Three years later, he made *Regeneration*, featuring three pieces by Thelonious Monk as well as three by Herbie Nichols, for Soul Note, another Italian label. It was his last complete album.

The people seated next to us at dinner turned out to be Catskills regulars, a couple in their early fifties, who informed us that the Granit was strictly Grade B, right down to the entertainment. "The Concord gets Paul Anka, the Granit gets Robert Merrill," the wife complained. "If you don't have to ask if somebody's still alive, they're too big for the Granit."

Maybe so, but I doubt that any other Catskills resort boasts a band capable of jamming so euphorically on "Mack the Knife." To my surprise Rudd wasn't the only band member with impressive professional credentials: the lineup also included Bobby Johnson, about whose trumpet solo on Erskine Hawkins's 1945 recording of "Tippin' In" Gunther Schuller wrote (in his landmark book, *The Swing Era*) that it was "so admirably conceived and executed" that "one assumes the presence of one of the great trumpet stars of the period, not the well-nigh forgotten Bobby Johnson." This missing person sang a few numbers in a swaggering voice reminiscent of Jimmy Rushing's and still played with effortless grace, despite appearing to be in his early seventies.

I actually enjoyed the show. Karen Saunders, a fine young singer whom I had never heard of, delivered a convincing "The Man I Love," with Rudd supplying a virile plunger obbligato on the slow intro. And Nipsey Russell broke up the band with a joke about a bygone Harlem jazz club where "they had an intermission every twenty minutes, to wheel out the dead and injured."

"I don't think Nipsey was having a good night, though," Rudd said, on joining us later in the Mystic Lounge. (The ivory tickler there *now* was Irving Fields, the composer of "The Miami Beach Rhumba," practically a Borscht Belt anthem, "Managua, Nicaragua," a number-one hit for both Guy Lombardo and Freddie Martin in 1947, and "Chantez, Chantez," a ditty popularized by Dinah Shore in 1957. And can you think of a better name for a songwriter than Irving Fields?) "He wasn't working the audience the way I've seen him do. He stuck to the usual order of his routines.

"Comedians are like the jazz musicians of the Borscht Belt," continued Rudd, who's closer to average in height and build than the yawp of his horn would lead you to expect. A caricature of him would emphasize his watery hazel eyes and his auburn and gray beard, which his wife says she would leave him if he ever shaved. "The high priest of comics here—the most original and articulate—is Mal Z. Lawrence. Then there's Ralph Pope, Jay Jason, Lenny Rush, and Mickey Marvin. I don't know if you've ever heard of any of them, but they're incredible. And they *do* improvise, within a set form. They work with a set number of variables—like a musician would with, say, twelve tones—and they shift the order of things according to how the audience is reacting. They usually start out the same and have a big thing they do at the end that brings it to a peak and lets them bow out gracefully. Like a final coda or cadenza. But in the middle, you never know where they're going next. That's the exciting part."

The following afternoon my companion and I drove to Accord, a few miles east, for brunch with Rudd and his wife, Moselle Galbraith. They live on a secluded dirt road, in a one-story house as narrow as a trailer and laid out like a railroad flat. The house, though less crowded than when the couple's son, Christopher, and Moselle's two daughters from a previous marriage still lived with them, is so small that Rudd wouldn't be able to extend his slide in it without poking a hole in the ceiling or knocking Galbraith's knickknacks off the mantelpiece. (Counting Rudd's grown son from his first marriage, he and his wife have four children—"his, hers, and theirs," as Galbraith puts it.) There wouldn't be room in the house for a piano. In order to practice or to compose music, Rudd has to go deep into the nearby woods, where he says he sings and chants and dances the notes out, in addition to "just letting it burn on my horn, which I have to be careful *not* to do on the job."

It soon became apparent that the house wasn't the proper site for an interview. Galbraith, who suffers from various respiratory and intestinal ailments, was having a bad day on account of the heat (she was unable even to lift her weight out of her chair in front of the air conditioner to change from her nightgown and to comb her matted hair). So Rudd and I spoke at length on the phone a few nights later, interrupted only when Moselle had him hunt for their Shih Tzu, the smallest of their four dogs, who had crawled underneath the sofa.

Rudd was born in Sharon, Connecticut, in 1935. Despite his Hotchkiss and Yale education, he doesn't come from money. A small inheritance long since spent was all that enabled him and his wife to relocate to the Catskills in 1982, two years after Rudd was denied tenure by the University of Maine. Both Rudd's parents were teachers in private schools, and his father—a record collector and avocational drummer—introduced him to jazz. One of his father's records that made an especially vivid impression on him was the Woody Herman Orchestra's recording of "Everywhere," featuring the tune's composer, Bill Harris, on trombone.

"It just killed me," Rudd told me. "I think a lot of it had to do with it being his own composition. It wasn't like he had to bring his musical personality to bear on somebody else's form. The song was *his*, and it was like I could tell that right away." (Rudd later reinterpreted Harris's ballad—half smoldering reverie, half drunken army reveille—as the title track on his first LP, in 1966). The other family member who helped to steer Rudd into music was his grandmother, "a Methodist church lady who was the director of her choir and who, on the out chorus of the hymns, would improvise a descant super libre in a high, pneumatic voice and just soar over the entire choir."

Rudd spoke with excitement about his grandmother (whom he once compared to the trumpeter Cat Anderson, the high-note specialist in Duke Ellington's band) and a number of other musical topics, including the marching bands in which he played French horn in as a teenager ("Your section was integrated into the other sections: a post–Industrial Revolution, urban hierarchical, almost Wagnerian kind of thing"), Greenwich Village jam sessions in the early sixties ("There would be as many as ten horns up there, and as a guy would be soloing, the other horns would be riffing behind him, harmonizing the riffs, and it would be like Duke Ellington used to do, only happening spontaneously"), and a love for battered upright pianos, with their weird overtones, which he inherited from Herbie Nichols, the maverick pianist who was mentor of sorts to him ("The last one I had, in Maine in 1982, just collapsed from the tension of the strings on a rotten frame").

Rudd's talk about music—which is probably all he would ever talk about if given a choice—made it obvious that he wasn't burned out on jazz and just going through the motions at the Granit. After talking with him, I still don't know the complete answer to how he got where he is. The long and the short of it might be that jazz brought him little fortune and only marginal fame. As tastes in jazz became more conservative, he found himself stigmatized, despite his consummate musicianship, as someone supposedly incapable of doing anything but making noise on his horn. He was already teaching part-time at Bard and working on and off for the folklorist Alan Lomax when the offer came along to join the faculty at Maine, in 1976. In Augusta his efforts to integrate raga and other improvisisational world music forms into a jazz curriculum displeased his department head, who, one assumes, wanted a real teacher, not a gifted eccentric. After relocating to the Catskills, where a friend had a handyman's special for sale, he worked sporadically in area clubs for a few years before successfully auditioning for David Winograd at the Granit, in 1986.

Rudd's wife, a native New Yorker often mistaken for Jewish, likes to joke that he's too "white bread" for the Catskills. But even though the only stretch of green visible from the Granit's lobby is the golf course, Kerhonkson itself is rural, and Rudd says he's always more at home in rural settings (his fondest memory of Maine is its green summers, which he says "just *raged* with life"). A self-described "White Anglo-Saxon Pythagorean," Rudd is the sort of unassuming fellow who gets along fine with everyone. My girlfriend didn't even mind his addressing her as "Doll," though I'd like to see anyone else try to get away with it. Rudd was one of the very few whites welcomed into the inner circle of militant black musicians amid the tumult of the 1960s. "At that time, in New York, a major topic of discussion was the reality of being black and playing this music versus the reality of being white and attempting to play it from a black perspective," Bill Dixon, a trumpeter and composer now tenured at Bennington, recalled during a recent conversation we had about Rudd. "But Roz fit right in because of his musicianship and, I would have to say, his personality."

Told how Rudd was now making his living, Dixon says, "It just proves that being a wonderful musician isn't enough anymore. But you know, in one sense, he's fortunate." Rudd could be driving a taxi or painting houses or working as a plumber, a carpenter, or a camp counselor—all jobs that he has held at one time or another. (His most interesting day job was with Lomax, helping to analyze "Cantometrics," which can be roughly defined as the measure of "song" in various ethnic musics.) Rudd's hotel job pays family health benefits, which were a blessing when he still had teenagers living at home, and are perhaps even more of a blessing now, given his wife's poor health. The job also gets him out of the house and lets him take pride in his craft. In some ways he's a better musician now than he was before. His sight-reading has improved, and he and his six bandmates have had a lot of practice in paring down big-band arrangements that some of the Granit's headliners bring along with them. He's come to place a higher value on showmanship. "No matter how tired they might be or how few people are in the audience, the performers here go on stage and deliver," he told me, admiringly. After speaking with Rudd, I saw his beloved Mal Z. Lawrence in a video excerpt from the show *Catskills on Broadway*, and thought he was nothing special. But even though Rudd might be giving run-of-the-mill Borscht Belt *tumlers* too much credit in comparing them to jazz improvisers, his enthusiasm for them suggests that he is one of those artists on whom nothing is wasted.

The drawbacks to the job at the Granit begin with the nagging feeling that a musician of Rudd's stature belongs somewhere else, doing something better. As the last member of Winograd's band to have been hired, he's the first to be laid off when business at the hotel is slow, as it was this past winter. Even when on full-time salary at the hotel, he has to drive a bread truck five mornings a week in order to make ends meet. A number of prominent jazz musicians live in Woodstock or nearby towns, but there's no local jazz scene to speak of— unfortunately for Rudd, whose essentially passive nature makes him one of those musicians able to blend easily into an existing scene but unable to start one around themselves. Bandleaders he worked with years ago still call him occasionally with offers to go to Europe for a few weeks, but because he's reluctant to leave his job unprotected and his wife uncared for, he routinely turns them down. He's said no so often that some musicians have wrongly concluded that he's just not interested anymore.

This June, however, Rudd surprised everybody—possibly including himself—by accepting an offer to bring a quintet to Italy for the Verona Jazz Festival. (His travel costs were defrayed by Arts International, an organization that provides assistance to American performers invited to participate in festivals overseas.) Rudd was scheduled to play outdoors, but rain forced his concert into an auditorium with no amplification. Nevertheless, Rudd returned in excellent spirits. "It was beautiful to play some music," he told me, implying a distinction between what he had performed at the festival—several of his own recent compositions, plus his arrangements of a few of Herbie Nichols's tunes and "Kid Ory's Creole Trombone"—and his nightly fare at the hotel.

He also said something that struck me as inconsequential at first but that I later realized summed up the unaccustomed elbow room the trip had afforded him. "At the hotel I'm sitting behind a music stand all night. It felt good to stand up, to do my little dance as I played. They'll be sending me a video of my set. It'll be a chance for me to see myself in flight."

One gig hardly amounts to a comeback, but there might soon be others, including a foreign tour by the reassembled New York Art Quartet, featuring Rudd, John Tchicai, the drummer Milford Graves, and the bassist Reggie Workman. In the meantime Rudd is at least playing music, even if it's only "The Look of Love."

(SEPTEMBER 1992)

The New York Art Quartet reunion never happened, and Rudd eventually lost his job at the Granit. The good news is that he's been working with the tenor saxophonist Allen Lowe (read on).

The Come-from-Behind Guy

Allen Lowe: *At the Moment of Impact* **(Fairhaven)**
Last year's most impressive jazz DIY came from a tenor
saxophonist whose day gig is in public relations for
New Haven's city administration. Julius Hemphill
blowing lustily in an open setting should be all the rec-
ommendation anybody needs, but there's more: Lowe's
darkly compelling writing, his tumbling solos, and
a degree of group interplay that speaks well of him as
a bandleader. Plus accordion on a couple of tangos, a
piquant taste of Don Byron's clarinet, and—courtesy
of Jeff Fuller—bass lines so propulsive you don't even
notice that the drummer sits out on about half of the
tracks. **A**

—"Jazz Consumer Guide," *The Village Voice*,
February 5, 1991

Thanks for your kind words," Allen Lowe wrote in response
to my enthusiastic review of his second release on his own
Fairhaven label.

"My situation is a little different from that of most jazz
musicians in that I'm a nine-to-fiver who's never done the
music thing full-time," Lowe went on to say in the letter, which
bore the official seal of the City of New Haven. "Which isn't
to say that there aren't plenty of musicians who work day gigs,
only that those I see as my peers generally have the sorts of jobs
they don't mind quitting to go on the road or to Europe, etc.
Musicians who go the serious day-gig route put limits, I think,
on their musical ambitions, and it's sometimes difficult to determine cause and effect—meaning, do they work days because

their sights are set lower, or do they set their sights lower because they work days?

"At any rate, part of my problem is that I didn't start playing music seriously until seven years ago, when I was twenty-nine," the letter continued. "I've had other artistic ambitions. I briefly attended Yale Drama School, also did some journalism. Playwriting was my first love, but regional theaters have become as hopelessly middlebrow as the mainstream theater they were supposed to provide an alternative to . . . . My tastes in drama run to Beckett, Brecht, Handke, and Büchner's *Woyzeck*, not Sam Shepard and John Guare (whom I lump together only because both of them represent a dead end, in my opinion).

"In jazz, I also tend to favor a kind of poetic realism shaped by theoretical aspects from literature (Robbe-Grillet's *Toward the New Novel*, Sontag's *Against Interpretation*, Beckett's profound notion that he was writing something, not *about* something). What these literary theories tend to do for me isn't to set up some sort of dogmatic musical ideology, but to strip away a lot of the outdated ideas I used to have about what jazz was supposed to be. . . .

"But in trying to find a place for myself in jazz, I'm encountering problems similar to those I encountered in trying to get my plays produced. It seems that in order to be noticed, you've either got to be a neoconservative like Wynton Marsalis or a postmodernist like John Zorn, who I do think is one of the musicians giving the music a new edge it desperately needed. But my own music probably isn't 'hip' enough for Zorn's downtown New York scene. Meanwhile, here in New Haven, I get virtually no calls for work because I'm not a fashionable John Coltrane/Wayne Shorter clone. So what's a musician like me to do? Produce his own records and find people like Don Byron and Julius Hemphill [both much better known than Lowe in jazz circles] who are open to trying something different."

★ ★ ★

Recently, over dinner in a quick-and-dirty around the corner from Carnegie Hall, Lowe said: "In New Haven I sometimes feel trapped. In the position I was in until just recently, I sometimes went weeks at a time without picking up my horn. Then I get a gig and by the third set my lip is falling apart and my brain is rattling around in my head from being so out of shape."

In New York just for the day, Lowe expanded on several issues in his letter. On January 2 John C. Daniels, New Haven's first black mayor, who had appointed Lowe public information director soon after taking office in 1991, promoted him to director of the Bureau of Cultural Affairs. In March, however, Lowe was one of more than two hundred city employees laid off to close the city's $6.2 million budget gap.

The layoffs were supposed to be temporary, but three months had passed without Lowe—the husband of a social advocacy lawyer and father of a three-year-old son—being reinstated. His reinstatement depended on New Haven's municipal union workers agreeing to a furlough plan that would have required them to take four days off without pay before the end of the fiscal year on July 1. In return, the unions were asking for a guarantee of no layoffs, which the mayor said he was unable to give.

"I guess that if I was younger and single, without a mortgage to think of, I'd probably try my luck in New York on the strength of my CD," Lowe said, about being left dangling. "I've always taken day jobs because I didn't have enough confidence in myself as a musician. But then I started getting day gigs I *liked*, that I felt committed to . . . .

"I oppose the wave of antiunion sentiment that came in with Reagan in 1980, and my feeling is that the unions in New Haven have been reasonable in their demands. On the other hand, having a job until July would have give me three months to plan my future, instead of the ten days I had after receiving my layoff notice."

It's understandable that Lowe would be torn between his

ideals and his self-interest in this dispute, given his political upbringing. His parents were "Hubert Humphery liberals who voted for Henry Wallace in 1948 and had friends who were blacklisted," and he himself helped to edit an underground newspaper in high school. He demonstrated against the Vietnam War in college at the University of Michigan and other schools (he attended ten in all, before receiving his degree in English Literature from the State University of New York at Binghamton in 1980).

Lowe was born and raised in Massapequa, Long Island (where his high school classmates included Jerry Seinfeld, Joey Buttafucco, and Phillip Johnston, of the Microscopic Septet), and remembers it as "a safe, suburban, white-cloistered place, with a mix of middle-class professionals, including my family, on one side of town and working-class ethnics, like Ron Kovic, on the other. My father taught elementary school elsewhere on Long Island, and my mother, who was a genius, though not in a show-offy, MENSA kind of way, went back to college after raising me and my older brother and sister, and eventually became the head of the department of library sciences at St. John's University, in Jamaica, Queens."

Lowe, who first became obsessed with jazz after hearing Sonny Rollins's recording of "There's No Business Like Show Business" around 1968, played in both jazz and rock bands as a teenager. "But I'm very bad in math, which you need in order to understand harmony, and not very mechanically inclined, which you need to be in order to get around your instrument. I became aware of my limitations, and that made me stop."

In his twenties, Lowe played gigs infrequently, always as a lark. But he remained active in the music in a number of other capacities. He taught courses in jazz history, organized festivals and symposiums, and wrote record reviews and artist profiles for *Down Beat* and various New England newspapers. Befriending such neglected figures as Barry Harris, Joe Albany, Al Haig, Percy France, Dicky Wells, and Dave Schildkraut, he wound up booking gigs for many of them. Before his appointment to city government, he worked at various times as an ad salesman, a reference librarian, and a book-review editor for a scientific journal. All the while he continued to send his plays off to indifferent regional theater companies.

In 1983, after a decade on the sidelines, Lowe began to play again in earnest. "I said to myself 'I have to give it a chance,'" he recalled. "I was hearing a lot of b.s. in jazz that I was sure I could do better than. I had always felt inadequate next to the machine-gun-fast tenor players I used to hear coming out of the Boston music schools, but I realized that maybe I had something they didn't have. For one thing, I had a more vocalized sound. And fortunately I was based in New Haven, far enough away from New York that you could get gigs before you had your chops together."

Three years later Lowe released *For Old B.B.*, an album of mostly slow bebop with an intimate, almost dreamlike slant. (The initials stood for Bertolt Brecht.) Between that album and *At the Moment of Impact . . .*, Lowe underwent a stylistic metamorphosis he attributes to a number of factors: his reading of books by Sontag, Robbe-Grillet, and the drama critic Richard Gilman; his discovery of the Argentine composer and bandoneon player Astor Piazzolla (the father of what's sometimes called "the new tango"); and the death of his mother in a 1988 car accident in which his father, who was driving and later admitted to having fallen asleep at the wheel, escaped with minor injuries.

Let Lowe make the connections. "From reading theoretical works which discussed the place of modernism in the arts, I realized that I was becoming a bit of a musical conservative. I was tight with Barry Harris, whom I love, but who a mutual friend of his and mine used to call 'a bebop nazi.' Barry thought if something wasn't bebop, it couldn't be any good. I wasn't quite that bad, because I still loved Ornette Coleman, Eric Dolphy, and that first wave of jazz avant-gardists from the 1960s.

But I had no use for the people that followed them, like Anthony Braxton and Anthony Davis. Everything I was writing was based on bebop chords, with bebop eighth-note divisions.

"Then around 1986 or '87, when I started listening to new-music composers like Steve Reich, that exposed me to different kinds of ethnic music, admittedly secondhand. Then I heard Piazzolla, and I realized that what I was looking for in my own work were melodies with flowing rhythms like his, but not necessarily melodies in the classic A-A-B-A popular-song form. At the same time I was still interested in chordal movement, so I began to try to combine the modalism of ethnic music and Ornette Coleman with the dense chord changes of bebop."

He wrote in his liner notes to *At the Moment of Impact* . . . : "My mother's death, in the midst of my realizing all of this, helped to focus me on what I wanted out of music and out of life."

Lowe agrees with the German novelist and playwright Peter Handke that, because there are no more new stories to be told, "the role of the artist at this point is to express levels of experience or to explore new worlds of consciousness. In the same way, I feel that the concept of the jazz musician 'telling a story' is outmoded. We've heard all the stories—now let's hear the sounds."

Lowe's literary allusions might give the impression that the music on *At the Moment of Impact* . . . is forbiddingly abstract, with few tender places. But his writing strikes an ideal balance of head and heart. His collection of altered blues, freebop marches, and vivacious near-tangos was one of the most refreshing jazz releases in recent memory, as well as one of the most individualistic.

"The further I stray from bop, the more I think of Barry and feel as though I'm cheating on my wife," Lowe said of his newest direction. "I think, 'Oh, I'm glad Barry's not here tonight to hear me doing this, because he wouldn't approve. But you gotta do what you gotta do. . . .

"It's just taken me longer than it does most people to get to where I want to be musically. I know I'll never be a virtuoso. I have more confidence in myself as a writer than as a improviser. From the technical standpoint, there are always going to be a lot of gaps," he admitted. "But maybe it's worked to my advantage, in a sense, not being a virtuoso. There are guys who can play anything they're asked to, but maybe that kind of adaptability has a price in terms of lack of originality. I think I've developed just enough technique to do what I feel I *need* to do, if you see what I mean."

(APRIL 1991)

Something peculiar is happening in jazz, an art music in which innovation has always been regarded as the young black man's burden. We assume that a wave of like-minded young brothers will arrive right on schedule, every ten years or so, to shake things up the way that Bird and Dizzy did way back when. So what are we to make of a generation of reverent black classicists embracing as its modest goal the preservation of jazz *as we know it?* Or that so much of today's boldest and most piquant improvised (or semi-improvised) music is being made by a radical fringe of men and women in their late thirties or early forties, a disproportionate number of whom are Europeans or white Americans? Insofar as it's possible to generalize, these beginning-to-wrinkle outsiders differ from the tadboppers (black *and* white) in not having spent their adolescence gazing at album jackets and practicing chords. Many of them were already in college, majoring in something as useless as art or English Lit (or as meaningful as drugs and politics), when they first picked up horns, moved to do so after hearing Sun Ra or the Art Ensemble of Chicago and wanting in on the noise. Their music reflects a fullness of experience missing from the etudes of those post-juveniles in whose hands jazz has come to signify the sound of no surprise.

Allen Lowe started out as a bebop supremacist, but otherwise fits the profile as a unproduced playwright and occasional jazz critic who became a full-time musician last year at the age of thirty-eight, after quitting his day gig as New Haven's director of cultural affairs. Don't be fooled by the billing on *Mental Strain at Dawn* (Stash), which lists Lowe's name below those of David Murray, Doc Cheatham, and Loren Schoenberg, the featured soloists in Lowe's Jack Purvis Memorial Orchestra (a ten-member ensemble cheekily named for the composer of the title track, an obscure white Satchmo adept of the late 1920s who was also a convicted gunrunner and South American mercenary). Recorded mostly in performance at the Knitting Factory last Easter and subtitled *A Modern Portrait of Louis Armstrong*, this is Lowe's baby all the way, and its charm lies in his tacit wager than he knows more about jazz tradition than those who wield it as a bludgeon.

Despite beginning with Lowe's transcription of Armstrong's cadenza on "West End Blues," this isn't another of those musical waxworks paying tribute to Armstrong by serving up his choruses verbatim. The snatch of "West End Blues" proves to be a fanfare for a bruising "La Cucaracha," a clue that Armstrong is going to be taken outside and generally subjected (as Fats Waller and Jelly Roll Morton will be, when their turn arrives) to the sort of affectionately rude treatment he himself gave Tin Pan Alley, feckless novelties and bona fide classics alike.

In deference to Murray and Schoenberg—and less sure of himself as a soloist than as a composer, arranger, and impresario of cross-generational dream bands, anyway—Lowe restricts himself to alto with the large ensemble. He unpacks his tenor (his best horn) only for "Dinah" and "Yodel Blues," studio duets with the bassist Peter Askim, the latter of which manages to suggest both Sonny Rollins at his most jocular and Jimmy Giuffre at his most rustic. The guest tenors tear it up on Waller's "Black and Blue," with Schoenberg (more versatile than his jazz rep credentials might lead you to conclude) holding his ground even as Murray aims for the ozone. The ageless Cheatham's period vibrato lends a touch of authenticity to several numbers, and if the dissonant reed cackle behind his theme statement on Purvis's "Copyin' Louis" fazes him, he doesn't let it show.

So it was a surprise to hear that Cheatham had sulked off complaining about altered chord changes following Lowe's opening set at Sweet Basil two weeks ago. Cheatham's absence was a blessing in disguise, because it meant that the trombonist Roswell Rudd, absent from New York clubs since 1983, was the band's senior member and reigning deity on the two nights he was featured (Don Byron and Jimmy Knepper guested earlier in the week, and Schoenberg was on hand all six nights). Rudd, an Ivy League Dixielander who wound up setting the pace for free-jazz trombonists of the sixties and seventies (partly by reminding them of the ax's comic potential as a projectile instrument), was in his natural element playing a music whose contrapuntal framework and wooliness of pitch suggested the New York Contemporary Five mauling a trad repertoire one moment and the Condon mob on a drunken jag the next. He added heft to the ensembles and practically levitated the rest of the band with his jubilant shouts over Ray Kaczynski's jungle snare patters on "La Cucaracha."

In the spirit of full disclosure, I should reveal that I played a minor part in bringing Lowe together with Rudd, whose talent is being wasted in his regular gig as a member of a Catskills show band. And my selection of two of Lowe's previous CDs as *Village Voice* Consumer Guide Pick Hits probably helped him to land his first week-long New York gig. So for a critic noticeably lacking in holiday cheer (I showed up at Sweet Basil the night after Christmas wearing a eye patch, after spending the afternoon in an emergency room awaiting treatment for a corneal abrasion—take my advice and be careful how you fold your Sunday Arts & Leisure), this was *It's a Wonderful Life*. But anybody brooding over the neglect of such a major talent as Rudd and the joylessness of so much of what passes for New York's hippest shit would have been justified in believing that the angels were on his side at Sweet Basil this Christmas.

(JANUARY 1993)

Out There

I'd left word with a friend of Charles Gayle's that I was looking for him, and he'd surprised me with a phone call. He was waiting for me, as promised, on the corner of Broadway and 10th, with his saxophone case by his feet. Even though I knew what he looked like from having seen him play, it took me a minute or two to spot him standing there by the curb away from the lunchtime crowd, completely inside himself, unnoticed and unnoticing. Maybe I was surprised just that he had shown up.

Although lunch was on the *Village Voice*, Gayle wasn't eating. He ordered a muffin, then hardly touched it as we lingered in a coffee shop on Astor Place, across from where the wretched of the earth dump old rags, shoes, and rained-on reading material on the sidewalk as though waiting for somebody to come along and bargain. (Who says capitalism no longer works?)

"Can I ask *you* a question," Gayle wondered at one point, after I'd turned off my portable cassette player at his request.

No actual question was forthcoming.

"A lot of people are working and I'm not. I don't know

why, and I don't know what to do about it," he finally said, after a pause, pointing a finger to his forehead and fixing me with a wary eye. "See, sometimes you can't get no work, you begin to think you must be terrible. Don't misunderstand me. I don't even know if I'm interested in that—the music business. It's just that I wouldn't mind working every once in a while. That's all."

This sudden plea caught me by surprise. Earlier in our conversation, after revealing that he earned just enough money for one meal a day by playing on the streets (his own music, he assured me, though he does take requests), he'd characterized that unprofitable form of self-enterprise as "the only honest alternative" for a black musician opposed to the almost exclusively white ownership of jazz venues.

Somehow, what he was saying now didn't strike me as a contradiction. What difference was one night at the Knitting Factory—or, for that matter, three nights there, like he said he had coming up on consecutive Sundays in December—going to make in the way he lived? I took a good look at him, noticing the gold cap over one of his bottom incisors, and the string tied around his right pinkie. If he hadn't mentioned that he would be fifty-two in a few weeks, I would have taken him to be at least five years younger, despite the gray on his chin. Gaunt, with long, expressive fingers more like those of a pianist than a tenor saxophonist's, he was neatly dressed in layers, with a blue denim jacket over a green plaid flannel shirt and a dark green T-shirt, and nobody was giving him a second glance.

"See, I still haven't solved the mystery of why anybody would want to listen to me," he'd said when we first sat down, trying to convince me that he wasn't going to be a very compelling interview subject, especially since questions pertaining directly to his past were understood to be off limits. "Wynton Marsalis can probably tell you who *he* is as a musician, and Sonny Rollins can tell you who *he* is, but I don't know who *I* am, because I'm not part of the music world, so I don't know how I'm regarded or if what I do even counts. I know there are some people who can hear themselves and evaluate whether they're good or bad. But I can't do that.

"I'm not trying to be modest. I just can't. I'm just a street person. I mean, I live in a squat in Bed Stuy. But I'm practically in the street. I will be again, soon."

After overhearing the part about the squat, our waiter rushed to refill our cups and assure us that the table was ours for as long as we liked.

I think that the first mention I ever saw of Charles Gayle was in Bob Rusch's interview with Buell Neidlinger, in a 1986 issue of *Cadence*. Neidlinger, who played bass with Cecil Taylor before joining the Buffalo Philharmonic in 1962 and eventually becoming a first-call L.A. session man, remembered Gayle "pushing televisions around in the Westinghouse factory" in Buffalo. "I brought him down to New York [for a concert] in '67 or something like that . . . Pharoah Sanders had his band, and Archie Shepp was playing. He blew them all off the face of the earth," Neidlinger said. According to Neidlinger, this mystery man had "stayed one day and went right back to Buffalo, [because] he couldn't deal with New York."

Rusch passed along the tantalizing information that Gayle was back in New York, "playing like a mother."

I heard no more about him until two years later, when Marty Kahn, whose Outward Visions handles Steve Reich, the Art Ensemble of Chicago, the World Saxophone Quartet, and other avant-garde fixtures, left me a phone message urging me to hear Gayle at the Knitting Factory. The gist of the message was that Gayle blew tenor with an intensity unmatched since Albert Ayler. What made the call different from any other I'd ever gotten from a bizzer was that it wasn't made on behalf of a client. Although circumstances prevented me from being there for Gayle's Knitting Factory debut, the euphoric word from friends who went was that Gayle's trio played unrepentant free jazz—

that his music was "out there," as we used to say way back when. I sensed the beginning of a genuine, street-level buzz, maybe the first for an unrecorded performer since Wynton broke in with the Messengers in 1980, or since David Murray started to make a name for himself in the lofts a few years earlier. But unlike Murray and Marsalis, both of whom were then teenagers, Gayle was a middle-aged man (roughly the age that Ayler himself would have been, in fact) with an element of uncorrupted Bunk Johnsonism enhancing his credibility—though not for me.

In its own era free jazz (nonchordal improvisation after Ornette Coleman, but especially the winged multiphonics and glossolalia that followed Ayler's *Spiritual Unity* in 1965) and the militant nationalistic rhetoric that usually accompanied it were blamed for scaring away what little had remained of the jazz audience. In punishment free has been banished from most academic histories and magazine trend pieces tracing the evolution of modern jazz from bop to fusion to bop again. In jazz the sixties have become the decade that never happened—or that never should have.

Yet I know (and so do you, if you get around enough) a type of romantic first-generation free jazz fan, now in his (always his) middle forties and usually (though not always) white, for whom free like it was in the 1960s, with indignant black men raising heaven's floor for hours at a stretch, is the only music that does the trick. Being first-generation myself (with the ESP Discs to prove it), I sympathize. But only to a point, because I suspect that this is my generation's moldy-fig primitivism.

I finally heard Gayle in Philadelphia, about a month after Kahn's phone call. As reported, Gayle's yawp was fierce enough to pin anybody's ears back. But as yawps go, it was a lot like Ayler's, though lacking both his melodic lurch and his thematic continuity. The concert was like somebody's foggy notion of a typical night at Slug's, circa 1966, with Dave Pleasant splintering drumsticks on his stripped-down kit, Hilliard Green plucking and bowing his bass with such force that it rocked, and Gayle scooping for high notes and bending from his waist for low ones. For its part, the audience got into the act by whooping and bowing forward rapidly as though *davening*, just like folks were said to do back when soloists measured their phrases by the breath, not the bar.

Say what you will about the superiority of live music, take-home is sometimes preferable for sparing you the inevitably misanthropic exercise of comparing your reaction to that of everyone else in the room. In the early spring of 1988, just weeks after I'd dismissed him as a shuck, Gayle recorded *Homeless, Spirits Before*, and *Always Born*, the three Silkheart CDs that, when finally released earlier this year, forced me to reverse that judgment. Both *Homeless* and *Spirits Before* feature Gayle's trio, with Sirone (of Phalanx, The Group, and the Revolutionary Ensemble) on bass in place of Green. Sirone is also on hand, along with AACM drummer Reggie Nicholson, on *Always Born*, on which Gayle faces off against John Tchicai (who played alto on Coltrane's *Ascension*, but sticks to tenor and soprano here).

In other words Silkheart's Keith Knox, perhaps hedging just a bit, surrounded Gayle and Pleasant, both virtual unknowns, with impressively credentialed sidemen. Sirone, in particular, merits raves for his miniature symphonies of slurs, strums, and artfully timed double stops. But Tchicai frequently gets hung up on repeated phrases, never quite entering Gayle's orbit. And though Nicholson does fine, Pleasant is terrific. A heedless basher in concert, or so I thought (Sunny Murray taught him drumming in a hurry), he heats up *Homeless* and *Spirits Before* with a personal amalgam of vintage free drumming styles, ranging from Milford Graves's tabla patterns behind Giuseppi Logan to Sunny Murray's unmetered cymbal synapses behind Ayler and Cecil Taylor.

Gayle himself is the mind-bender, though. His longer solos are crapshoots, sometimes testing your patience along with his endurance (*Spirits Before*'s title cut, for example). But others—

typified by *Homeless*'s "Then Creations," almost Monklike in its gradual enlargement of a three-note theme—rivet you with their energy, control, and endless ripple of ideas. Gayle at his most impressive is Gayle at his most "accessible"—nothing wrong with that. The track I keep returning to is "Lift Ev'ry Voice and Sing," J. Rosamond Johnson's "black national anthem," here mistitled "Lift Every Voice" and consigned to the public domain. Fortified by Pleasant's lashing cymbals and Sirone's rolling bass, Gayle ravages the song, subjecting it to about six minutes of convulsive variations before allowing the melody to emerge in all its hardscrabble dignity, then brings it to a prolonged climax that's simultaneously turbulent and serene.

Published in 1900, with lyrics by James Weldon Johnson, the composer's brother, "Lift Ev'ry Voice" was a popular sign-off theme on black radio stations in the 1970s, which is probably how Gayle knows it. The only nonoriginal on the three CDs, it begs comparison as an anthem to many of Ayler's humble little themes, and Gayle underscores the similarity by stretching his intervals and fluttering melismatically at the end of phrases. But the resemblance to Ayler is flattering enough to Gayle to seem circumstantial rather than the result of direct influence. "We must have been drinking from Lake Erie around the same time," Gayle quipped when I asked him about the Ayler connection. "He was from Cleveland, you know, and I'm from Buffalo."

Did Charles give you his political rap?" a fellow critic asked me, alluding to the strange night at the Knitting Factory last June when Gayle spent most of a set haranguing whites for attempting to play jazz, pretending to appreciate it, and controlling its presentation. (Remember, Amiri Baraka's preferred term for "free jazz" was "the new black music.") That night has since become part of Gayle's legend, along with the time he supposedly requested a jar of baby food as his preconcert dinner.

The rap I got—maybe by virtue of facing Gayle across a table rather than being one white face among many in a darkened room—was softer and sadder. He told me that he was part Cherokee and that he had grown up in a Buffalo neighborhood in which all of the stores were black-owned-and-operated. "You could walk all over the city and feel that you were coming home to something that belonged to you," he said.

This was as autobiographical as he got. A friend of mine, who once worked as a graduate assistant in the Department of Adult Education at SUNY Buffalo, had told me that one of her co-workers there had been involved in a stormy relationship with Gayle. "That was my wife's name," he said when I mentioned the woman my friend remembered. But the silence that followed made it clear that he wasn't going to open the door any wider.

From talking with a few current and former upstate musicians, I did find out that Gayle himself once taught at the university, inheriting the jazz course from Charles Mingus in 1969. Somehow that piece of information wasn't as surprising as the news that one of his students was Jay Beckenstein, who later founded the wretchedly successful fusion group Spyro Gyra.

"I recall a funny scene with Charles trying to teach Jay how to play the blues," said the saxophonist Paul Gresham, another of Gayle's students and later a member of his band. Gresham, who's still active around Buffalo, remembered Gayle as "the kind of musician who could pick up any instrument and play it well. When I was in his band, with both of us playing saxophone, he would often play piano behind my solos."

On the other hand, another Buffalo musician who requested anonymity told me that he thought Gayle "played free from start to finish, with no tonal center" because he was a late starter who never mastered chord changes or saxophone technique— an accusation that dogs every free musician. But according to Gresham, Gayle was "like Eric Dolphy in that respect. He would play inside the changes, but so fast and so completely that it might go right by you. It was inside, but it sounded outside."

Did Gayle have an audience upstate? This also depends on whom you ask. Gresham remembers him always packing the house, "whether it was some hole-in-the-wall club or a concert at the university." Then again, how often would a free player like Gayle have worked? Buffalo was a hotbed of avant-gardism in the early 1970s, with Robert Longo showing at Hall Walls; an experimental video scene forming around Steina and Woody Vasulka; Lukas Foss conducting the Buffalo Philharmonic and commissioning works by John Cage, Morton Feldman, Lejaren Hillyer, and others; John Barth and Robert Creeley on the university faculty; and Allen Ginsberg in town for a drug symposium every other month or so. "But jazz was never included in that," says the drummer Bobby Previte, who grew up in nearby Niagara Falls. "The jazz scene was owned by the boppers. It must have been brutal for someone like Charles Gayle, coming out of late Coltrane and Albert Ayler. It was for me. That's why I'm in New York."

It wasn't just Buffalo. There was no audience for that kind of music all over, except maybe New York," Gayle told me, visibly considering but finally unable to answer the question of when he moved to New York, "because I was going back and forth for a long time."

Gresham remembers hearing Gayle in Greenwich Village with the drummer Rashied Ali's band around 1973. Otherwise, the years between Buffalo and now are a mystery.

As a general rule of thumb, neglected geniuses bear some complicity for their neglect. But I don't know what skeletons Gayle has in his closet, and he wasn't about to tell me. Still, we could talk about music. As we walked east on St. Mark's Place, I asked him why hardly anybody else was still playing free. I have my own pet theories, of course, one of which is that many of the style's originators are now too waddled in middle age to take many risks anymore, and another of which is that they grew so weary of hearing not just their musicianship but their sanity questioned that they themselves must have begun to wonder how many times they could go to the edge before forgetting their way back (Ayler wound up in the East River, after seeing flying saucers).

"It was just a fad," Gayle said, surprising me. "It didn't start off to be, but you know very well that it became that. They couldn't continue because it wasn't in them to continue. It was just the *time*."

What about him?

"It's just something in me. It's a fate that challenges you until it becomes very natural. You have to dig inside your soul and keep creating. You have to fight your memory, because it's easy to recapitulate. You keep pushing, because it's there, and you don't know what it is. You just keep going."

I asked him if he needed anything—a taxi to where he was going next, maybe?—but he wouldn't take my money.

Two days after our meeting, Gayle flew to Amsterdam on a one-way ticket bought for him by one of his admirers. He'd heard that a musician could make a decent living playing in the streets there. A few weeks later I heard that he was back in New York again, inclement weather having prevented him from earning very much money. This bit of hearsay was from someone who knows someone else in New York so passionate about Gayle (the ultimate jazz cult hero, famous for longer than fifteen minutes, but known to only fifteen people) that she kept track of the weather in Amsterdam the whole time he was there. Again, I left word for him to call me, but he never did. In the library a few weeks ago, while researching another story, I considered looking up "Gayle" in the Buffalo telephone directory, to see if he still had relatives there. But I didn't have the heart.

Gayle showed up at the Knitting Factory for his gig the Sunday before Christmas, along with Dave Pleasant, Hilliard Green, and about two dozen late-niters, including me. Thirty years ago Ornette Coleman, just in from California (some said the moon), confounded New Yorkers by not counting off his tunes. Gayle doesn't count off, either. He announced his presence with a sustained renal shriek, the first of many during the next forty-five minutes, which ended with him jackknifing into oblique staccato phrases that, given a different rhythmic underpinning, could have passed for R&B. Remember when reviewers used to complain that the problem with free jazz was that you could drop the needle down anywhere on the record and hear the same thing? To anyone ducking in and out of the club every five or ten minutes, Gayle's performance might have sounded as monomaniacal. But if you stuck with him, he overpowered you with his soaking emotionalism, his flying dynamics, his lovely and unexpected sobs of melody. It was free jazz not just like you remembered it, but like you always wished it could be.

(JANUARY 1991)

Gayle now works frequently enough to rent a small apartment.

Mischief

Sun Ra, Himself

Like most musical road warriors, Sun Ra and the entourage of instrumentalists, singers, and dancers he calls his Arkestra (sometimes the Myth Science Arkestra, sometimes the Cosmo Jet Set Arkestra, but always the Arkestra) often find themselves car-bound in the middle of the night, when traffic is light but nobody's as wide awake as he should be. Bessie Smith, Scott LaFaro, and Clifford Brown, among others, died from injuries sustained in car accidents, and practically every musician you ask—including Sun Ra—can tell you about a close call. But not surprisingly, Sun Ra's recollection detours into the preternatural.

The Arkestra was recently was on its way to the airport after a gig in San Francisco, Ra explained as we sat in the front room of his three-story home on Morton Street, in the Germantown section of Philadelphia. The since-banished Danny Thompson, then one of the Arkestra's saxophonists and Ra's de facto public relations man, who was driving, assured Ra that he wasn't tired, even though he'd already racked up considerable mileage driving to Los Angeles and back to see relatives earlier in the day.

"We were on the highway, right up on the car in front of us, with another car right behind us," Ra said in his Southern-accented monotone. His hair was tinted copper around the chin and temples, and he was wearing a black, knee-length, glitter-dusted tunic over shirt and trousers, with a matching scarf knotted in a point above the crown of his head—an eye-catching outfit, but prim compared with his on-stage motley. "All at once, I heard June [Tyson], the vocalist with us, say 'Danny!' because he was asleep with his eyes wide open, and he was goin' to hit that car in front. He woke up, but if he put the brakes on, the car behind was going to hit us.

"That was the situation, very dangerous," Ra continued, in

a matter-of-fact voice. "But we was saved because the car ahead of us shot straight up in the air and got into the next lane."

Wait a minute. The car *levitated*?

Ra smiled and nodded in affirmation. "You need a lot of protection on this planet."

Sun Ra pioneered the use of African percussion and electronic instruments in jazz. He showed that a big band could play hard bop and free, footloose styles supposedly exclusive to small groups. An innovative force in jazz for over thirty years as a keyboard player, bandleader, and composer, he rivals John Cage as America's most venerable avant-gardist.

But all of this is like saying that a rhinoceros is pointed at one end and round at the other: it doesn't begin to describe what's so peculiar about the beast. This is a man who once said, "Knowledge is laughable when attributed to a human being," and who, when asked if he considered himself human, answered, "No. As a man thinketh, so shall he be."

The New Grove Dictionary of Jazz says that Ra was born Herman "Sonny" Blount in Birmingham, Alabama, in May 1914. But the name and date are guesswork. According to Ra, he wasn't born, but "arrived on earth," presumably from somewhere else, on an unspecified date "outside the division of time that man has." He's forthcoming about his early life, albeit in his own fashion. He first evinced musical talent, he says, when his mother bought him a piano for his "so-called birthday" and he began transposing—by ear—the violin sonatas a school chum who lived next door would bring to him.

After studying music in high school under Professor John Tuggle Whatley, whose other students included Erskine Hawkins and Jo Jones, Ra won a scholarship to Alabama A&M, where he led the student band and majored in education, until, he says, he was kidnapped by extraterrestrials who took him to Saturn.

"I had to go up like this," he explained, demonstrating with his elbows meeting over his paunch and his fingertips clasping his shoulders, "because if I touched anything outside my body, I wouldn't be able to return.

"Did you ever see *Star Wars?*" Ra asked me. "It was very accurate."

After showing Ra around the galaxy and commanding him to alert mankind "there was goin' to be great trouble from the teenagers in high schools," they convinced him that a great destiny was in store for him: "When the world was in complete chaos, then I could speak and the world would listen, but not until then."

Asked if that moment had yet arrived, Ra smiled and said, "Well, I just got back from a jazz festival in Russia, and they declared me an international citizen, because they said I represent friendship." Also, while still in college, he decided to "try to reach God," who told him that "He wanted to find one pure-hearted person on this planet—just one." And that was Sun Ra? "Must have been." He said he once had "proof" of these experiences in a diary he was forced to "abolish" when he found his college bandmates "havin' a real good time readin' [it] on my bed. But I still retain the memory."

After college, Ra landed first in Nashville, where he recorded with the archetypal rhythm and blues singer and guitarist Wynonie Harris, and then in Chicago, where he worked with Fletcher Henderson, Stuff Smith, and an obscure blues singer named JoJo Adams, "a Chuck Berry type who had this knock-kneed dance that he would do," and performed what Ra describes as "X-rated" blues in top hat and tails, sometimes dressing his sidemen as Revolutionary soldiers. Chicago's jazz musicians nicknamed Ra "the moon man," not merely for predicting that man would one day go to the moon, but also in puzzled admiration of his far-out chords.

"They didn't understand what I was doin', but they were fascinated by it," he explained, with no false modesty.

Those musicians who were especially fascinated became the nucleus of his Arkestra, which he formed in the early 1950s. But

Ra began to attract widespread attention only after relocating the Arkestra to New York in 1961 and recording collective improvisations and pure "sound" pieces that demonstrated his kinship with John Coltrane, Albert Ayler, Cecil Taylor and others involved in what was then called "free" jazz. Ra, however, has never marched in step with any movement, and in response to the question of how much he thought his music of that period had in common with theirs, his answer was typically expansive but cryptic.

"That was when I was having my argument with God, because I didn't want to have to be the one to have to save the world," he explained. "I told him 'Let a minister do it! Let an intellectual do it! Let a millionaire do it! Let a Muslim do it!'"

In 1969, he moved his headquarters to Philadelphia, because "to save the planet, I had to go to the worst spot on earth, and that was Philadelphia, which is death's headquarters. This is where liberty started, but the bell cracked on them, because liberty wasn't what it's cracked up to be. And that's why you have so many teenagers here smoking crack."

Actually the Arkestra seems to have moved here because member Marshall Allen's family signed over the deed to the house. These negative sentiments about his adopted hometown might have given pause to the mayor's representatives, who were planning to award Ra with a Liberty Bell before one of his performances a few nights hence. Then again, much of what Sun Ra says seems designed to give *someone* pause.

He blames Jesus Christ for "the reign of death" on earth. "Jesus said, 'I come to cast fire on the earth.' It's happenin' everyday, atomic bombs, people trapped in fires, can't get out. They don't believe nice, meek Jesus would do that. But he is." Ra's distrust of Christianity dates from childhood. His mother wasn't a churchgoer, but his grandmother was devout, "and I never could understand why if Jesus died to save people, why people still had to die. That seemed ignorant to me. I couldn't equate that. That's how I felt as a child, and I never changed."

He also blames Jesus for introducing mankind to drugs, "on account of Him asking for drugs on the cross." (He expanded on this with something I couldn't quite follow, about how the legend "IHS" nailed above Christ's head was "shit" spelled backwards. It does if the cross was the "T," I guess.)

A case could be made for Ra as jazz's first Afrocentric. The rhymes chanted by his musicians during his shows from the late 1950s on proselytized about the wonders of ancient Egypt and foretold a future in outer space. In a sense, the songs about rocket ships taking off for Saturn were as Afrocentric as those about mythic sunsets on the Nile. Both came across as expressions of his conviction that he was from somewhere else and had little in common with most of those around him—a sense of cultural displacement shared by many African-Americans, but taken to extremes by Ra.

Yet, though Ra was among the first American jazz musicians to perform in African regalia, he scoffs at the concept of black pride, observing that "pride goeth before the fall." He also criticizes African-Americans for being too materialistic: "Black folks too close to slavery. They worked four hundred years, don't have nothin' to show for it. They tryin' to make up for that. It's about money, money, money.

"Black power, black pride. Actually, I prefer the word 'dark.' Black folks used to be darkies. 'A darky's born, he ain't no good no how, without a song,' I take that as my song. God didn't give the black man anything but his music."

On the other hand, Ra believes—as do an increasing number of academics, both black and white—that the fundaments of Western thought, usually credited to the Greek philosophers, in fact stem from ancient Egypt. (The case was argued most persuasively by Martin Bernal, a white professor at Cornell University, in his *Black Athena: The Afro-Asiatic Roots of Classical Civilization*, which was published in 1987. But it was first argued in *Stolen Legacy: The Greeks Were Not the Authors of Greek Philosophy, but the People of North Africa, Commonly Called the*

Egyptians, a crackpot text published by the renegade black scholar George G. M. James in 1954. Ignored by the white academic establishment, James's book reached an avid black readership, possibly including Ra.) According to Ra, "the black races were in touch with the real creators of the universe at one time, in perfect communication with them, but they lost it. So they go to church, take dope, do all sort of things to try to regain that state. The white man never had it."

In West Germany recently, Sun Ra, who cautions his bandmembers "to never leave me alone with any nation," was "kidnapped" by an interviewer and a photographer, who took him to a planetarium and asked him questions that even he thought were strange. "Like how did I intend to get black people off of this planet. What kind of ship was I going to use. What kind of rocket fuel. I told them I wasn't using any gasoline. I'm usin' sound. Scientists haven't reached that stage yet, where you can run your car or heat your home with a cassette. But it will happen—with the right kind of music, of course." (Ra isn't the only one who's proposed tapping his music for the greater good: Norman Mailer, after being blown away by the Arkestra in Chicago thirty years ago, speculated that Ra's music could probably cure cancer.)

Ra likes to give the impression that he's deliberately been withholding his most visionary music from a species not yet prepared for it. "For years, I been tellin' John [tenor saxophonist John Gilmore, who joined the Arkestra in Chicago in 1963 and remains with it to this day], 'play and don't play. Play your best, but retain something the world has never heard before. And one day, I will tell you, John, OK, play it.'" For whatever reason, after orbiting the outer limits for much of the 1960s, Ra's music has returned to earth in the decades since. An entire set might now be given over to his offbeat arrangements of jazz and pop standards, or even to numbers from the Walt Disney songbook (the Arkestra now sometimes takes its traditional march around the auditorium to the tune of "Hi Ho, Hi Ho,

It's Off to Work We Go"). In Philadelphia recently, he says, a fan thanked him for playing "that sixth-grade music," meaning music that even someone with only an elementary school education could follow. Thanks to an outrageous persona more befitting a rock and roller than a jazzman, he's even begun to attract an audience on the edges of pop: last year's *Blue Delight*, his first major-label release after close to two hundred independent albums (counting those on his own Saturn label) was played on college alternative rock stations, alongside Camper Van Beethoven and REM.

The most common misconception about Ra's music—the only one that irks him—is that its dissonances are a matter of happenstance. "They say, 'Does the band have music or do they just play?'" he said mockingly, rummaging around on the top of his piano and producing a densely notated page of sheet music for my inspection. This score-in-progress was about the only thing that Ra wanted to show me that he was able to put his hands on quickly. He wobbled around his workshop trying to find newspaper clippings and books of his poetry amid the clutter of record albums, hand drums, and artworks given to him by admirers (the most striking of these were a vibrant painting of him as a Pharaoh, with a headdress of piano keys, and a metal sculpture of the Egyptian sun god in which Ra had stuck his phone bill for safe keeping). He apologized for the funky asceticism of his digs by way of an analogy: "If there's no sawdust in the carpenter's workshop, no work is gettin' done."

The Ra house, on Morton Street, is weatherbeaten, but not an eyesore by neighborhood standards, despite the blue paint on the window frames and the thick strips of plastic hung to keep out the cold. (Twenty-one years ago, when Ra and his men moved here, their black neighbors were frightened of them. Now Ra and his men are becoming increasingly frightened of their younger neighbors.) Ra, who also maintains a nearby apartment for business purposes, lives here with a fluctuating number of his most devoted sidemen. The house ban on drugs and alcohol also applies to female cohabitation, which is unfortunate, because the place could use what my mother refers to as a woman's touch.

"It's more than one man can do," Sun Ra complained at one point. "I got to write my music and take care of the bookings, plus worry about the men's health, make sure they eat properly and everything."

Ra's sidemen, who were studying their sheet music and warming up on their horns as they waited for him to begin rehearsal, chatted happily about the Super Bowl and the Publisher's Clearing House Millionaire Sweepstakes notification that one of them had received in the morning mail, as Sun Ra gabbed just as casually about interplanetary travel and the secrets of antiquity. It seemed like a good time to ask him about his earthly needs. "I have to eat properly," he said. "But I sometimes forget to. I have to cook for myself, because I have to have everything just so. I like my food real done. Everybody likes my moon soup. I have to choose the vegetables real carefully—the corn, the tomatoes, the okra—and heat it at just the right temperature, so you taste each vegetable individually. Not a soup where you can't taste none of the ingredients in it."

I asked him something I was dying to know: Had he ever gone, during his years in Philadelphia, to watch the mummers strut up Broad Street in their feathered capes and sequined headdresses on New Year's Day? The annual parade is Philly's version of Mardi Gras, and it, too, is African derived, right down to that fluid, hips-and-shoulders strut the mummers do to "Oh, 'Dem Golden Slippers" (composed, it just so happens, by James Bland, a black man, though the parade itself, which dates to the turn of the century, has traditionally been lily-white; in addition to carrying banjos, its participants wore minstrels' blackface in the parade's early days).

He sure had, Sun Ra said, many times, in fact. "All that work for one day, and competitive, too," he said, admiringly.

But don't look for Sun Ra to show up in costume on Broad

Street on New Year's Day anytime soon, even if invited to. "I have to keep something of a low profile," he said, "because what I'm doin' is earthshaking. I don't want to panic anyone."

(FEBRUARY 1990)

Sun Ra left this planet, as he might put it, in 1993.

Dog Wild

For decades newspaper reporters have been asking Dizzy Gillespie why he's called Dizzy, why his horn is tilted, and why he puffs up his cheeks so big when he plays. In talking to Lester Bowie—Gillespie's heir apparent as clown prince of the trumpet—the question you can't avoid is, "What's the significance of the physician's lab coat?"

Make that coats, plural, because though Bowie (who pronounces his last name as Jim did, not as David does) wears medical whites as a member of the Art Ensemble of Chicago, standard bearers for the jazz avant-garde for close to a quarter of a century now, he opts for technicolor as the leader of Brass Fantasy, a ten-piece group including two percussionists, tuba, French horn, two trombones, and three trumpets besides his own.

"I wear a sequined lab coat with Brass Fantasy, because that's a glitzier band," Bowie explained during a recent interview from his home in Brooklyn. "I even got 'em in gold and silver lamé."

Shades of Liberace?

"Yeah, well as a matter of fact, you know what the guys in Brass Fantasy call me?" Bowie asked, before delivering the punch line. "*Nigger*-achhi."

But seriously, folks. "Everybody in the Art Ensemble dresses up, because of the theatrical aspect of playing music. I used to be a lot of different characters in that group. I used to dress up like a janitor or a housepainter. I was a construction worker in a hard hat. I finally settled on the lab jacket mainly because it's light, easy to carry.

"Plus, it stands for research—the technical aspects of playing the trumpet, the science of it, how certain sounds affect people. I consider the stage to be, like, my laboratory. I want to see what reaction a certain note, a certain pitch, a slightly different inflection will get. Like, if I play an E one way, then what sort of reaction do I get if I repeat that same E, but pressing the valve only halfway down?

"I notice their surprise. Sometimes, maybe, their disgust," explained Bowie, whose measured technique—developed at a time when most young trumpeters were striving for long, fast, continuous lines in the manner of Freddie Hubbard—enables him to squeeze notes into vulgar, sidesplitting imprecations. "I just like getting a reaction."

That's the difference between Bowie and your garden variety jazz experimentalist: he acknowledges that his audiences have a stake in the outcome. Dressed as a doctor, he—and Brass Fantasy—have discovered a cure for anhedonia (fear of fun, in layman's terms).

Brass Fantasy's five albums, beginning with *I Only Have Eyes for You* in 1985, have included their share of band-generated originals—by Bowie, Bruce Purse (the band's producer), and such former or current members as Craig Harris, Steve Turre, and E. J. Allen. These have made imaginative use of the band's unusual instrumentation: Allen's Iberian-tinged arrangement of Purse's "After Thought" on the new *My Way* (DIW), for example, with tuba and trombones gracefully shadowing the higher-pitched horns. More to the point, though, Brass Fantasy have also torn apart and reassembled a veritable jukebox worth of oldies and more recent pop hits, including Fats Domino's "Blueberry Hill," Lloyd Price's "Personality," the Four Seasons' "Oh, What a Night," Michael Jackson's "Thriller," Bobby McFerrin's "Don't Worry, Be Happy," Whitney's Houston's "Saving All My Love for You," and James Brown's "I Got You" and "Papa's Got a Brand New Bag."

Not to mention "My Way," loser Paul Anka's treacly anthem for winner Frank Sinatra. Taking what amounts to the lead "vocal," Bowie doesn't completely lampoon the song. "I just identify with its message. Doing it *my* way, not kissing anybody's ass," Bowie replied when asked what could possibly have drawn him to the song. "Plus I get a big kick out of taking a song that was made famous by a singer and doing it with a brass ensemble, so that it's totally different but you can still feel the presence of the original."

Postmodernism in a nutshell.

Brass Fantasy's immediate forerunner was the New York Hot Trumpet Repertory Band, an unrecorded group with five trumpets and nothing else that Bowie formed in the late '70s. And in high school, he led a band called the Continentals, which played "a combination of doo wop, bebop, Dixieland and boogie woogie, with Sousa influences, similar to Brass Fantasy in a way, with a sousaphone in the rhythm section, instead of a bass."

But the band's lineage can be traced as far back as the Bartonsville Cornet Band, the marching band to which Bowie's father and at least four of his uncles once belonged in Frederick, Maryland, Bowie's birthplace. As Bowie pointed out during the interview, his hometown, about forty-five miles west of Baltimore, is "a little bit famous, on account of the Civil War and John Greenleaf Whittier's 'Barbara Frietchie.'" (One of the most memorized American poems of the nineteenth century,

"Barbara Frietchie" recounts the legend of an elderly Frederick woman who defiantly waved the Union flag at a squadron of Confederate horsemen commanded by Stonewall Jackson.) In some circles, Frederick is just as famous as the site of the annual Bowie-Thomas Family Reunion, which has been attended each August since 1963 by as many as five hundred of Bowie's close and distant relatives. It includes picnics, concerts by Bowie's various bands and those of his brothers, Byron (an alto saxophonist) and Joseph (a trombonist and leader of Defunct), and services at an African Methodist Episcopalian Church built on ground donated by Bowie's great-grandmother in 1880.

Bowie's immediate family continued to summer in Frederick even after relocating first to Little Rock, Arkansas, in 1943, when he was two, and then to St. Louis a year or two later. William Lester Bowie, his father, now eighty-five and back in Frederick year round, directed the concert and marching bands at Washington Vocational Tech in St. Louis until his retirement some twenty years ago. But at his insistence, his three sons attended the more academically oriented Sumner High School, said to be the oldest black high school west of the Mississippi.

"He decided to let us cause problems for somebody else," Bowie cracked—in this case, Sumner's C. J. Wilson, in Bowie's estimation, "one of the many great high school band directors of that period who might have been an excellent classical musician, except for the racial situation. So they became teachers and passed their love of music on to people like me."

After his graduation, Bowie enlisted in the Air Force. "To travel, right? But I wound up spending the whole three years in Texas, first San Antonio, then Amarillo." Told that no positions were open in the Air Force Band, he became an M.P. "I could have been in the bugle corps, but having played solo cornet with the all-city student orchestra in St. Louis, I considered bugle to be beneath me. Being a policeman sounded like more fun." Besides, the pistol he was permitted to carry even off duty gave him a sense of security in the blues clubs he jammed in on weekends, which he describes as "straight-ahead Texas ghetto get-your-throat-cut-quick kind of rough, with people gettin' shot up and cut up every night."

That wasn't the last that he saw of raucous crowds. Following his discharge and two years of college, at Lincoln and North Texas State Universities, Bowie—eager to become a jazz musician, but more eager "to become a musician, period, which meant learning to feed myself with my horn"—hit the road with the Leon Claxton Harlem Revue, an old-fashioned midway show with "a sword swallower, a bearded lady, a two-headed man, a Viking giant, some three-legged calves, all kinds of rides and games of chance, and dancing girls we played for who doubled as prostitutes after closing—regular carny-type stuff. We worked six days a week, fourteen hours a day, for fifty-nine dollars a week. That was around 1962."

Around the same time, Bowie also traveled the midwest with a variety of blues and R&B singers, including Jackie Wilson and Little Milton, and "played all of those little dirt-floor clubs in Central Missouri" with an obscure act called Jack Harris and the Arabians, with whom he made his recording debut, in Chicago. (Attention, discographers: Bowie doesn't remember the label or the exact date, but the title of the group's single was "Dog Wild." And, yes, the leader sometimes wore a turban.)

According to Bowie, midwestern musicians "don't even think about New York. They want to go to Chicago." He moved there as music director for Fontella Bass (then his wife) in 1965, as her record of "Rescue Me" was zooming up the charts. "I did a lot of session work in Chicago at first. Jingles and sessions for Chess and Brunswick Records, with singers like Jerry Butler, Gene Chandler, and Sugarpie DeSanto. But even though I loved doing that kind of work, I was getting kind of bored with it."

After he had been in Chicago for a year or so, a fellow musician took him to a rehearsal of Muhal Richard Abrams's Experimental Band, the renegade workshop ensemble that eventually spawned both the Art Ensemble of Chicago and its parent organization, the Association for the Advancement of Creative Musicians.

"That was where I met everybody, and I had never seen so many weird cats with instruments in one room in my whole life. It was a revelation."

The rest of jazz was in for a revelation just a few years later, when the Art Ensemble provided its own alternative to the fulltilt "energy" style then in fashion in New York. "We added humor, theatricality, the changing of moods," Bowie explains it. "We liked what was happening in New York, but it was monochromatic. We wanted to utilize it as one possible color among many, like the blues."

The secret of the Art Ensemble's longevity, in Bowie's opinion, is that its five members are not only free to moonlight, but encouraged. "What we say if there's a momentary conflict is, 'You want your own band? Then start your own band.'"

Bowie's own bands have included the "jumbo-size" Sho' Nuff Orchestra and the jazz-and-gospel hybrid From the Root to the Source, featuring vocals by Fontella Bass, her mother, Martha, and her stepbrother, David Peaston (now a hot item in pop, following his appearances on TV's *It's Showtime at the Apollo*). Of Brass Fantasy, the most popular and durable of his enterprises, Bowie remarked, "People sometimes don't even realize until they think about it a few days later that we didn't have keyboards, bass, or any saxophones up there. It's very subtle."

Thankfully no more subtle than you'd expect from a man with a tattoo of a trumpet emitting flames on his right arm. Listening to Brass Fantasy accelerate the tempo and escalate the dynamics toward the end of their version of "My Way," you imagine the drums and horns crisscrossing at the fifty-yard line, like the Grambling State University Marching Band.

"Hey, that was my father's world," exclaimed Bowie, now married to a graphic artist, with five children of his own ranging in age from eight to thirty, and a three-year-old granddaughter. "I'm the original halftime kid. I used to watch football on TV just to hear the halftime music."

So Brass Fantasy takes him back to the beginning?

"Right. And maybe one day, I'll put up a tent on stage, start my own carny."

(JANUARY 1991)

Bagels and Dreadlocks

You wanna hear the tune of Mickey's that's the hardest of 'em all to play?" Don Byron asked, fast-forwarding the home cassette of *Mickey Katz Plays Music for Weddings, Bar Mitzvahs, and Brisses* he said I could take with me when we left.

"This is it," he said, landing on the beginning of something he identified as "Frailach Jamboree." It was one of the tunes he'd taught his band in preparation for a tribute to Katz at the Knitting Factory a few nights later.

"Listen to them motherfuckers! They're puttin' some *swing* on the *thing!*" he shouted over the woofing clarinet, the hot-as-salsa trumpet, the Schlomo Grappelli violin. "You hear that tempo, B.?"

"B." was short for "Homeboy," which is what Byron calls you once he decides you're OK. I said that such a lickety-split tempo must be difficult not to screw up.

"Don't say that, man," he pleaded, looking at me as though I was hopeless. "Don't put the jinx on me."

Don Byron is probably sick and tired of people joking that

he doesn't *look* Jewish. Maybe it's the dreadlocks, har, har, har.

Klezmer, a Yiddish word borrowed from Hebrew, literally means "instrument or vessel of music," or just "musician." But it was also the name for the *kind* of music—party music, really—that Eastern-European Jews brought with them to this country from the *shtetls* about a hundred years ago. Musicologists say that it was an instrumental secularization of medieval cantorial singing, a theory that makes sense once you've heard Byron or any of the older klezmer clarinetists he admires uvulating fervently up and down a note.

As one of very few klezmers of color (the only others I can think of offhand are Al Patterson and J. D. Parran, both of whom are in Byron's band), Byron might seem to be in a position analogous to that of a white bluesman. There are obvious differences, though, beginning with the fact that it's par for the course for whites to perpetuate fading black styles, but virtually unheard of for a young black musician to revive a white ethnic minority's rara avis. And unlike some of the white boys who play that funky music, Byron isn't on a race-switching trip. "I'm not Mezz Mezzrow in reverse," he told me, referring to the fabled Jewish clarinetist and drug dealer of the 1930s, who convinced himself and the French jazz critics (if nobody in Harlem) that he was black underneath the skin. "It's not like when I play Yiddish music, I close my eyes and forget that I'm a black man, not a Jew. And I'm not pretending that I'm in the middle of a field somewhere in Poland in the nineteenth century, like a lot of the Jewish kids who're playing klezmer."

Even when jamming with their idols, white bluesmen usually wind up doing their stuff for fellow white blues fans. But Byron regularly faces audiences who think of klezmer as theirs, not his. "A few weeks ago, we were doing Mickey Katz's 'Trombenik,'" he told me on the afternoon that I took the number 6 local up to Elder Avenue in the South Bronx, where he met me on his bicycle and escorted me over to his place on 187th Street. "The title is Yiddish for a no-goodnik, and you pronounce it 'Trum-BENIK.' I know that. But as a joke, I announced it as 'Trum-BONE-nik,' because it features the trombonist. Do you know, about a dozen Jewish cats yelled out '*Trum-BENIK! trum-BENIK!*'"

This wasn't at a synagogue or Jewish recreation center, mind you. It was at the Knitting Factory, a nondenominational temple where, as *The New Yorker* never tires of pointing out, "beat and melody are optional [and] 'music' and 'noise' [are] relative terms." Actually, the joke was on the pedants who yelled out, as though correcting a bar mitzvah boy. According to Leo Rosten, a *trombenik* is somebody who blows his own horn. So Katz, in featuring his trombonist, was making a pun.

Even so, Byron isn't taking any more chances. "You all can rate me on my pronunciations," he announced the last time I heard him perform "Trombenik." "Like the Olympics. 'Five-point-five from the Rumanian judge.'"

"Do you mind if I put the TV on in the other room and let it blast while we talk?" Byron asked after pouring me a glass of cherry seltzer. "*Video Music Box* is on, and you can never tell when they might play 'Big Ol' Butt' by L. L. Cool J. I wanna tape it if they do."

Byron's one-bedroom apartment is on the second floor of a three-story walk-up owned by his parents, who live across the hall, "and who first turned the key in that door downstairs the day my mother's water broke." The apartment is indifferently furnished and littered with *tchotchkes*—movie posters ("That describes my current relationships," he said, pointing to one for something called *Three Murderesses*), Sports Flix baseball cards ("This one of Tom Seaver in a Red Sox uniform is going to be worth money someday"), rare LPs by both Mickey Katz and James Brown, toy footballs, and a 1950s viewmaster Byron clinked absentmindedly as he talked.

Byron, who's thirty-one and doubles on baritone saxophone, is a postmodern eclectic in good standing: one of Marc Ribot's Rootless Cosmopolitans, and the leader of a strings-

and-woodwinds, Schoenberg-and-beyond chamber group called Semaphore. He's interpreted Scott Joplin with Gunther Schuller's New England Conservatory Ragtime Ensemble, and Duke Ellington with the ghost band led by Ellington's son, Mercer (in which he took the part of the mighty Harry Carney—"an Arnold Schwarzenegger gig").

But he keeps coming back to klezmer. Eleven years ago, as an undergraduate at the New England Conservatory of Music in Boston, he was a charter member of (and one of a handful of non-Jews in) the Klezmer Conservatory Band, the brainchild of Hankus Netsky, and just one of several Yiddische revival ensembles formed around that time in various parts of the country. He stayed with the KCB until 1986, by which time he'd begun to make a noise in jazz as a sideman with such younger eminences as Hamiet Bluiett, Craig Harris, and David Murray.

In fact, it was right after Byron had been fired by Bluiett, at a New York club called Carlos I in 1988, that I first introduced myself to him. Bluiett's Telepathic Orchestra (Leaving Too Much to Telepathy would have been more fitting) had just finished murdering Wayne Shorter's "Footsteps," and a frustrated Bluiett had waved Byron and another member of the reed section off of the bandstand, throwing a stool in their general direction for good measure. Byron said that this was a typical night with Bluiett—including the firing, which didn't necessarily mean that he was excused from playing the second set.

I learned something else from him that night. I assumed that the KCB had been just a gig for him—a way of getting his chops together for the big time. But he told me that he was now working Jewish affairs with his *own* band.

"Yeah, even though I was playing with all the heavy cats," Byron said, when I reminded him of that first conversation. "See, I left the KCB because it's difficult to be in a band with fourteen other people and get along with everybody year after year. But I was afraid that I would never play klezmer again, and

I didn't want to lose that skill. I felt like one of those track-and-field cats who has nowhere to go after the Olympics. Ingrid Monson, one of the trumpeters in the band, who's Swedish, was leaving, too, and she felt the same way. I mean, it wasn't like the rabbis I met with the KCB were going to be calling *me* up and asking if I could make a gig at their synagogue. So Ingrid and I made a band together. No concert gigs, just weddings. She did the bookings, and I took care of the music.

"Nobody had a book like us. In fact, you gotta take a look at it, B.," Byron said, fetching a bound volume of arrangements from the other room. He leafed past the klezmer transcriptions and the Israeli material to the Motown tunes. "I had twenty, maybe twenty-five Motown transcriptions, with those bad James Jamerson bass lines that bring the sound right out to the people on the dancefloor. Plus things like 'Downtown,' 'Judy's Turn to Cry,' 'Cold Sweat, Part 2' . . ."

What about the Jewish stuff?

He flipped back to "Ayhar Nach Mein Chassene." "You know that one? It means 'a year after our wedding.' Let's hear *you* pronounce it, B."

I admitted that my Yiddish wasn't so good.

"Mine, neither," he said. "But when *I* say it wrong, it's supposed to be cute," he added in a dour voice, revealing just the proper amount of cynicism toward those audiences who find the idea of a black man doing that old yi-diddle-diddle just too adorable for words.

"I heard all sorts of music around here when I was growing up," Byron said. "Now the neighborhood is mostly black and Hispanic, but there used to be a lot of Jewish families. That church on the corner," he said, gesturing toward the window, "used to be a synagogue. If you look close, you can still see the star above the door. I used to hear Jewish music on the radio, on *Bagels and Lox: Art Raymond's Sunday Simcha*, on WEVD, 'the station that speaks all languages.' My folks were almost militant about me checking out all different kinds of music, whether it was Dizzy at the Village Gate or Leonard Bernstein's Young People's Concerts. You used to watch them on TV? Well, I was in the audience for some of them."

Byron's father is a retired mailman who, though not Jamaican, once played bass in New York calypso bands. "My mother's not a musician, but she's likely to sit down and play 'Clair de lune' on that piano over there whenever the mood strikes her. She worked for the phone company, as one of the first generation of Adam Clayton Powell–installed blacks hired to do more than just sweep up the floors. She's retired now, but you still can't say anything bad about the phone company around her.

"Before clarinet, I played little knickknacky instruments, like recorder. What happened, we had a dog that I was allergic to, and the allergy developed into asthma. So the doctor recommended as therapy either swimming or a wind instrument. I have a phobia about going into the water, so I inherited a clarinet from the family pool of instruments."

Byron pointed to a copy of Lawrence Welk's *Save the Last Dance for Me* thumbtacked to the wall. "He had the only TV show where you ever saw anyone playing clarinet. That was my ambition—to play in his band and with the Conservatory Ragtime Ensemble, which I must have seen on PBS." Because I wanted to give Byron the benefit of the doubt by chalking some things up to camp, I had restrained myself from asking about Welk—and about the Neil Diamond song on his answering machine. But I did ask about the color poster of a dignified gentleman identified as Guy Deplus.

"Guy Deplus!" Byron exclaimed, and began to read the legend under the photo. "*Professeur de Clarinette du Conservatoire National Supérior de Musique de Paris!* My idol! Mister New Music. The clarinetist on the original recording of Messiaen's 'Quartet for the End of Time'!"

Jimmy Hamilton, Tony Scott, and Artie Shaw were Byron's favorites among jazz clarinetists. "Until Paul Gonsalves joined

Duke, nobody in that band was playing any hipper shit than
Hamilton. He was the hippest cat in a section of hip cats. Artie
Shaw was bad, man. He was a better legit player than Benny
Goodman, whose classical recordings are a joke among people
who know that music—whether or not they'd want to say that
in print. But it's not like I can steal lines from Artie or any other jazz clarinetist, because we're talking about an instrument
that's been dead in the water since 1960, as far as jazz is con-
cerned. I listen to saxophonists and pianists. Joe Henderson is
really my man.

"You know, even before I started playing jazz, people in
school had me stereotyped as a jazz player because I didn't look
or talk Bryant Gumbelish, the way that most brothers in classical music tend to do. When I got into jazz, my friends were [the
alto saxophonists] Greg Osby and Donald Harrison, from the
Berklee School of Music. They were the baddest young cats in
Boston at that time. For a while I wanted to do what they were
doin'—get in front of a too-loud drummer and sound like
Coltrane. But I was also running down to New York every
chance I got to hear punked-out bands like Defunkt and James
White and the Blacks.

"Klezmer was the first old music I ever responded to. Before
that, I was one of those guys who wouldn't even watch silent
movies, because I start thinking how most of the actors in them
were probably dead and that would depress me. Hankus Netsky
recruited me for this band he put together to play three
klezmer tunes for a NEC faculty concert called 'Contemporary
Dimensions of Twentieth-Century Jewish Music,' or something
like that—the other faculty members played stuff by Leonard
Bernstein and George Rochberg, but Hankus wanted to do
something different. That was the beginning of the Klezmer
Conservatory Band.

"At first, my attitude was, OK, you put a piece of music in
front of me and I can deal with it. But I responded immediately to the *mischief* in that music: the place on each of the old

records where the clarinetist would play the most *out* thing he could think of. It's not like in jazz, where a guy gets hot and takes another chorus. There might be just one exciting trill, but that's where the creativity was. Most of the young cats playing klezmer are just trying to sound like the old 78s. But those guys on the records were taking risks. That's what I think I brought to klezmer that excited the rest of the band. Maybe some of the stuff I played was inappropriate, especially in the beginning. But at least I was doing something new. And as time went by, I developed my own voice in that language."

Lately Byron has channeled his interest in klezmer into the music of Mickey Katz, a clarinetist, singer, and noveltymeister of the 1950s, for whom indigestion was the ultimate Jewish experience—or so you might think from his "Bagle Call Rag," "Don't Let the Schmaltz Get in Your Eyes," "How Much Is That Pickle in the Window," and his devastating Mel Brooksian *schlemiel*ization of Tennessee Ernie's "Sixteen Tons":

> *To eat a piece* kishke
> *you must have* koyech.
> *Just like a* shtayn,
> *it lays in your* boyech.

I knew that Katz, who died in 1985, once was an arranger for Spike Jones, and that he was Joel Grey's father and Jennifer's grandfather. What I wanted Byron to tell me, as he walked me back to Elder Avenue, was (a) whether he got all of Katz's Yiddish and Yinglish jokes, and (b) whether it was true what other klezmers told had told me, that there were two Mickey Katzes: the *tumler* of the parodies and the maestro responsible for the scintillating *Music for Weddings, Bar Mitzvahs, and Brisses.*

"Nobody gets all the jokes, man, because nobody knows that *much* Yiddish anymore," claimed Byron, whose Mickey Katz band includes Patterson on trombone, Parran on reeds, Tony Barrera on trumpet, Mark Feldman on violin, Lee Musik-

er or Uri Caine on piano, Mark Dresser on bass, Richie
Schwarz on drums and Mr. Bones xylophone, and Loren
Sklamberg on vocals—sidemen whose collective credentials
range from Ellington, Basie, and *Black and Blue* to Anthony
Braxton, Steve Reich, Frank Zappa, and John Zorn.

"And no, you can't say there were two different Mickey
Katzes, because that's one of the few instrumental albums he
made like that, with just incidental vocals and patter. The rest of
his stuff is the parodies, which are very, very funny, including
one called 'Paisach in Portugal' that I won't do in concert
because it's got an awful *faygelah* joke. But on almost every
record he ever made, that instrumental genius bursts through,
usually when the band goes into that hora thing in the middle
of the parody.

"The first time I heard him, it was 'Mickey's Dreidel,' one
of the records from Hankus's collection, and I thought, 'What *is*
this? This stuff is *bad*. And whoever is on that clarinet sounds a
little like *me*.' Because his playing had that athleticism I like.
Getting a band together to play his music is something I've
wanted to do for a long time, but I didn't know where I was
going to find the musicians to do Mickey justice until I was on
the road with Mercer Ellington. The lead trumpeter was Tony
Barrera. Big, macho, Latino cat. We became running buddies. I
asked him if he ever heard of Mickey's trumpeter, Mannie
Klein. And he yelled, '*Mannie Klein*! That's my *man*!' "

Somebody recently asked me if Byron was in klezmer's
"mainstream." What a foolish question. Counting his there are
perhaps only about half a dozen active klezmer bands, and the
question worth asking about the rest of them isn't "mainstream
or fringe?" but "Orthodox, Conservative, or Reform?" Klezmer
is absolutely secular: for dancing, not *davening*. As Byron points
out, "If religion is mentioned at all in the lyrics, it's usually to
say, 'Oh, look at the rabbi. He's making a fool of himself by eating too much,' or something like that." But for many younger
Jewish musicians, including those in the KCB, klezmer has

become a source of cultural identity, growing desecularized in the process. These days, if you don't lock arms for the hora at the end of a KCB concert, you're worse than a spoilsport—you're probably a gentile (which I, in fact, *am*, though I know Jews who feel the same way). These bands make klezmer mirthless fun.

Byron doesn't have a sanctimonious bone in his body. As a non-Jew he responds to klezmer strictly as music (significantly, a style of music in which clarinet is undisputed king) and asks that his listeners do the same. Does his brand of klezmer smack of opportunism, all the same? Not at all. It's not as though there's much demand for this music even at catered affairs, where you're likelier to hear a mix of Motown, current Top 40, *Fiddler on the Roof* ("Sabbath Prayer" has become a favorite of with-it cantors who accompany themselves on electric guitar), and Israeli folk tunes (Hebrew is where the action is now). Besides which nobody—black or white—is going to make a bundle performing Mickey Katz, full appreciation of whose lampoons requires not only some fluency in Yiddish, but also some familiarity with (and maybe a peculiar affection for) that dreck-filled period of popular music between the demise of the big bands and the official birth of rock and roll—a period so forgettable that not even Casey Kasem has a name for it.

Even so, Byron commands a loyal following, if only in New York. In April he filled the Knitting Factory to at least twice its fire capacity (standing room only, and not much of that): the people you think you always see there (guys with ponytails from the *last* time men wore them) rubbing elbows with people who looked as though they had metaphorically crossed Delancey just for this. I suspected that word had leaked out that Joel Grey was going to be singing three of his father's parodies with Byron that night. The bartender said the club was always like this when Byron did Mickey Katz.

At any rate, unlike most klezmer audiences, this one was hip enough not to throw off the musicians' timing by attempting to clap along. My own entourage included a friend from Boston, a music critic specializing in rock and world beat who knew nothing about Byron and even less about Katz. I was curious to see his reaction. "This is delightful," he said over the amen ending of "Mazeltov Dances," echoing my sentiments exactly, but surprising me with his word choice (he usually indicates approval with words like *feral*). The music hooked him, as it had me, with its contrapuntal oomph. It was like the MJQ, but with wailing horns, ethnic charm, and a dab or two of Jelly Roll Morton and John Philip Sousa. Delightful was the word for it, all right.

"This is Jewish hip-hop," Byron deadpanned in introducing Katz's "Litvak Square Dance." "Hope its's klezmer def and klezmer fresh enough for you. Know what I'm sayin'?" In addition to Katz's originals, parodies, and traditional arrangements, Byron also played a piece of his own called "Tears," accompanied by just Mark Dresser's bowed bass and Uri Caine's tolling piano-in-octaves. It was a lament for Katz combining elements of traditional Yiddish *doyne* and a cool meditation on the overtone series, with a slowed-down and deliciously extended quote from "Kiss of Meyer" (Katz's send up of Georgia Gibbs's "Kiss of Fire") toward the end.

"My father would have loved you!" Joel Grey told Byron when he joined him to sing "Tickle Tickle" ("Tico Tico"), "Geshray of de Vilde Kotcke" ("Cry of the Wild Goose"), and "Haim affen Range" (you shouldn't have to ask). Joel Grey at the Knitting Factory? I had seen Grey perform live once before, in a road show of *Cabaret*. And I do mean *seen*, not heard: suffering from laryngitis, he'd lipsynced his numbers while a backstage stand-in did the actual singing. But hearing him with Byron's band was like hearing *Cabaret* for real, if only because it revealed how much of his father's mocking delivery Grey had borrowed for his role as the Kit Kat Klub's master of ceremonies—especially for the S.S. favorite, "If You Could See Her Through My Eyes (She Wouldn't Look Jewish at All)."

Grey exuded the right sort of theatricality, milking the laughs without overdoing it, pausing just long enough between jokes for the punch lines to sink in and not a second more. Between him and Byron, you had no doubt that you were hearing the definitive reinterpretation of Mickey Katz.

On the way home, I listened to the Mickey Katz tape that Byron had given me and found myself thinking about how Byron's musical ecumenism made him a kin of sorts to the first American klezmers. Like most professional musicians, then as now, klezmers were naturally curious about other ways of making music and prided themselves on their ability to deal with anything put in front of them. Take Mannie Klein, for example. In addition to working with Katz, he also played Goodman and Dorsey, backed Frankie Laine on "That's My Desire," and dubbed bugle for Montgomery Clift in *From Here to Eternity*.

I remembered something Byron said about klezmer á la Mickey Katz: "It wasn't folk music, man. It was some *nasty, urban, ethnic* shit, B." Then I flipped over his cassette to find that he'd recorded King Curtis and Champion Jack Dupree on the other side.

(JULY 1990)

"Zorn" for "Anger"

John Zorn, whom John Rockwell of the *New York Times* has called "the single most interesting, important and influential composer to arise from the Manhattan 'downtown' avant-garde

scene since Steve Reich and Philip Glass," is the only musician
I've ever considered suing. I'm not entirely joking. In 1989,
when Zorn (whose name in German means "anger"), wearing
a T-shirt that read DIE YUPPIE SCUM!, was playing Ornette
Coleman tunes on alto saxophone with his band Spy vs. Spy at
the Painted Bride Art Center in Philadelphia, he put me and
everyone else in the small auditorium at risk of permanent
hearing loss by recklessly turning the volume up as high as it
would go.

I'm not ordinarily squeamish about loud music, but Spy vs.
Spy's opening downbeat was so brutal that I thought I felt my
eardrums break. Thirty seconds into the first tune my head was
spinning as though I had been drunk and awake for days on
end, and my stomach began to churn in reaction to the music's
velocity, which I decided was almost as senseless as the volume.
Zorn and Spy vs. Spy—the alto saxophonist Tim Berne, the
bassist Mark Dresser, and the drummers Joey Baron and
Michael Vatcher—were grinding Coleman's music down into a
feelingless, monochromatic din. They treated his compositions,
which are benchmarks of free jazz, as though they were speed
metal (bohemianized heavy metal, without the oversized stage
accouterments) or hard core (the most dystopian contemporary
mutation of what used to be called punk). Although intended
as homage, the concert amounted to heresy, presenting Ornette
Coleman without swing, sensuality, and blues-based *joie de vivre*
that make even his own forays into rock and funk recognizable
as jazz and identifiable as his.

All around me people were fleeing with hands over their
ears, while a handful of mostly younger audience members,
there for the duration, sneered. I should have fled, too, but a
combination of shell shock and journalistic instinct kept me
glued to my seat. (Someone, maybe an infuriated Ornette
Coleman fan, overturned a sales table of Zorn albums and
compact discs on his way out.) Who would have thought that
a quintet without a single electric instrument could inflict such

pain? As though to add insult to injury, the bandmembers chatted among themselves between salvos but didn't address the audience until about twenty minutes and nine or ten numbers had passed. When Baron glanced up from his drums (rather dazed-looking himself, I thought) and asked "How ya doin' out there?" I didn't hear anybody answer him.

This nightmare was still on my mind when I spoke with Zorn in New York last spring. "A lot of people were outraged when they first heard Ornette play his music in the fifties and sixties," he said, in defense of his similar junking of Coleman on his 1989 album *Spy vs. Spy* (Elektra Musician). "The speed and the power and the volume, those are elements that admittedly were not part of Ornette's original conception. But those are essential elements in bringing it up to date, in giving it the same impact it had then. Volume is an important parameter. It's visceral. Physical."

Granted, with practically anything now permissible in the name of music, the threat of physical damage posed by unreasonable volume might be the last remaining shock. But shouldn't a musician be wary of longtime effects on his own hearing? "Forget about it," said Zorn, a mild-looking New Yorker in his late thirties with a long, narrow face, stylish eyeglasses, and, when I last saw him, the beginnings of a ponytail. "My ears are blown already. I've been playing loud music for a long time." But he admitted that some of his sidemen wear earplugs. "That's the loudest situation they've ever been in," he said, referring to Naked City, yet another of his bands, which, in addition to jazz tunes and movie themes, also plays old surf hits and Zorn's own hard-core originals—a repertoire for which, I told him, top volume does seems appropriate. When I heard Naked City perform live, they were less painfully noisy than Spy vs. Spy.

That observation brought a hoot. "We probably weren't loud enough then," Zorn said.

By Zorn's current standards, probably not. One of those

New Yorkers who gives the impression of being as proud of that city's murder rate as Iowans are of their corn (the cover of Naked City's eponymous debut, released earlier this year, is Weegee's famous photograph of a corpse face down on the sidewalk with his revolver a few feet away), Zorn delights in his self-cast role as the bad boy of Manhattan's eclectic fringe. By this point, it's part of the identity he brings onstage with him.

In 1989 when the Brooklyn Philharmonic performed his "For Your Eyes Only" as part of New Music America, an annual showcase for avant-garde music that's staged in a different city each year, he used the space allotted to him for a biography in the festival brochure to attack NMA for annually sponsoring "the same tired names [and] pompous, overblown projects." (Most reviewers lambasted Zorn for taking the money if he felt that way, but—in all fairness—his piece had been commissioned by the Brooklyn Philharmonic, which considered the piece its own to perform whenever it wished.)

Zorn once wrote a piece for the Kronos Quartet that called on the members of that resolutely with-it but essentially straightlaced string ensemble to bark and growl like dogs. This was an example of his humor at its most lighthearted, but it can be heavy-handed, too. He once faxed a message to an Austrian concert promoter requesting that his trio be billed as ZOG—an acronym for "Zionist-Occupied Government," which is a rallying cry for The Order, the Aryan supremacist group that murdered the Denver talk show host Alan Berg in 1984. The trio, which Zorn describes as "the world's first all-Jewish heavy metal band," and whose other members are guitarist Elliott Sharp, a veteran free improviser, and drummer Ted Epstein, from Blind Idiot God, Zorn's favorite speed metal group, ultimately decided on the name Slan, after a monster in a 1950s science fiction novel.

Zorn, in short, is exactly the sort of rude, overgrown adolescent you would go out of your way to avoid, if only he weren't so . . . well, interesting, important, and influential (at least potentially). A decade ago he seemed just a minor figure in the New York avant-garde—not innovative, just eccentric. At that time his work consisted mostly of his "games" pieces: prankish, discontinuous, Zorn-"cued" group improvisations with titles like "Archery," "Rugby," and "Soccer." These sounded like frathouse Stockhausen and qualified as Zorn "compositions" only in the sense that a party can be said to belong to the person who throws it.

Then Zorn sprang a delightful surprise with *The Big Gundown* (Nonesuch/Icon), a 1986 album on which he "covered" the film music of Ennio Morricone, an Italian composer best known in this country for his soundtracks to Sergio Leone's spaghetti westerns. But Morricone has a much greater range than that, as Zorn showed. The album would have been notable if only for rounding up a veritable subterranean Manhattan who's who, including the keyboard player Wayne Horvitz and the guitarists Bill Frisell and Fred Frith, all of whom subsequently joined Naked City. With its kinesthetic mix of musical styles and its equivalent of jump cuts, wipes, fades, and dissolves, *The Big Gundown* played like a witty essay on the relationship of music and film—the perfect salute to its subject. In an obvious parallel with contemporary painting, the album established Zorn as a composer by acquisition, capable of altering a work's meaning by shifting its context. He gave new significance to the word "cover," traditional record business parlance for slavish emulation of another artist in an attempt to tap a new audience (in the 1950s, for instance, Pat Boone and other white artists "covered" Fats Domino and Little Richard). In Zorn's terms, reinterpretation in another style is simultaneously transgressive and the ultimate act of homage.

A year later, he followed up with *Spillane*, an album whose lengthy title track so successfully evoked the testosterone-and-bile ethos of its pulp-novelist namesake that, as Zorn complained to me, it was accepted as another of his covers rather than as an original work. With these back-to-back releases,

Zorn helped to clarify a previously murky new aesthetic: "avant-garde" as an *attitude* toward music and as an eclectic, self-contained genre, rather than simply a vanguard movement in classical, jazz, or pop.

Zorn also called attention to an audience whose values were identical to his as a performer, and that had just been waiting for someone like him to come along—something usually true of only the biggest pop stars, and almost never true of avant-gardists. "In general, my generation and younger, this is how we grew up," Zorn, who was born in Manhattan and raised in Queens, told me. "We had an unprecedented variety of music available to us, because of the availability of everything on LP."

Zorn's mother, a professor of education, liked classical music and world ethnic recordings; his father, a hairdresser, listened to jazz, country, and French chansons. "And through my brother, who's seven years older and wanted to be a greaser in the fifties, I was exposed to doo wop and the Silhouettes, groups like that." Around the age of fourteen, Zorn says, he immersed himself in Stravinsky, Webern, Ives, Varèse, and such contemporary experimental composers as Stockhausen and Mauricio Kagel. "But all through that period, I was listening to the Doors and playing bass in a surf band." As a high school student commuting daily from Queens to Manhattan, he also spent a lot of time in Manhattan's repertory movie houses, sometimes staring at the screen so long that he had to sleep at a schoolmate's apartment in Manhattan to avoid taking a subway home at a dangerous hour.

By practically living at the movies, he says, he was avoiding his squabbling parents, who are still together today, though not on very good terms with their son. But Zorn also found himself spellbound by film music—"the many [different] styles a film composer has to know in order to complement the images. In that sense I think the great film composers are the precursors of what my generation is doing today." In addition to Morricone, Zorn's pantheon includes Bernard Herrmann,

John Barry, Dimitri Tiomkin, Jerry Goldsmith, and Henry Mancini. His biggest formative influence of all, though, was Carl Stalling, whose music for Warner Bros. cartoons he worshiped, he realized later, for its discontinuity and use of Stockhausenlike "sound blocks"—not to mention the antic sound effects.

Stalling is suddenly in vogue. Last fall, in New York, *Bugs on Broadway* featured Bugs Bunny cartoons accompanied by a live orchestra playing Stalling's original music. The best of his soundtracks for Bugs, Daffy Duck, Road Runner, and others in the animated menagerie have now been collected on *The Carl Stalling Project: Music from Warner Bros. Cartoons 1936–1958* (Warner Bros.). Zorn, in the liner notes, praises Stalling for "following the visual logic of screen action rather than the traditional rules of musical form," thus creating "a radical compositional arc unprecedented in the history of music."

After high school Zorn briefly attended Webster College, in St. Louis, "a very small hippie liberal arts school that let you study whatever you wanted to and was the only college that would accept me." It was there that he "got turned on to the jazz scene seriously," through live exposure to Julius Hemphill, Oliver Lake, Hamiet Bluiett, and other then-local musicians who had bonded in a collective called BAG, for Black Artists Group. "I knew I didn't have a place in that, but I didn't really want a place. Jazz was just another kind of music I studied and learned from, like classical or rock."

When trying his hand at straight jazz, Zorn can be controversial without even trying. On *News for Lulu* (Hat Art), a 1987 trio session with Frisell and the trombonist George Lewis, Zorn plays compositions by Sonny Clark, Kenny Dorham, Hank Mobley, and Freddie Redd—unsung jazzmen associated with Blue Note Records in the late fifties and early sixties, a period and sound also favored by hard boppers Zorn's age and younger. But Zorn's approach is the antithesis of that of these neoconservatives. To begin with, his instrumentation is unorthodox (no rhythm section), and his choice of tunes was non-canonical. And instead of zipping through the chord changes of the tunes, he pays careful attention to their melodies and rhythms, finding in them improvisational possibilities that even their composers overlooked.

Not everyone appreciates Zorn's fresh slant on hard bop. Some reviewers dismiss it as his desperate attempt to mask his lack of conventional musicianship. Such criticism irks Zorn, although he swears it doesn't. "Some people say I can't play the changes, some people say I can't play in tune, and some people say I can't play the saxophone," he told me. "My basic response is I'm doing the best I can. You can spend your whole life, like Frisell has, learning to get inside the chords. I don't do it that way."

Zorn's way still includes free improvisation. Last May he gave a three-night retrospective of his "games" pieces—each involving a different group of improvisers—at the Knitting Factory, in lower Manhattan, a few blocks from his apartment. I was in the audience the first night, sitting behind two musicians awaiting their turn to go on stage. "Which piece is this?" one asked the other during Zorn's "Rugby." "I don't know. Don't they all sound alike?" the second musician replied. I had the feeling they'd had this conversation many times before.

A truism about free improvisation is that it's fun to play but murder to sit through. Another truism is that you gotta be there: it doesn't work on disc. At the Knitting Factory the rowdy fraternity of Zorn's music won me over, especially the trio piece "Rugby," performed by the cellist Tom Cora and the violinist Polly Bradford, with Zorn on saxophone and duck calls. (Apparently more considerate of audiences on his home turf than of those on the road, he warned that "Rugby" would be "excruciatingly loud," though it wasn't.) But I hesitate to recommend even *Cobra* (Hat Art), arguably Zorn's most successful record in this genre, which I listened to immediately upon receiving it in 1987, and have had no interest in listening to since.

Along with *The Big Gundown* and *Spillane*, the best introduction to Zorn's work is *Naked City* (Elektra/Nonesuch), on which he takes genrebending to delicious new extremes. Zorn being Zorn, *Naked City* tries your patience with a cluster of eight ear-numbing rants by the band and the screaming singer Yamatsuka Eye, none lasting more than thirty-eight seconds. My advice is to skip selections ten through seventeen when programming the CD, because the other eighteen tracks justify the effort. Zorn atones for *Spy vs. Spy* with a crafty reinterpretation of Ornette Coleman's "Lonely Woman" loaded with verbatim Coleman quotes over a this-means-business bass line appropriated from John Barry's "The James Bond Theme" (which is itself transformed into a Jimi Hendrix-style rave-up a few tracks later). It shouldn't work, but it does. The most satisfying of the disc's several movie themes are Georges Delarue's "Contempt" (done as an art-rock symphony, à la Glenn Branca) and Morricone's "The Sicilian Clan," on which Zorn's improvisation takes the form of an edgy but apposite countermelody.

Of the Zorn originals the one that stays with you the longest is "Saigon Pickup." Just under five minutes long, it comes at you in sections (as Fred Astaire said of a femme fatale in the Mickey Spillane parody sequence in the movie *The Bandwagon*): a minimalistic, almost Philip Glasslike piano theme; then Zorn squalling over an Asian-sounding scale; then a country and western pastiche; then back to the piano theme, this time reinforced by string synthesizer; then more squalling, followed by more C&W; then some lounge jazz; then some psychedelic organ and reggae drumming; then a gleeful, Ornette Colemanlike melody; then more country, more squalling, more minimalism, and the final fade. The miracle is that it isn't a hopeless audio collage. You never feel as though as though you're being given a smug demonstration of what's currently hot in music, as you sometimes do with Zorn (on this album's "Graveyard Shift," for example).

Zorn's breadth is such that he tends to fragment the intrepid audience he already has, which would seem to put masscult adulation out of the question. But on tracks like *Naked City*'s "Latin Quarter," "Reanimator," and "Batman" (a Zorn original, not Prince's movie or Neal Hefti's TV-show theme), the group rocks out so hard that some of his fans have begun to think of it as Zorn's "boogie" band—his ticket to commercial success. Guess again. Naked City's second release, due later this year, will consist of what Zorn calls "classical covers" of works by Debussy, Ives, Scriabin, and others. It's all part of Zorn's effort to take listeners by surprise. Let's hope this one doesn't hurt.

(JANUARY 1991)

Grand Guignol, *Naked City's album of classical "covers," was eventually released by Avant, a subsidiary of the Japanese label DIW, after Zorn severed his ties with Elektra/Nonesuch. Zorn, who no longer gives interviews, now lives part of the year in Japan and seems to have reembraced Judaism, to judge from such recent works as* Krystallnacht *and his series of albums with his band* Masada.

For Aesthetes of All Ages

T ime to sit down and be quiet, Caitlin," a mother of four seated in front of me at a performance of "Moscow Circus— Cirk Valentin" at the Gershwin Theatre last month instructed her youngest, who appeared to be about six and was standing in her seat for a better look at a rouged clown who was winding up a large mechanical dog and setting it loose on stage (it turned out to be a costumed man). "I expect big-girl behavior from you tonight."

The poor woman had no way of knowing that Bobby Previte and I would be setting a bad example with our unceasing whispering.

How I came to be at the circus with Bobby Previte is a long story. Taking self-inventory this fall, after rebounding from my forty-fifth birthday, I realized with a jolt that there were two things I still hadn't done. I'd never seen Frank Sinatra in person, and I'd never been to the circus. Pop Culturalists say that first-hand experience of certain phenomena is unnecessary. I can vouch for this. I "remember" Sinatra at the Paramount Theater in 1942, as though I'd witnessed him there through my own eyes. I've even dreamed of him. He died in one dream, and in memory of him, nearby church bells chimed "Saturday Night Is the Loneliest Night of the Week."

As for circuses, my actual knowledge of them begins with the episodes of *Circus Boy* I watched as a kid and ends with *Wings of Desire* and *Fellini's Clowns*. But never having been under a big top didn't stop William Butler Yeats from employing "stilted boys," a "burnished chariot," a "Lion and woman and the Lord knows what else" as (literally) metaphors-to-end-all-metaphors in "The Circus Animals' Desertion," and it's never stopped me from joking about clowns in trick cars on finding myself squeezed into a Toyota or VW with too many fellow passengers.

I finally saw Sinatra from the uppermost tier of a Philadelphia sports arena whose unreasonable scale combined with his faltering memory to diminish him somehow. This was in early November, a few nights after I attended a performance of the Moscow Circus with Bobby—my friend in the business, as it were.

Bobby, a drummer and composer who grudgingly admits

to being forty but objects to the label "downtown" even though that's his usual orbit, had written a new score for the Moscow Circus, working closely with its director, Valentin Gneushev, and his troupe in Moscow in August, during the failed coup. Bobby's departure from Moscow on the first night of Gorbachev's detention, when the city was under strict curfew and all of the main roads to the airport were blocked by tank guards, is a story in itself, possibly involving bribery on the part of his translator. On his return to New York, he recorded *Music of the Moscow Circus* (Gramavision) with a few of his regular associates, including the pianist Steve Gaboury, the trumpeter Herb Robertson, the violinist Mark Feldman, and the guitarist Jerome Harris.

Bobby leads two different bands and, generally speaking, composes two very different kinds of music: knotty jazz for the septet Weather Clear, Track Fast; and technoeclectic for Empty Suits, his other band, and for special projects like this circus. And generally speaking, I prefer the knotty jazz—call it unbop—to the techno, which can be overcalculated and spacey. But techno or not, parts of Bobby's circus album, including his brief interludes for the clowns, were so energetic they might have been shot from a cannon.

I think I first realized what an terrific musician Bobby was one night about five years ago when listening to him accompany the alto saxophonist Marty Ehrlich. Bobby wasn't just keeping time behind Ehrlich, or even just sounding out counterrhythms. The best jazz improvisers, including Ehrlich, are those who have internalized their own drummers, and it was as though Bobby was engaging Ehrlich's inner drummer in a sizzling, stroke-for-stroke duet. I hoped he would do the same for me, but verbally. I wanted him to sit next to me and give me the inside dope on Gneushev's circus for aesthetes of all ages.

"Cool," Bobby said, but warned me that opening night was out, because he planned to man the sound table himself until the Gershwin's engineers got the hang of it. He showed up in the seat next to me the following night just as the houselights went down and the stage filled with puffs of colored smoke. Trim and fit in a sleeveless black T-shirt and gray slacks, with a trace of dark stubble on his face, he looked as though he himself might be an acrobat or juggler.

"I've got to cut the cord sometime, so it might as well be tonight," he said, then pointed to the four Russian musicians—a guitarist, a bass guitarist, a drummer, and a keyboard player—who had taken their places on risers behind a scrim. "They're very, very good," he whispered, "though I can't tell you much about them, because all of my contact with them was through a translator. But the other day, I was in one of the music shops on 42nd Street having a drumhead repaired, and when I mentioned the drummer's name to the guy behind the counter, he said, 'Oh, yes, *Boldyrev!* He's one of his country's best.'"

Except for Bobby's fanfare (the traditional "Thunder and Blazes" electronically phased and deconstructed) and a surrogate ringmaster who looked like the Grim Reaper in a bright red hat (he was actually supposed to be the puppeteer who pulled the other performers' strings, I found out later), nothing that happened in the show's first five minutes challenged my secondhand memories of Ringling Brothers and Barnum & Bailey. Then came "The Russian Bar," which Bobby, sucking in his breath, informed me was "the most dangerous act in the circus." I soon saw what he meant. To Bobby's cadenced, trancelike solo piano score, two ballerinas—twin sisters, Bobby said—each toed a Plexiglas beam balanced on the shoulders of two men, then bounded in the air over and over again, soaring higher with each leap and executing a perfect split before miraculously landing back in point position on the narrow beam.

"Whew," Bobby said, watching this as intently as I was, even though he had seen it numerous times before in Moscow over the summer. "It really puts what I do as a performer in perspective. I might drop a stick or accidentally turn the beat around. But even if I embarrass myself, I still have my *body*.

"In this country, we tend to confuse circus performers with carnival people—cardsharks and bearded ladies, and like that. But in Russia, where every big city has its own circus building, like we have symphony halls, these people are regarded as artists. Which they most definitely are."

I told Bobby that what fascinated me about the act (and what his music effectively underscored) was the inner concentration on each sister's face as she prepared to leap: a ballerina *on* the bar rather than at it, contemplating the void. "Right," he said. "Just before they jump, there's a moment when time stops, what Valentin refers to as a 'frozen moment.' And somehow or other, time has to stop in those piano cadences, too. I love movement as an idea, and I've always enjoyed writing for dancers, but modern dance is becoming so static and predictable. So I jumped at the opportunity to write for a circus, when this offer came along through Steve Leber, Valentin's American producer. Before commissioning my score, they used canned music, a mixture of classics and pop, even some rap. Would you believe 'The Russian Bar' once had loud, blaring, upbeat music behind it?

"I tried not to listen to much traditional circus music or many Russian composers, but some of that stuff was probably lurking around in my unconscious. It's lurking around in everybody's. You'll hear 'Thunder and Blazes' again at the end, this time arranged as a ballad. It really sounds beautiful that way. The composer was a man named Julius Fucik, who apparently never wrote anything else that anybody remembers.

"Valentin gave me a free hand, but some of the artists were very skeptical of me at first. The one who accepted what I was trying to do immediately was Yuri Borzykin, a juggler who does his act standing on a big ball. You'll see him later. But some of the performers, including those in 'The Russian Bar,' were afraid that replacing the music they were used to would undermine their concentration and put them in great danger, which I can understand. The most skeptical of me were the clowns, and they remain the most skeptical, because they're still not using what I wrote for them. They're the most particular, and you'd think that they'd be the least particular, wouldn't you?"

Before I could answer, the lighting changed, and so did the music—to slithery, hormonal funk, like something a topless dancer might writhe to. A man and a woman in tight matching leopard skins came rolling out of the inferno-red smoke in a wheel. After releasing themselves from it, they proceeded to use it as a brace for their gymnastics. At one point, while balancing the woman on his feet, the man did a handstand atop the wheel on stilts. Then still balanced precariously, the couple formed a right angle, with the horizontal man caressing his vertical partner's hip. The two performers seemed to eye each other libidinously whenever they clung. Their movements reminded me, as did Bobby's music, of that line from the newest Prince album, about "twenty-three positions in a one-night stand."

"You're not imagining it," Bobby said. "Anatoly and Yelena are husband and wife, so there's obviously a physical attraction between them, an intimacy with each other that they project as part of their act. It's very physical, very sweaty, very erotic. They were using Ravel's *Bolero*, but I thought the act demanded something that had a succession of climaxes instead of building to just one."

As Bobby spoke his eyes darted from one end of our row to the other. "It's the music," he explained. "It's just not *loud* enough. Last night we had a real Broadway opening-night kind of audience, including a lot of older people who complained about the volume. I wish they had given us aisle seats so I could run back up there and tell the guy on the board to turn it up. But I guess there's nothing I can do about it until intermission."

Before intermission, there were four more acts, including the juggler Bobby had mentioned (he paddled Sisypheanly on his sphere) and "Angel," an incredible twelve-year-old male gymnast in a loin cloth, with a shoulder-length, Pre-Raphaelite mane, who flew over the first few rows of the audience in a sling (talk about breaking down the fourth wall). I was going to have to wait to find out what the visual correlative was for "Rattango," my favorite piece on *Music of the Moscow Circus*—a slambang tango that doesn't spoil the fun with undue claims for authenticity. (It turned out to be a collaboration between an art deco acrobat in top hat, white tie, and tails, and a white rat who might be the most talented white rat I've ever seen.) When intermission arrived Bobby beat a path for the sound table behind the back row.

I spent intermission by the bar in the lobby, from which one could buy, depending on one's craving, either a bag of cotton candy or a Jack Daniels on the rocks. Bobby found me at the bar trying to decide which would be less damaging to my metabolism. He said he'd decided to stick close to the sound table for the rest of the night. But before fleeing, he told me a little bit about his days in Niagara Falls, as a veritable preteen Harry Partch.

"My father was a barber, and he had a deal with my aunt and uncle, that he would come over once a month and cut my cousin's hair. That used to take about twenty minutes, and while he was doing it, I would be allowed to practice on my cousin's drums. Twenty minutes a month, man! That's all I had, because my parents couldn't afford to buy me a set of my own. So when I was about twelve years old, I built my own set. I turned an old iron trash can on its side. That was my bass drum. Then, I had two pieces of linoleum and, between them, a coat hanger wound into a spring. That was my beater. I had aluminum pie plates as cymbals and plungers as stands. Plus a metal box with a bunch of old junk in it that would rattle when I struck it. That was my snare. I even got to play with a neighborhood band using that set, although they fired me and hired a kid with a set of real drums. That was the saddest day of my life. Maybe I should have held onto those drums, though. I'd be all the rage on the downtown music scene with them."

I ran into Bobby again on my way out. "You hear that?" he asked, referring to the exit music. "'Thunder and Blazes' again, but this time arranged as a ballad. Doesn't it sound beautiful that way? It's too bad you weren't seeing all of this in a big circus arena, the way I did in Moscow. Remember 'Angel'? Well, it's even better in a big arena, with the audience surrounding him on all four sides, and him flying over their heads. It's fantastic, man."

I argued that seeing a circus in the relative intimacy of a Broadway theater provided certain compensations—being able to watch the performers' faces as they stared down danger, for one thing. Then again, I admitted, maybe I didn't know what I was taking about. After all, I reminded Bobby, I had never seen a circus before.

"You still haven't," he said.

(DECEMBER 1991)

Les Paul Standard, Rebuilt

The scene is Fat Tuesday's, a low-ceilinged club on the northern tip of Greenwich Village. Les Paul, whose trio has been the Monday-night attraction here since 1984, has finished his first set and is now greeting well-wishers at the bar.

"Les, my parents played that album of yours with 'How High the Moon' on it the whole time I was growing up, and I've been meaning to get here to see you—and now I have!" a guy about forty says to Paul, who, with his piercing blue eyes and rooster's comb of hair, looks like a wholesome William Burroughs or a wizened, less self-absorbed George C. Scott.

"Why, thank you," Paul says, shaking the guy's extended hand. "Where you from, anyway?"

"Staten Island," the guy says.

"That's not so far away, is it?" asks Paul, never at a loss for words on or off the bandstand. "You should have been here sooner."

It's happened on each of the two recent occasions that I've dropped into Fat Tuesday's to hear Paul's trio, with Gary Mazzeroppi on bass and Lou Pallo on rhythm guitar. Midway through his first set, Paul asks the audience if there's anything it especially wants to hear. As if on cue someone requests "How High the Moon," and Paul gets a laugh by deadpanning, "Does anyone know what key that's in?"

G-major, as a matter of fact, though it doesn't stay there very long, which must explain its enduring appeal to musicians, because it has no melody to speak of. Written by Morgan Lewis and Nancy Hamilton, a partnership whose only other profitable copyright was "The Old Soft Shoe," it was introduced by Alfred Drake and Frances Comstock in the Broadway revue *Two for the Show* in 1940, and popularized that same year by Benny Goodman (vocal by Helen Forrest, arrangement by Eddie Sauter, and inferior cover versions by Larry Clinton and Mitchell Ayers). Billy Eckstine crooned it more engagingly than anybody before or since with the Metronome All-Stars (featuring Roy Eldridge, Warne Marsh, and Lester Young) in 1953, five years after Stan Kenton brought it back on the charts as an instrumental.

It's one of those tunes practically everybody knows. Yet when was the last time you heard anybody but Les Paul actually *play* it? For jazz musicians, it's just a blueprint for improvisation, thanks to Charlie Parker, who subverted its chord changes into "Ornithology" in 1944. Insofar as it continues to exist as a song, the credit goes to Paul, whose benchmark hit of it with vocals by his late ex-wife, Mary Ford, top of the pops for nine weeks in 1951, is more remembered as a *sound*—one of very few pop hits of that period that you can listen to today without inventing evil scenarios of Perry Como buttoning his cardigan and blissfully mowing his lawn as Elvis and Jerry Lee Lewis snarl and zip up their leathers and kick start their bikes on the outskirts of town. Not rock and roll by a long shot, this and Paul's other chartbusters of the late forties and early fifties—those with Ford, like "Vaya Con Dios," "Bye, Bye Blues" and "The World Is Waiting for the Sunrise," as well as those without her, like "Nola" and "Brazil"—nonetheless pioneered the technology that made rock and roll possible.

Paul's name has become synonymous with electric guitar because it's been on so many of them, beginning with the Les Paul Model, introduced by Gibson in 1952 and soon renamed the Les Paul Standard. But in addition to fathering the first solid-body electric (he unsuccessfully approached Gibson with a prototype eleven years earlier), Paul also designed the first multitrack tape recorder (an eight-track marketed by Ampex in '52, which W. C. Fields, one of Paul's old cronies, suggested calling "the octopus") and was overdubbing direct-to-disc before tape recorders of any sort were in general use.

Multitracking was only the half of it. Working in his garage, which was probably better equipped than any studio of the time anyway, Paul also used echo, reverb, delay, and in-the-red dynamics to multiply Ford into the Boswell Sisters and himself into a guitar army. (He thus became the first to bang his head against modern pop's central dilemma: how to sound as good on stage as you do on record. Paul's solution involved touring with a bassist not on his records and miking Ford's soundalike sister in the wings. "She wore headphones, and if Mary laughed, she laughed," Paul, who keeps vampire's hours, told me during a recent crack-of-dawn telephone conversation. "If Mary coughed, *she* coughed, just to convince the audience that they were hearing only one girl. And hearing more than one voice, they would also think they were hearing more than one guitar, like on the records.")

Because he's such a Mr. Wizard, you believe Paul when he boasts that he's rebuilt every guitar he's ever owned practically from scratch (at Fat Tuesday's, he plays a Les Paul Standard with a curly-maple finish and an ivory trim, fortified with pickups from a Les Paul Recording Guitar, which he molded to specification in his own oven). And you believe him when he claims to have started work on what would have been the first keyboard synthesizer in 1948, following a car wreck that put his future as a guitarist in jeopardy. If it was a short leap from Paul to Duane Eddy and Link Wray, it was an even shorter leap from his "sound on sound" to Phil Spector's wall of it.

Ironically, the revolution-in-sound that Paul helped to engineer instantly antiquated him. Compared with, say, Eddie Cochran's "Summertime Blues," or any of Elvis's Suns, Paul's hits sound like pure pop for then people—quintessential Music of Your Life. Even so, Spector has been to Fat Tuesday's to pay homage to Paul (accompanied by his hired muscle, no doubt), and Jeff Beck, Steve Miller, and Jimmy Page are among those who've sat in with him there. (On my visits, the only rockers in the quiet-to-the-point-of-reverent, all-ages audience were a few anonymous guys with Long Island cover-band shags.) Paul McCartney once made a pilgrimage to Les's home in Mahwah, New Jersey, to pick up the left-handed guitar that Les custom made for him, and told Les that the Beatles auditioned for one of their first gigs by playing "The World Is Waiting for the Sunrise." And Jon Bonjovi and members of Aerosmith provided the free entertainment at Paul's seventy-fifth birthday party at the Hard Rock Cafe last year.

At this point, Paul's career is a tribute to the physicians who have pieced him back together over the years. The aforementioned car wreck almost cost him his life, and did cost him seven inches of tendon near his right elbow; at his request, the doctors reset his arm at a right angle ideal for strumming but little else. He has two artificial eardrums, and underwent quintuple bypass surgery ten years ago. But chronic arthritis might be his most serious handicap as a musician, and when he starts spinning yarns between numbers at Fat Tuesday's, you suspect it's a charming ploy to give his aching fingers some rest.

Fortunately, Paul is in a class with Hope and Carson as an ad libber. In response to a request for "something from *Chester and Lester*," his 1977 Grammy-winning album of bowlegged duets with Chet Atkins, he quipped "Chet couldn't rock and roll, you know. He could never learn that third chord." Introducing his sidemen, Pallo and Mazzeroppi, he joked that with names like that, they must be in town for the Gotti trial. In a devilish mood the second time I heard him, he tried to distract Pallo, who sings in a clear, shy tenor in addition to his no-nonsense chording, with homophobic taunts that had me in stitches despite myself. "I knew it was over between Lou and me when I found that purple condom in his sock drawer," Paul told the audience as Pallo went on singing. "He told me never to wear purple, said it wasn't my color!"

Paul gabs incessantly on the bandstand and at the bar afterward but doesn't announce tunes. No need to: his nicely balanced sets consist of such instantly recognizable items as "Avalon," "Caravan," "Over the Rainbow," and "Exactly Like You." This songbook is a giveaway to what Paul's been up to on Third Avenue these last seven years. Though given his due in *The Rolling Stone Illustrated History of Rock and Roll*, he's unlisted in *The New Grove Dictionary of Jazz*, the logic for which omission escapes me unless it has something to do with crossover usually buying a one-way ticket. He's racked up so many recording-industry firsts that some of them have been forgotten, but his gig at Fat Tuesday's is a forceful reminder that he participated on the first commercially released jazz concert recording: the inaugural *Jazz at the Philharmonic* gathering from

1944, on which he and Nat Cole (another early crossover) hooked up for a chase sequence that was an exercise in crowd-pleasing subtlety.

Paul achieves a comparable simpatico with his sidemen at Fat Tuesday's, especially when they play follow-the-leader with him on Django Reinhardt's "Nuages." He also remains in touch with the wistful, Eddie Langlike lilt he displayed behind Bing Crosby on "It's Been a Long, Long Time" in 1946. When a performer reaches his seventies, an element of nostalgia clings to everything he does. But Paul treats his current audience to interpretations it only *thinks* it remembers hearing somewhere before. This is the sort of venue he might have played and the sort of band he might have led in the 1950s, if his hits had never happened. Avoiding postbop brow-knotting and muscle-flexing, he adheres closely to the melodies in his improvisations, decorating them with what might be dismissed as clichés or personal tics—that hiccup across the frets, for example, or those long, reverberating phrases that end by dissolving a chord into its component notes—if not delivered with such a gratifying combination of simplicity and flash.

And, yeah, he honored the requests for "How High the Moon," on both occasions starting it unaccompanied at a quiet, contemplative rubato before inching it uptempo like on the record, though not like on the record at all. The second time I heard him do it, he eventually turned it over to Mazzeroppi with an incongruous, in-your-face rock and roll guitar move, to which Mazzeroppi responded with a quote from "Ornithology." I'd jotted down a note to ask Paul if he ever tired of "How High the Moon," the way performers often do when obliged to include a song identified with them every night from here to eternity. But after hearing him reinterpret it so lovingly, there was no reason to ask. I guess the secret is not merely playing a song, but playing around with it, the way you would with one of your own inventions.

Paul, who was born Lester Polfus in Waukesha, Wisconsin,

just outside of Milwaukee, in 1915 (not 1916, as some reference books say), tends to recount events that happened more than fifty years ago in a slangy present tense—a sign of the born raconteur. The sort of man who isn't happy unless he's doing something with his hands, he's built everything from his own pirate radio stations to an outhouse—"a three-holer with a half moon on the door and everything"—as a joke on his friend Jack Paar, who could never find the bathrooms in Paul's twenty-six-room mansion in Mahwah, New Jersey.

Apart from stationing Mary Ford's sister behind the curtain, Paul rarely tried to conceal his magic. He even provided a step-by-step demonstration of it on an episode of *At Home with Les and Mary*, the daily network radio show he and Ford hosted in the late 1940s.

"Instead of explaining it technical, which would be boring, I made up something called the Les Paulverizer," says Paul, who years later actually did invent a remote control tape recorder he named that. "I said 'Mary, with the Les Paulverizer, I can make your voice into a glee club and my guitar into an orchestra.' She says, 'Those gadgets of yours are going to put us both in the nuthouse.' I sez, 'But wait till you hear what I can do with it.' So she laughs, and I multiply her into sixteen people laughing. Applause? I sez, 'The two of us can clap and I can turn us into a hall of people clapping. Now, let me add echo and see what happens.' She says, 'Les, you and your inventions!' and goes on washing the dishes."

They say that necessity is the mother of invention, but biological mothers sometimes play a part in it, too. Paul began his experiments in multitracking after his mother complimented him and Ford on a radio performance they never gave.

"I said, 'Mary and I weren't on radio last night, Ma.' She said, 'Somebody's imitating you, then.' I said, 'Jeez, Ma, a *lot* of them are imitating us,' and she said, 'Well, you ought to come up with something that isn't so *easy* for them to imitate.'"

Paul's first love was the blues, and his first instrument was

a harmonica given to him by a black ditchdigger in Waukesha.
"I heard him playing it on the street, and I guess you could
say I *stared* him out of it. He said, 'You like it so much, you take
it. I got another one.' And my mother, people being how they
were in those days, boiled it in hot water for a week before she
would let me put it in my mouth."

His fascination with guitar was a side effect of building his
own crystal set as a newspaper delivery boy, back in the cat's-
whisker era of radio.

"That was in Waukesha, on a mound that was supposed to
be a Indian burial site in Cutler Park, which is now Les Paul
Park. The first station I brought in was playing the Mills Brothers, and I loved that. But then I heard a guitar player, who
turned out to be a local musician named Gene Emerald. A few
years later, after I started playing guitar myself, I met him and
told him about hearing him when I was a kid. He asked me if
he could borrow my guitar, and don't you know, that son of a
bitch skipped town with it."

Paul's gig at Fat Tuesday's is his interpretation of doctor's
orders. Following quintuple bypass surgery in 1980, his physician told him that the key to recovery was to keep busy.

"I asked myself what did I enjoy doing. Well, it wasn't playing for presidents or governors or at Radio City Music Hall. I
wanted to find myself a little joint."

So after woodshedding in a North Jersey tavern, Paul
approached the owner of Fat Tuesday's about doing Monday
nights there. "He said, 'We're closed Mondays.' I said 'Well, I
know, that's why I'm asking, and I'll play for nothing if you
want me to.' He said, 'You start next Monday,' and I said, 'You
know, I was half kidding about playing for nothing . . .' My girlfriend said if you play there, I'll never come to New York to see
you. That was seven years ago, going on eight, and she never has
been there to see me. Because she thinks it's a sewer."

In fairness to Fat Tuesday's, as sewers go, it's practically
swellegant. The important thing is that Paul likes it there. "I turn

down just about everything else, because I'm retired and I just want to play one night a week," said Paul, who still receives a royalty on every guitar bearing his name sold by Gibson. "I don't practice at home, either, although I might work fourteen hours at a stretch on my electronics. I keep to my diet and I allow myself one beer a day. I used to be able to drink a whole case. I'm a big popcorn eater, and it's no good without a beer to wash it down. My mother, who died just last year in a nursing home while listening to me being interviewed on *The Larry King Show,* was a beer drinker to the very end. Thought it had vitamins. In fact, she had her doctor write her a prescription saying that she was allowed to have four bottles a day. The people in the nursing home were reluctant to go along with that, but they did. She kept count, too. You'd go to visit her, and she'd say 'Do you think I could have my fourth one a little early today?'

"With the kind of bypass I had, you're supposed to be good for five to seven years; some go ten. My doctor calls me, says, 'You're overdue for tests, you should be having problems by now.' I know he's right, but I would hate like hell to know something was wrong and have *that* cloud hanging over my head. It's better for it to be, like, 'clunk'—it just happens. Right now, I don't worry about it very much. My mother lived to be a hundred and two, so I ought to be good for at least a hundred, wouldn't you think?"

(JUNE/AUGUST 1991)

Words and Music

Real Stuff in Life to Cling to

If it's possible to seem unpretentious dressed in black tie and surrounded by a chamber symphony on stage at Carnegie Hall, Tony Bennett did when I heard him there last spring. The show began without announcement: Bennett just walked onstage, where the pianist Ralph Sharon, his longtime music director, sat waiting for him, and sang "Taking a Chance on Love." On the line "I walk around with a horseshoe," he pointed a thumb at his chest and lifted one foot off the ground, as though proud enough to strut. He followed with "My Foolish Heart," slowly shaking his head "no" on the line "For this time it isn't *fascination*," turning palms down on the offending word for good measure. He and Sharon were then joined by the bassist Paul Langosch and the drummer Joe LaBarbera, and eventually by the horns and strings. But in keeping with his self-image as a glorified saloon singer, Bennett stayed close to the piano, sometimes unselfconsciously resting an elbow on it. (Now and then Sharon would play something that let you imagine sawdust and peanut shells under Bennett's feet.)

This expert but understated stagecraft goes along with Bennett's reputation as a consummate entertainer who also happens to be the decent sort of man you'd be happy to find on the next barstool. Frank Sinatra might own the patent on that persona, but Bennett gives the impression of being that way for real (with his jutting nose and jawline, he even looks the part of best friend, not leading man). He was in good voice at Carnegie, despite what sounded to me like an inadvertent key change on the fortissimo ending of "I Left My Heart in San Francisco," at the climax of a far-from-perfunctory medley of his greatest hits. The evening's only real clinker was promotional, not musical. The concert, which also featured songs from *Astoria: Portrait of the Artist* (Columbia), Bennett's ninety-first album in a career dating back to 1950, was being subsidized by the Gitano Group, Inc., which meant that Bennett had to sing his 1963 hit "The Good Life" to footage of young marrieds and their children romping outdoors in the sponsor's sportswear.

I know that corporate underwriting of live music is a necessary evil at this point (chamber symphonies cost money), but by presenting what amounted to a TV commercial onstage, Gitano was crossing one of the few remaining lines. (In ending with the printed slogan THE SPIRIT OF FAMILY, the ad was politically objectionable, too. Doesn't anyone at Gitano know or care that the fundamentalist right has corrupted "family" into a buzzword in its war on sexual and procreative choice?) The whole thing was unworthy of Bennett, and I was glad that he seemed a little embarrassed by it. "This is my commercial," he said in introducing "Lost in the Stars"—his third and final encore, after "Fly Me to the Moon" and "How Do You Keep the Music Playing?"—and then explained to the audience that the song was from a 1949 Broadway adaptation of the South African novel *Cry the Beloved Country*, and that he found its message of brotherhood still timely.

But Bennett had already given the audience something to think about with "Fly Me to the Moon." He often does this song as his encore (probably because it allows him to exit after singing the final words, "I love you," and pointing to the front rows), and he frequently asks that his microphone be turned off when he does it in nightclubs. Still, it was a surprise to hear him make the same request in a hall as large as Carnegie.

"Musicians' shoulders go back when they walk onstage there," he told me a few days later, during an interview in his business office, a few floors down from his apartment in a midtown Manhattan hotel. He meant that he had wanted to prove himself still worthy of Carnegie Hall, at sixty-three, by bouncing his unamplified voice off its walls.

Actually, there were moments during the song when you

could barely hear him, but his lung power wasn't what made the stunt remarkable. Bennett was breaking down pop's fourth wall (how often these days, even in concert, do we hear a singer's actual *voice*, minus echo, reverb, and artificial sibilance), and thus exposing his style to closer scrutiny. I was finally able to put my finger on something I had always thought of as curious: his way of elongating the final words of certain phrases and assigning each of them several different notes, a melismatic touch that I (perhaps owing to my own ethnic background) associate with Irish crooners, not with an Italian-American singer like Bennett.

"Ah, that's Crosby," Bennett said when I mentioned this. "You see, my uncle was married to an Irish lady, and they both adored Bing." Then, indirectly, Bennett pinpointed one of the secrets of his own appeal. "He loved to sing and you could hear it. That's something that you can't buy. Either you have it or you don't. It had nothing to do with the money he made. He had a natural love for it. Just like a guy in a barroom. You say, 'Come on, sing us a tune.' And he sings."

In a 1965 article for *Life* magazine in which he found most vocalists wanting in one way or another (the piece bruised as many egos in show business as Norman Mailer's "Evaluations: Some Quick and Expensive Comments on the Talent in the Room" had in literary circles when published in *Esquire* six years earlier), Frank Sinatra called Bennett "the best in the business . . . . the singer who gets across what the composer had in mind and probably a little more." These words from on high have since acquired the air of prophecy, no matter how dubious they must have sounded at a time when Sinatra himself was still very active.

To gain a measure of Bennett's musical growth over the decades, all you need to do is compare the new version of "The Boulevard of Broken Dreams" on *Astoria* with the 1956 version included on *16 Most Requested Songs* (Columbia), a CD-only compilation of Bennett's hits of the fifties and early sixties. The original version's Apache dance of an arrangement, for which Bennett can't be held accountable, isn't the only problem. There's also Bennett's vibrato, which doesn't know when to stop, and his overzealousness in punching up each note, even at the expense of lyrical message and rhythmic flow.

The new version, with spare but effectively atmospheric accompaniment by just Sharon, Langosch, and LaBarbera, demonstrates Bennett's mature willingness to let a song breathe. The lower key, though obviously dictated by Bennett's diminished range, amounts to an advantage: it's more in keeping with the rueful mood of Al Dubin's lyrics, which Bennett manages to make seem almost worthy of Harry Warren's lovely melody, virtually sighing that silly but delightful line about "gigolo and gigolette." *16 Most Requested Songs* also includes Bennett's back-to-back number one hits from 1951, the quasi-aria "Because of You" and his clueless pop crossover version of Hank Williams's country hit "Cold, Cold Heart."

On the albums of standards he made with jazz musicians in the fifties and sixties, you can hear Bennett on his way to becoming the singer he is today. A reissue from this period worth seeking out is *Basie/Bennett* (Capitol/Roulette). Although Basie plays piano on only two tracks, his band is present throughout. Sharon did the arrangements, including an especially lovely version of Lerner and Loewe's "I've Grown Accustomed to Her Face" from *My Fair Lady*.

But I think that Bennett reached a turning point in 1972, when he was dropped by Columbia Records after twenty-two years on the label, his departure hastened by his reluctance to do more albums like *Tony Sings the Hits of Today*, from 1970, on which he sang cover versions of rock and roll tunes for which he had no genuine feeling. At least Bennett was assigned songs by Stevie Wonder, Burt Bacharach, and Lennon and McCartney—unlike his labelmate Mel Torme, who was given "If I Had a Hammer," "Red Rubber Ball," and "Secret Agent Man." When I spoke with Bennett in March, he likened his disgust at being pressured to do "contemporary" material to that of his mother, a seamstress, when she was forced to work on a cheap dress.

Although Bennett was off the hit parade, appealing mostly to listeners beyond record-buying age, he continued to fill nightclubs and concert halls. The confidence that he was going "to make a buck no matter what" seems to have encouraged him to strengthen his relationship with jazz; he recorded an album of voice-and-piano duets with Bill Evans for Fantasy, and two collections of Rodgers and Hart with the guitarist George Barnes and the cornetist Ruby Braff for his own label, significantly named Improv (for which he also recorded another album with Evans). On the road constantly, he became a kind of traveling salesman for American popular song. He also began to enjoy success in his second career, as a painter, signing his works "Anthony Benedetto" (his real name) and selling them for as much as $40,000 each (though you have to wonder if collectors are paying for the paintings or his signature).

It was during his banishment from Columbia that Bennett developed what's since become his most endearing vocal trait: bearing down on the key words of a lyric and sometimes delivering them in what's practically a stage whisper or a shout, like a man thinking out loud while singing *con brio*. The effect is too fleeting—too intimate and too much Bennett's own—to be characterized as sprechsteme or parlando. In addition to making a virtue of the slight huskiness that's crept into his voice with age, it gives his performances an autobiographical depth comparable to that which Sinatra achieved in his late prime, in the 1950s. The most striking instance of this is on Bennett's recording of "Make Someone Happy" with Evans. "'Fame if you win it, comes and goes in a minute. Where's the *real stuff* in life to cling to?'" Bennett sings, and you sense that the real stuff to which he's holding fast includes the song itself and others like it.

After going nine years without a new release, Bennett resigned with Columbia in 1986. His three new albums since then have been produced by his son, Danny, and delivered to the label as finished products. *The Art of Excellence* featured mostly newer, nonrock songs of Bennett's own choosing; although the emphasis was on such dolorous, overblown ballads as "How Do You Keep the Music Playing?" and "Why Do People Fall in Love," Bennett sang them beautifully. On *Bennett/Berlin*, Bennett did with "White Christmas" what might have seemed impossible, putting the song across with gentle barroom yearning in place of the family-around-the-fireplace smugness with which it's usually sung. *Bennett/Berlin* captured Bennett at his absolute best, with flawless support from his trio and cameo appearances by George Benson, Dizzy Gillespie, and Dexter Gordon.

Astoria, with Bennett's trio, plus an orchestra conducted by the arranger Jorge Calandrelli on all but two of the fourteen tracks, is what used to be called a concept album: a musical "autobiography" (though Bennett wrote none of the songs) and a celebration of the working-class section of Queens in which the singer grew up and for which the album is named. (Given this, *Astoria* bears a superficial resemblance to Bennett's long-out-of-print 1958 album *Hometown, My Town*, whose unifying, extramusical subject was Manhattan's exhilarating pace.)

Although a song from the 1930s called "Just a Little Street Where Old Friends Meet" ("and greet you in the same old way") successfully evokes the front-stoop culture that Bennett remembers, *Astoria* finally amounts to an uneven collection of vintage and recent songs. The older songs are fine: aside from "The Boulevard of Broken Dreams," the best performance here might be "Body and Soul," if only for the pleading edge which with Bennett renders the line (which most singers find nearly unsingable) "My life a wreck you're making." Bennett also fares well with "Speak Low," "The Folks That Live on the Hill," "A Weaver of Dreams" (interpolating it with "There Will Never Be Another You"), "The Man I Love" (which Bennett sings as "The Girl I Love," using Ira Gershwin's alternate lyrics), and the

Billie Holiday-associated "It's Like Reaching for the Moon."

The problem is that whereas these older songs are about love, friendship, ambition, heartbreak—the works—*Astoria's* newer songs tend to be about little more than older songs. This is true usually only in terms of mood but quite literally in the case of P. J. Ericson and Buddy Weed's "Where Did the Magic Go?," whose lyrics pine for "Francis Albert," "The King of Swing," and the "Dorseys' sound," as well as "Spencer playing Katherine's beau" and "Fred and Ginger dancing slow." (The lyrics also rhyme "Hemingway" and "Courvoisier," reducing educated taste in literature, movies, and song to consumerism with class.) Bennett puts the infernal song across with such snap that I find myself humming along despite myself. I suppose that what really bothers me is that songs like this (and the cultural conservatism presumed to go along with them) provide ammunition for those who would dismiss Bennett and the songs he does best as irrelevant to contemporary life.

"All this music is written and sung in the style that dominated popular song before rock and roll—which means before the '60s, before what we've come to accept as the dawn of modern life," Greg Sandow complained in his review of *Astoria* in *Entertainment Weekly*.

> Men, in those days, were men; marriage was forever; woman comforted men and cooked their meals. No, Bennett never explicitly sings that here. But every time he does sing about marriage . . . the very sound of his music drags me back to an age when wives were expected to spend their time keeping house. And that, I'm afraid, tells me why the classic American popular song might be going out of style.

To spot the illogic in Sandow's argument, you don't need to know that he's a former classical music critic (arguably the best ever on the subject of the classical avant-garde), who now writes with a convert's zeal about rap and heavy metal, genres whose lyrics hardly tend to be enlightened in their view of women. Sandow is forgetting that music and the emotions it calls into play don't have to be raw in order to be real. He's also not giving Bennett—who's twice divorced and (like so many of the singers and songwriters now associated with pop's disdainful upper crust) a product of the ethnic working class—credit for realizing that life doesn't always work out the way it did in the great old songs, and for knowing that might be the best reason to go on singing them.

Some of Bennett's supporters wind up hurting his cause. "All of this only two years ago, right out there, front and center, on a Bruce Springsteen planet," Jonathan Schwartz, a writer and New York radio personality with a past as a progressive-rock disc jockey to recant, wrote in praise of *Bennett/Berlin* in *Wigwag* last year. Bennett's own pronouncements often don't help, either. In summing up the difference between rock and his kind of pop, he smugly told me, "One is marketing, the other is good music."

But why should it be necessary to choose between Tony Bennett and Bruce Springsteen? Bennett conveys as much urgency as Springsteen does, though it's of a different sort. Often written about as though he were Sinatra's exact contemporary, he's eleven years younger, the difference of at least a generation in pop. The lost magic that Bennett mourns on *Astoria* was already vanishing by the time he began his career: jazz and pop were no longer close kin, Broadway and Hollywood were entering what everybody must have sensed would be their last decade of providing durable new songs, and rock and roll was just around the corner. Forty years later, Bennett has become the best singer of his kind, but he must sometimes feel like an ambassador from a country that's fallen off the map.

(AUGUST 1990)

This was written a few years before MTV adopted Bennett as its token adult (I don't think, by the way, that his audiences have gotten any younger; it's just that the people who've always liked him now feel better about themselves). I keep waiting for him to make a fool of himself, to break an egg on his head and crow "Cock-a-doodle-doo," like Emil Jannings in The Blue Angel—*but so far he hasn't. I guess class tells.*

Rosie

A jazz singer is like a jazz musician. It's all about improvising. It's something in your heart, and something that is you. You know, they call Rosemary Clooney a jazz singer. This woman never improvised in her life. She sings a song exactly the way it's written."

So whined Carmen McRae, still upset about not winning a Grammy for her Thelonious Monk album, in a recent *Down Beat* interview in which she also had harsh words for Betty Carter, Anita Baker, Dianne Reeves, Harry Connick Jr., and even Ella Fitzgerald.

"Carmen has reached a stage in her life where she feels overlooked and has become cranky about everything," Rosemary Clooney sighed when I read McRae's remarks to her during a phone chat from her home in Beverly Hills. "Which is a shame, because she is so good she ought to just relax and enjoy herself. But what's so strange about what she says about me now is that in one of the very first articles *Down Beat* ever did on her, back in the early 1950s, they asked her who her favorite singers were, and the list she gave them began with me. So we've come a long way, haven't we?"

What about yourself, Rosie (she wouldn't hear of "Ms. Clooney")? Do you consider yourself a jazz singer?

"I wish," she replied. "But no, I don't. I don't have that—oh, that sense of chord structure that Ella or Mel or Diane Schuur has, that tells them where they can take liberties with a melodic line. They're all such good musicians. Me, I'm never really sure enough of myself to do what they do."

No need to be so modest, Rosie, because it's all semantics anyway. It reminds me of how the essayist Ellen Willis once characterized the position of antiporn feminists: what turns me on is erotica, what turns you on is smut. What I enjoy is jazz, what you like is banal pop.

Indeed, the distinction between who sings jazz and who merely sings is so murky that the same people who'll tell you that the only *genuine* jazz singers are those who scat happily agree with you when you contend that the greatest female jazz singer of them all was Billie Holiday, who never scatted in her life—at least not on record or that anyone remembers live. The key was her phrasing: her ability to sing a melody more or less as written while locating the depth (or, when she was younger, the *joie de vivre*) in even the slightest lyric.

Not to put Clooney in Holiday's class, but that's her secret, too. The case against calling her a jazz singer begins with her 1951 hit "Come On-a My House," the first in a string of dialect novelties forced on her by her producer, Mitch Miller. Written—would you believe it?—by the novelist and playwright William Saroyan (a Pulitzer Prize winner for *The Time of Your Life*) and his cousin Ross Bagdasarian (as David Seville, the brains—so to speak—behind Alvin and the Chipmunks), "Come On-a My House" and its follow-ups undermined this nice Irish lass's credibility, even while landing her on the hit parade.

The case *for* Clooney as a jazz singer—if any proof be needed beyond *Blue Rose,* her lovely 1957 collaboration with Duke Ellington, on which she turned in what might be the definitive vocal "Sophisticated Lady"—pivots on her dozen or so Concord Jazz albums since 1976 (including a get-together with Woody Herman and the best composers' songbook series since Ella's) and shows like the one I saw her do in a Philadelphia concert hall last summer.

(She's supposed to be even better in cabarets, "where I can at least see the people I'm singing for. I put my glasses on in a larger room, but I'm so nearsighted, it doesn't help.")

Introducing "These Foolish Things," she described it as "the most evocative of all the ballads I've ever sung," then proceeded to give Holt Marvel's poetic lyrics the most evocative interpretation imaginable. Although she did the durable "Hey There" as well as "Come-On-a," "just to help you remember which one I was," she sang mostly Cole Porter, Rodgers and Hart, and material from *For the Duration* (great title), her 1990 concept album of love songs popular during World War II. Smoothly supported by the cornetist Warren Vaché (from the Concord stock company) and the tenor saxophonist Larry McKenna (a Websterish local subbing for Scott Hamilton), she sang everything with sincerity, sophistication, and an absolute lack of showbiz vanity. If it was obvious that, at sixty-three, she can't slide a note the way she used to, it was just as obvious that her phrasing now rivals that of Sinatra or anybody else you can name.

Besides all of which, people used to tell my mom she looked like her.

Clooney sings with that elusive but quickly recognizable quality that McRae identified as "heart." She speaks from the same place. During our chat, she discussed a range of topics at length.

Clooney on her childhood in Maysville, Kentucky, a little

town on the Ohio River: "My grandfather, who was a jeweler, was mayor of Maysville at one point. I left there for Cincinnati when I was in about the sixth grade. My mother and father were divorced by then, and my brother and sister and I took turns living with one parent or the other, or with one of our sets of grandparents.

"My mother had a performer's personality, very outgoing, but she didn't have any talent. She sang *at* songs, because she had terrible time. She just couldn't figure out where the beat was, at all. When I was a little girl, singing around the house, she would ask me, 'Why do you wait so long between words?' I was intuitively counting the beats in the measure, but I couldn't explain it at that age. So I'd just tell her, 'Because you're supposed to.'"

On hitting the road with her kid sister, Betty, as singers with Tony Pastor's Orchestra, in 1947: "We were lucky. Big bands were dropping by the wayside then, so we made it in right under the wire. I was only eighteen, and being so young, I could sleep anywhere, even on the bus if need be. So I'm glad it happened for me exactly when it did. The guys in the band had one another to hang out with, and thank goodness I had Betty for company. Without her, I would have been very lonely. Plus, our Uncle George traveled with us as Betty's legal guardian, because she was only fifteen, three years younger than me.

"Three years later, when I went out on my own, Betty made it very, very easy for me. I was free to quit the sister act because she said *she* was quitting show business. She said she missed being with people her own age. To this day, I don't know how much of it was the truth and how much was her letting *me* go."

On Miguel Ferrer, thirty-five, the eldest of her five children from her dissolved marriage to the actor José Ferrer, and a member in the cast of *Twin Peaks* (he played Albert, the supercilious federal agent Sheriff Truman decked in an early episode): "Sensational news! There's going to be a feature film of *Twin Peaks* [called *Fire Walk with Me*] and Miguel is in it. So Albert lives! And there's another David Lynch project that

Miguel is the star of. It's called *On the Air* and it's about a 1950s TV variety show. My son plays the head of a network, and they've already done the pilot. I tell you, I'm so proud of him."

On the barbiturate habit that contributed to the 1968 nervous breakdown she detailed in her 1977 autobiography, *This for Remembrance*: "I liked downers, seconal and all of those things. I wasn't unique. Years ago, when a woman would see a doctor, the attitude used to be 'Give her all the sleeping pills she wants, all the equinil and librium, whatever will keep her quiet.' It was like popcorn. My mother was addicted, too, when she died."

On *For the Duration*, released just days before George Bush's Television War for People with Short Attention Spans: "My brother, Nick [a columnist for the *Cincinnati Herald*], thought of the title. Those songs, like "Sentimental Journey" and "I'll Be Seeing You," are almost too much for people who lost someone close to them in World War II. They felt very immediate to me when I recorded them, because I learned most of them from my Uncle George, who died last July, right before the sessions. That's him in his Air Force uniform on the cover, his graduation photo from flight school.

"[Before the album was released] I was performing at the Pebble Beach Golf Tournament in Monterey, and Tommy Smothers asked me what songs I was going to do. When I told him, he said, 'Oh, sure, we're about to go to war, and you rushed in and recorded old war songs.' I said, 'Do you think people are really going to *think* that?,' and Tommy said, 'What else are they going to think?' I thought, should I do a disclaimer? Because here was my brother writing newspaper columns condemning the president for the bombings and calling for his impeachment. And me with an album of war songs. So in one way, it turned out to be good timing for the album, though I wish to God it hadn't."

On the Betty Clooney Center for Brain Injuries, in Long Beach, California, named after her sister, who died of an aneurysm in 1976, at the age of forty-five: "After getting over being mad at her for dying on me, I wanted to keep her name alive, because she played a very important role in my life. Then, my cousin's daughter had a boating accident and was in a coma for twelve years, before coming around to the point where she could at least spend her days sitting in front of the TV, just staring.

"Three years ago, when we opened the center, we intended for it to be a full-time residence, but that was beyond our means. So it's a daytime-only facility where youngsters with brain injuries can come to relearn physical skills. It's funded, in part, by Meet the Songwriter, an annual concert a bunch of us put on out here every spring.

"I can't spend as much time at the center as I would like, because I'm working all of the time now—fortunately. But sometimes I feel badly about that. Do you know what I mean? I go as often as I can, but it never feels like enough."

(JUNE 1991)

The Song's the Thing

You have to know the story before you can tell the story
.... And I *tell* the story. That's all.

—Barbara Lea

Before I heard Barbara Lea sing "Begin the Beguine" on National Public Radio's *Fresh Air* and then again at the main branch of the Free Library of Philadelphia as part of last year's

Mellon PSFS Jazz Festival, the only version of the Cole Porter tune to stir my imagination was Artie Shaw's 1938 hit, on which Shaw's band sounded like the one Porter had in mind when he wrote "and down by the shore, an orchestra's playing." Most vocal renditions of "Begin the Beguine" brought back unpleasant memories of operatic baritones on 1950s television variety shows, shouting out Porter's lyrics as though their cummerbunds were on too tight. (Was it always Ezio Pinza, or did it just seem that way?)

Lea *felt* the song. She sang the first chorus slowly, hushed and a cappella, increasing the volume only slightly, and the tempo not at all, after her piano accompanist joined her on the second chorus. Despite giving no line of the lyric undue emphasis, she made it the story of a woman *recalling* moments divine and raptures serene, not anticipating them. The song was *about* something for a change, and despite the unorthodox nature of Lea's interpretation, you felt as though you were hearing "Begin the Beguine" exactly as its composer had intended it to be sung.

"I didn't yet have the whole story of the song in mind when I began doing it that way about ten years ago," Lea confessed last week, during an interview from her New York apartment. "Starting off a cappella was more of a challenge at first than anything to do with the lyrics. I just started doing it, and the story gradually took place in my mind. I never worked on it. I never 'work' on songs. If they mean something to me, I do them."

But songs obviously "work" on Lea, a stylish woman who has been singing professionally since the 1950s but who declines to reveal her age. If lyricists such as Porter, Ira Gershwin, and Lorenz Hart have been twentieth-century America's Shakespeares—the source of so many of our aphorisms and so many of our attitudes toward life and love—our greatest dramatic actresses have been cabaret singers such as Lea and the late Mabel Mercer and Sylvia Syms. If the play's the thing for members of England's Royal Shakespeare Company—"presentational" actors devoid of self-indulgent mannerisms, who put themselves at the service of a text—the song's the thing for Lea.

"Often, what passes for great acting on the part of singers amounts to their ability to put *themselves* across," Lea said in response to a question about possible affinities between acting and singing. "They misinterpret the tune, but they don't care. If they're belters, they belt every tune. If they've been taught to smile, they flash a big smile when they're singing about heartbreak. And sometimes, even singers who think they're dramatizing a lyric are just overemoting. For example, Nancy Wilson singing 'Guess Who I Saw Today' with those tortured gestures and her head thrown back. That's bad acting, as well as bad singing."

In light of such comments, it's no surprise to learn that Lea has acted. Her stage credits have included roles in *Follies*, *Company*, and *Who's Afraid of Virginia Woolf?*

"I initially studied acting to help my singing," she recalled. "And it did. I was terribly shy when I started singing. I could sing very musically, but I had no stage presence, and that held me back from getting work. When I studied acting, I just fell in love with it."

Originally from Detroit, Lea grew up in a family in which everyone was musically gifted, but one in which a career in show business was deemed somehow improper.

"My mother would have wanted me to be a secretary and then a housewife, as she was. My father [an assistant attorney general for the state of Michigan] would have preferred me to be a brilliant, intellectual something or other, maybe even a concert pianist. But no way. I started out extremely well on piano as a child, until I ran into kids who were more talented than I and willing to practice all the time on top of that."

At Wellesley, Lea majored in music theory, and "had visions of doing a little composing, which came to naught. But that's OK. The training was good for me as a singer. The first singers

I really loved were Lena Horne and Dinah Shore, who were on the radio all the time when I was growing up. Then I heard Billie Holiday and fell for her like a ton of bricks. Then Mildred Bailey and Lee Wiley," said Lea, naming the singers whose voice hers most resembles, though it's a shade deeper than either of theirs.

Among male singers, she liked "instrumentalists who also sang, beginning with what I guess you could call the big three: Louis Armstrong, Jack Teagarden, and Fats Waller. The male singers who were really singers, I never really liked very much. People are shocked when they find out I don't absolutely worship Frank Sinatra. It's just that, to me, ballad singing has always been a woman's art, somehow."

Lea recorded for labels such as Prestige and Riverside in the 1950s, when the line separating cabaret from jazz was less defined than it is now. As to whether she now considers herself a jazz singer, Lea said, "It depends on what they're hiring. If they're hiring jazz singers, absolutely. If they want a cabaret singer, that's what I am.

"In the 1940s, when Lee Wiley and Mildred Bailey were active, I would have been accepted as a jazz singer, no questions asked," said Lea, who, in addition to her cabaret engagements, is the vocalist with the tenor saxophonist Loren Schoenberg's New York-based jazz repertory orchestra (and whose latest CD release is a collection of songs from Duke Ellington's ill-fated 1966 Broadway show *Pousse-Cafe*, with Ellis Larkins playing piano and the show's lyricist, Marshall Barer, singing the male parts). "But jazz singing has become equated with scatting and with improvising on the melody and tearing it to shreds. I'm just not that kind of singer. I don't like it when I hear it, so I'm not motivated to do it."

For eight years beginning in 1965, she didn't sing at all, except around the house.

"I used to give an elaborate answer when someone would ask me why I quit, until I figured out that the actual reason was that nobody was hiring me. The world had gone completely rock and roll crazy, and there was no room for a singer of my type who wasn't already a name. I had just begun to establish myself when the bottom fell out."

During her hiatus, Lea returned to college for her master's in drama and taught at Hofstra University and the American Academy of Dramatic Arts. She spent two years of this time in Philadelphia, moving there when the computer company for which her third husband worked transferred him to Camden (they've since divorced).

On her return to singing, she gathered momentum from the New York cabaret renaissance of the mid 1970s. Cabaret is supposed to be experiencing another such renaissance now, but Lea is skeptical.

"I have found, to my great regret, that the public will come out for Irving Berlin, for George Gershwin, for Cole Porter, and for Rodgers and Hart," she said. "They won't come out for Jerome Kern, and they won't come out for Harold Arlen.

"They want only the big, big, *big* names, and why that makes me sad is that there are wonderful songs being written today that I would love to be able to do, by people whose shows open and close very, very quickly Off-Off Broadway or not at all. If *I* were a bigger name and could draw a huge audience no matter what I sang, I could introduce these songs to the public they deserve. Not *being* a big name, I've got to stick with the big names."

During her reign as cabaret's queen bee, the late Mabel Mercer used to tell interviewers that she never sought to express her own emotions while singing—she sought to express the emotions of those listening to her. Though speaking only of herself, Mercer thus defined the appeal of every great American popular singer from Ethel Waters and Bing Crosby on.

Mercer's words came to mind earlier this week, during Barbara Lea's tribute to George and Ira Gershwin at the Free Library. Lea sang twenty great Gershwin tunes in all, swinging effortlessly on such uptempo numbers as "'S Wonderful" and "Soon." But her ballad interpretations were in a class by themselves, and she turned "But Not for Me" into great theater without subjecting it to vulgar theatrics. She sang the first few verses in a merry tone meant to suggest a shallow woman laughing off a failed love affair. Then, with her piano accompanist, Bill Charlap, following her unerringly, she gradually slowed the tempo and softened her delivery, making the lyrics' glib dismissal of romance ironic. With Lea singing it, the song didn't seem to be unfolding up there on stage. It seemed to be unfolding in the heart of each member of the audience—the most fitting of all dramatic settings, as Mercer also knew, for a song about unrequited love.

(JUNE 1992)

A Bit Much

Ever hear of "Barbra Strident"? There's a card for her in the female vocal section of Medium Rare, a second-hand-record store just off Castro Street, in San Francisco. It follows one that reads: BARBRA STEISAND, ALL TITLES 1963–1973, PLUS *THE WAY WE WERE, FUNNY LADY, CLASSICAL BARBRA, THE BROADWAY ALBUM* AND *YENTL*. "You can't say she's ever lost her touch," says Michael Mascioli, the store's co-owner, in explaining the not strictly chronological distinction. "She's always gone back and forth."

Mascioli might have to take a hacksaw to *Just for the Record . . .* (Columbia), a new, four-CD box set on which Streisand herself traces her career from the beginning. Or from *before* the beginning: the first disc (one of two subtitled *The '60s*, with the seventies and eighties getting one disc each) opens with a 1955 acetate recording of Streisand, then only thirteen and accompanied by a studio pianist-for-hire, singing "You'll Never Know" in the style of Alice Faye. For the set's finale, Streisand lowers the needle on the scratchy disk again, this time singing a duet with her younger self until the earnest teenager's voice fades away and we're left with only the mature Streisand and strings.

Just for the Record . . . —a title that says more than it wants to, given that Streisand long ago abandoned regular in-the-flesh performances to become a Hollywood Hallucination, almost entirely a creature of the sound stage and recording studio— weighs in as this year's major act of artistic self-indulgence, topping even Norman Mailer's *Harlot's Ghost* for can-you-believe-it chutzpah despite a white-lace-and-pink roses cover and booklet motif that blushes modesty (a friend says that the packaging reminds her of one for a feminine hygiene product). A handful of Streisand's most famous recordings are here, beginning with "People," her 1965 breakthrough smash from the score of *Funny Girl*. But for the most part, Streisand presents unfamiliar versions of the songs most associated with her, frequently employing segues designed to call attention to her creative process—as when, for example, a demo tape of her strumming "Evergreen" on guitar blossoms into the full orchestral version from the *A Star Is Born* soundtrack, complete with Paul Williams's sticky lyrics.

Including demos, rare live performances, TV archives, numbers from *Funny Girl* taped in the theater, home recordings (including one of her mom singing "Second Hand Rose" with a trill that's itself a relic), and tracks left off of albums for sundry reasons, about two thirds of *Just for the Record . . .* is previously unreleased. There are numerous gems here, none of which outsparkles a "Happy Days Are Here Again" that predates and is even more dramatic and oddly moving than the celebrated (and hitherto definitive) reading on *The Barbra Streisand Album* (1963). This "new" version is from a "That Wonderful Year" segment of *The Garry Moore Show*, broadcast in the spring of 1962, when Streisand was first making her mark on Broadway as Miss Marmelstein, the put-upon secretary in Harold Rome's *I Can Get It for You Wholesale*. Guesting on *The Tonight Show* later that same year, she gamely attempted Tommy Wolf and Fran Landesman's "Spring Can Really Hang You Up the Most," a tricky lament that's thrown any number of singers, including (just recently) Bette Midler. But even here, you find yourself applauding the younger Streisand's good taste in material, further proof of which was the generous amount of Harold Arlen in her repertoire (her bravura interpretation of his "When the Sun Comes Out," for starters).

Along with her avid gay following, an appreciation of Arlen was one of the things that Streisand shared with Judy Garland, the singer to whom she was most frequently compared when she was starting out. Strange, then, that neither Streisand's duets with Arlen (from the out-of-print *Harold Sings Arlen*) nor her Arlen-heavy medleys with Garland (from a 1963 TV broadcast) produce many sparks. But Streisand's appearance with Garland at least qualifies as a powerful nostalgia item, as do sincere, on-air testimonials from Moore, Johnny Carson, and Ed Sullivan on behalf of a talented young singer whom many of us first encountered on television. But old TV material also supplies many of *Just for the Record . . .*'s most egregious indiscretions, including Streisand's at first endearingly kooky but gradually cloying Emmy and Oscar acceptance speeches (the accompanying ninety-two-page booklet, in addition to Streisand's own liner notes and hundreds of photographs tracing her metamorphosis from schnozzy hoyden to leggy cover girl, also provides a year-by-year summary of every citation she's ever received) and an overwrought "Hatikvah" to which the only sane response is "Oy!" This last item, from *The Stars Salute Israel at 30*, a 1979 showbiz celebration of Israel's thirtieth anniversary, follows a telephone conversation between Streisand and Golda Meir in which the two women seem to be talking to each other not just from different countries, but from different planets. "How do you manage all these years to have such energy," the singer and movie star asks the former prime minister. "Do you take vitamins or a special diet or go jogging every morning?"

Just for the Record . . .'s ostensible storyline is Streisand's growth as an artist as she conquered one medium after another. But the set is more revealing than she might imagine. It suggests that she might never have become a star without her appearances on TV variety and talk shows, where she could put everything she had into one number and still leave viewers wanting more. In addition to demonstrating her discomfort at being close to an audience, eight tracks recorded at a New York cabaret in 1962 also show that her Garlandlike tendency to turn all but her novelty tunes into three-minute therapy sessions could wear thin pretty quickly.

Though her musical values align her with an earlier generation, Streisand is actually eleven months younger than Bob Dylan and almost a year-and-a-half younger than John Lennon would have been. On *Just for the Record* . . .'s first two discs, she emerges as an irresistible anomaly: an impudent young woman, petit bourgeois and proud of it, whose respect for her music-business elders accounted for a good deal of her charm. But by the end of the 1960s (and of disc two), when most in her generation were letting it all hang out, Streisand was squeezing herself into a bustle and starring as Dolly Levi in a white-elephant movie musical. She seemed not just anachronistic but irrelevant, which no doubt explains why her record company pressured her to record "contemporary" material, such as the halfhearted 1970 cover version of Laura Nyro's "Stony End" included on disc three.

She was soon applying her own pressure. On the face of it, the 1970s were Streisand's most successful decade. With *The Way We Were* (1973), she established herself as a credible romantic lead as well as a funny girl, and the title song from that movie took her to the top of the charts for the first time. But the material on disc three finds her drifting uncertainly between pop and rock vocal styles for most of the decade. On "Crying Time," a duet with Ray Charles from the 1973 TV special *Barbra Streisand . . . and Other Musical Instruments*, she even resorts to imitating Aretha Franklin, despite being perhaps the only major postwar American pop singer with no discernible black influence. A 1971 TV duet of "Close to You" with Burt Bacharach, the song's composer, and an interpretation of Paul Williams's "We've Only Just Begun" left off of the 1971 album *Barbra Joan Streisand* show that, even after toning herself down, she still was too much the belter to be fully comfortable singing fluffy seventies pop.

Just for the Record . . . has a surprise ending, though, and arguably a happy one. Disc four starts off badly with Streisand and Neil "America's Vibrato" Diamond groaning "You Don't Bring Me Flowers" on the 1980 Grammy Awards. But "Guilty," a duet with Bee Gee Barry Gibb from the same year, is as disarmingly lighthearted as it is lightweight, and then Streisand reaches a turning point of sorts with *Yentl*, her 1983 directorial debut, represented here by a work tape of Streisand reading a plot synopsis and calling on the skills she had by then acquired as an actress to bring unexpected shadings to three of the songs written for the movie by Michel Legrand and Alan and Marilyn Bergman ("A Piece of Sky," the final song, segues into the full soundtrack version). Much of what follows—including a live rendition of Arlen's "Over the Rainbow" from the 1986 album *One Voice* and a previously unreleased 1988 interpretation of Frank Loesser's "Warm All Over"—suggests that there's nothing wrong with Streisand that decent material can't fix. From a technical standpoint she's singing better than ever, having tamed her vibrato and refined her upper register to such an extent that she's now able to hold and extend notes that she once would have shouted out staccato.

The downside is that the modulated Streisand often sounds mannered and lacking in the sort of immediacy that used to be her trademark. Our friend in San Francisco to the contrary, it was at the beginning of Streisand's career that she was often guilty of being "Barbra Strident," a singer unable to deliver a torch song without immolating herself and anyone within earshot. But it was just such excess that made her so exciting. The difference between boffo and so-so Streisand often boils down to the difference between much too much and a bit *much*. The latter describes *Just for the Record . . .*, despite its many felicities.

(OCTOBER 1991)

Full of Foolish Song

Miles Davis, on his first visit to London, in the late 1950s, supposedly remarked that he wasn't much enjoying himself, because it pained him to hear English spoken that way. It sometimes pains me, on listening to a show album, to hear Jerome Kern, Cole Porter, George and Ira Gershwin, Irving Berlin, or Richard Rodgers and Lorenz Hart performed "that way"—by which I mean as show tunes rather than as jazz. I feel this even though I realize that the fusty sopranos and rhythmless baritones making me cringe were usually the very singers for whom these songs were crafted. Insofar as Broadway was the point of origin for most of the songs now regarded as standards, musical theater is American popular song's mother tongue. But

Broadway's most recognizable dialects are those of vaudeville and Viennese operetta, turn-of-the-century idioms that sound stilted to ears used to the relaxed pulsation of a Frank Sinatra or Ella Fitzgerald.

By virtue of removing songs from their theatrical context, these and other superior jazz and pop singers gain the further advantage of needing to project only themselves, not scripted characters. The fact that in practically every instance I happened to hear their interpretations first probably explains my preference for them. But another possible explanation is my having entered adolescence in the early 1960s, as part of the first rock and roll generation—a generation convinced (and not unreasonably so, on the basis of *My Fair Lady*, *The Music Man*, and *The Sound of Music*) that Lerner and Loewe, Meredith Willson, and Rodgers and Hammerstein were synonyms for "square." A decade or so later, Broadway attempted to woo us by turning up the decibels with such frizzy monstrosities as *Godspell* and *Hair*, but this only succeeded in widening the breach. And though a soft spot for showtunes is an enduring gay stereotype, most of the gay men my own age I knew in the 1970s were more inclined to spend their weekends in discos than singing along in piano bars.

Things have changed since then. Broadway musicals are no longer categorically dismissed by arbiters of hip as bourgeois self-indulgence at its most ostentatious. Over lunch one day last year in New York, a journalist friend of mine in his late thirties who can always be counted on to know the latest buzz (as a staffer at one of the slicks, he usually has a hand in starting it) asked my companion and me if we planned to see any of the new shows while we were in town. This is a question he might once have asked only of an aunt and uncle in from the burbs for the proverbial Rotary convention. Also last year, in an edition of his *Village Voice* Consumer Guide, Robert Christgau—the rock critic most closely read by others in the field—wrote that only his preference for the original *Guys and Dolls* prevented him from choosing *Guys and Dolls: The New Broadway Cast Recording* (RCA Victor) as one of his Pick Hits. Studio restorations of George and Ira Gershwin's shows of the 1920s, such as the recent *Lady, Be Good!* (Elektra/Nonesuch), are accorded the same respect as new recordings of Beethoven and Stravinsky, and greeted with only slightly less curiosity than greets collections of previously unissued Bob Dylan. And people who see George C. Wolfe's *Jelly's Last Jam*, about the life of Jelly Roll Morton, leave the theater debating the show's racial politics, just as they do after seeing a movie by Spike Lee.

My generation's belated embrace of musicals past and present (and of singers such as Tony Bennett, Chet Baker, and Jimmy Scott) is generally taken to be evidence that we now require a roomier fit in our music as well as in our jeans. Maybe so, though as someone who has always held Elvis and Frank Sinatra in more or less equal esteem and who enjoys much of the rap and alternative rock that's supposed to baffle people our age, I can hardly offer myself as living proof. My own experience is probably atypical, but one aspect of it is probably typical enough. Until persuaded otherwise by *Sweeney Todd*, massive doses of Kurt Weill and *West Side Story*, and a revival of *Oklahoma* that somebody dragged me to in the late seventies, I had no use for Broadway. At around the time I discovered that there were musicals I enjoyed as complete scores (and not just as mulch for the Fitzgeralds and Sinatras), I also realized that what had spoiled Broadway for me—along with rock and roll's frank adrenal pitch—were those awful film adaptations of the hit shows of the fifties and sixties.

These movies, which amounted to the only exposure to Broadway that many of us had, tended to be implausibly cast (*Oklahaoma*, with Rod Steiger as a ethnicized Jud who'd read *An Actor Prepares*, is one example among many), and to overextend the big production numbers to the point of tedium. Much worse, in order to "open up" a show for the screen and thus prevent it from being perceived as uncinematic, its producer or director would often change into matter-of-fact dialogue talk that was originally used only to telegraph songs.

The point lost on these filmmakers was that musicals are inherently stylized, not naturalistic. The musical theater scene that most persuasively sums up the medium's reason for being—and best reveals its capacity for magic—might be the one in Frank Loesser's *Guys and Dolls* in which Sky Masterson and Sister Sarah, just back from Havana and strolling through a quiet and nearly empty Times Square a few hours before dawn, serenade each other (and us) with "I've Never Been in Love Before," as luminous a song as any ever written for the stage. The crapshooter and the Salvation Army worker, tipsy with lust and unembarrassed to be "full of foolish song," could be singing this duet for all of Broadway's brimming-over couples, all the Curlys and Laureys and Tonys and Marias likewise so full of foolish song that giving voice to it becomes their only practical recourse. In drama as in life, crapshooters, street gang members, and ranchers and farmers who should be friends don't celebrate falling in love by bursting into song. In musicals they do, and when the songs are as seductive as the best of those in *Guys and Dolls*, we happily buy into the make-believe—an opportunity not offered to us by even the greatest recorded performances of Sinatra and Fitzgerald, who always are exactly who they are.

Naturally, "I've Never Been in Love Before" was omitted from Joseph L. Mankiewicz's 1955 movie of *Guys and Dolls*. So was "My Time of Day," the ode to nightlife that in Loesser's score amounted to the introductory verse to "I've Never Been in Love Before," and whose wide intervals were presumably too great a stretch for Marlon Brando, Mankiewicz's improbable Sky. But though hardly equal to the numbers he does warble, Brando manages to use his shy whisper of a singing voice to externalize the flamboyant Sky's hidden softness and decency, the qualities that prevent him from taking advantage of Sister Sarah after getting her soused on rum in Havana. Legend has it that Brando, once he found himself in a position to demand script approval, would insist on being shot or beaten up at least once in every movie, in order to enlist sympathy for his character. You can't help feeling sympathy for his Sky, whose wavering intonation and puzzled relationship to the beat are the aural equivalents of a bloodied nose or an arm in a sling.

Besides, there's never been an entirely satisfying stage production of *Guys and Dolls*, either—at least not in terms of the singers chosen to interpret Loesser's songs. In saying this, I realize that many will think me guilty of heresy. The LP of the original 1950 production (now available as an MCA compact disk) is one of the most cherished artifacts of the early original-cast-album era. Robert Alda and Isabel Bigley as the romantic leads, and Sam Levene and Vivian Blaine as their comic counterparts, the floating-craps-game operator Nathan Detroit and the showgirl Miss Adelaide, are generally believed to have set a standard to which the cast of the current Broadway revival can only aspire. But this lofty reputation strikes me as borrowed magic, a side effect of the realization that the unapologetic contemporary American accent of Loesser's melodies and lyrics represented a real breakthrough for Broadway.

From the vantage point of four decades later, Bigley is nondescript, Blaine a little brassier than her role calls for, Alda close to tone-deaf, and Levene phlegmatic in the laryngological as well as the dispositional sense (a singing postnasal drip). The only member of the original cast who gives a performance that you sense in your bones couldn't possibly be bettered is the inimitable Stubby Kaye as Nicely-Nicely Johnson, the tinhorn who's so good at conning himself that his nag can't lose that he cons himself into believing his dream about needing to change his wicked ways. This, of course, is "Sit Down, You're Rockin' the Boat," the biggest of the show's production numbers, delivered by Kaye in a voice as stout and unmannered as Jimmy Rushing's and preserved in the film version. (Seemingly wider than he is tall and therefore just made for Cinemascope, Kaye steals the movie; you can see the look of preternatural bliss on his face as he sings.) There's never going to be a comparable Nicely-Nicely, but on the cast album of the new *Guys and Dolls*, an eager beaver named Walter Bobbie sets the nerves on edge by whining "Sit Down, You're Rockin' the Boat" instead of singing it. I wish the role had been given to J. K. Simmons, who joins Bobbie on "Fugue for Tinhorns" and the title song, and whose voice is similar to Kaye's in amplitude as well as timbre.

In nearly every other instance, however, the new cast members outshine their predecessors, with Faith Prince and Josie de Guzman scoring especially high marks as Adelaide and Sarah, and Edward Strauss's orchestrations bringing out a jazzy shimmer in Loesser's melodies that wasn't always apparent on the first cast album. Prince's skills as both singer and actress are such that what for once comes across in "Adelaide's Lament" is the wit of Loesser's lyrics about the perils of a girl remaining single, instead of just the character's Brooklynese. The challenge in singing the role of Sarah is that it demands two completely different voices—a prim and yearning soprano for "I'll Know," and a horny, openly amazed-at-itself slur for "If I Were a Bell." De Guzman is believable at both, perhaps because she has the wisdom not to overdo either.

As his gambler namesake, Nathan Lane relies more on comic timing than on vocal prowess, which is okay, because no role originated by Sam Levene requires much in the way of vocal prowess anyway. The role of Sky does, and Peter Gallagher isn't always up to the task, though his voice does curve handsomely under de Guzman's on their two love duets. A studious actor for whom singing is an acquired skill, as it was for Alda and Brando, Gallagher isn't bad, just unsure of himself. He's a Sky lacking in self-confidence, and this cannot be. The RCA CD includes a few of the spoken interludes leading up to the songs, and Gallagher frequently seems determined not to speak in his natural voice, much less sing in it. Just when he seems to be doing fine, he becomes Gordon MacRae.

Gallagher is said to have developed a cold (as Miss Adelaide might put it) just before the recording session, and this could be the reason he sounds so strained. But friends who've seen this new production tell me that Gallagher failed to live up to their mental image of Sky. One friend quipped that Gallagher comes across as so much the eighties yuppie that the show's producers should have updated the book and had him beseeching Lady Luck to favor him in a leveraged buy out, rather than at craps.

My friend's unkind remark reminds us that actors who sing on Broadway are seldom cast for their singing abilities alone. They also have to look the part, and it helps if they're able to move and to deliver their spoken lines with some amount of grace. In a way, cast albums are no more than one-dimensional souvenirs of the shows they allegedly preserve. The exceptions are those albums on which a cast was assembled for the sole purpose of recording. These are usually not just revivals, but anthropological digs restoring to *status quo ante* songs discarded at one point or another during a show's early run. The masterpiece of this genre is John McGlynn's 1988 restoration of Jerome Kern and Oscar Hammerstein II's *Show Boat*—a more "theatrial" experience than most stage productions of the show, largely owing to the chill provided by Teresa Stratas as the mulatto Julie and McGlynn's retrieval of an ominous, quasi-gospel number called "Mis'ry's Comin' Aroun'."

Not every vintage show benefits from, or even justifies, this archival approach. A case in point is *Lady Be Good!* (Elektra/Nonesuch), the latest in Tommy Krasker's series of Gershwin restorations, following *Strike Up the Band* and *Girl Crazy*. As presented on Broadway in 1924, *Lady Be Good!*—the Gershwins' first smash—as less an organic whole than a series of star turns for a variety of the period's top performers, including Fred and Adele Astaire and the vaudevillian Ukulele Ike. In addition to the title song, the score introduced "Fascinating Rhythm" and "The Half of It, Dearie, Blues." It also introduced a number of period novelties there seems little point in recording now, especially with performers lacking the charisma of the Astaires. (An actual stage revival, with the songs complementing the action and vice versa, might be another matter.) On "Fascinating Rhythm" and "Little Jazz Bird," the singer and guitarist John Pizzarelli, this production's Ukulele Ike, exudes a carefree swing that six decades of jazz interpretations of the Gershwin brothers have conditioned us to expect from all performers of their songs. But Lara Teeter and Ann Morrison, though faithful to the composer's intentions, sound hopelessly dated in the roles originated by the Astaires.

There have been studio recordings of *Guys and Dolls*, but nothing like today's meticulous, carefully cast restorations. My own dream cast recording of *Guys and Dolls*, featuring singers past and present, would include Stubby Kaye and Faith Prince. My choice for Nathan would be none other than Frank Loesser, whose singing voice resembled Gene Kelly's in its regular-guy-ness, though his phrasing was far more relaxed than Kelly's—like a jazz instrumentalist singing a few choruses for his own enjoyment. I base this judgment on *An Evening with Frank Loesser* (DRG), a CD collection of recently discovered "demonstration" versions of songs from *Guys and Dolls*, *The Most Happy Fella*, and *How to Succeed in Business Without Really Trying*. No one else has delivered Nathan's lines (from "Sue Me") "All right already, I'm just a no-goodnik . . . it's true/So nu?" with as much charm as the composer himself.

Frank Sinatra as he was in 1955 is the only man fit to play Sky, his credibility as a high roller enhanced by his long-alleged links to organized crime. Wasted in the role of Nathan in the movie of that year, presumably because Hollywood still considered him too much of a toothpick to woo a leading lady, Sinatra got his revenge eight years later as first among equals on an album of songs from *Guys and Dolls* by the Reprise Repertory Theatre (actually an ad hoc gathering of Rat Packers and their fellow travelers). This *Guys and Dolls*, reissued last year on a Reprise CD, is truly a crapshoot. Sinatra sings "I've Never Been in

Love Before" so beautifully that you're willing to forget that the song is supposed to be a duet, and his bravura "Luck Be a Lady" (with Billy May's punching high brass taking the place of a chorus of crapshooters urging Sky to "Roll the dice!") has since become one of his trademark numbers. It's such a definitive performance that many of us now think of the song as Sinatra's, not Broadway's. Sammy Davis Jr.'s "Sit Down, You're Rockin' the Boat" is brash fun, and Jo Stafford's "I'll Know" is just about perfect (harmonizing with the orchestra where Sarah usually does with Sky, she interpolates the male respose into the bridge). On the other hand, the McGuire Sisters' "A Bushel and a Peck" is sheer torture, as are Debbie Reynolds and Allen Sherman as Adelaide and Nathan. Your affection for Sinatra's half-juiced singalongs with Dean Martin and Bing Crosby will depend on your sociological interest in the bonding habits of affluent middle-aged males in the early sixties.

You could do worse than Jo Stafford or Josie de Guzman as Sarah. But if we decide to go for shock value (and the guarantee of friction between the romantic leads), the choice would be Sinead O'Connor, the Irish bristlehead who Sinatra said deserved "a kick in the ass" for refusing to allow "The Star Spangled Banner" to be played before one of her concerts a few years ago. Who better to play Sarah as a woman of spiritual conviction than O'Connor, a "recovering Catholic," who has likened herself to Saint Joan, and who epitomizes as much as anyone on the fundamentalist right the intolerance of the pious. O'Connor's *Am I Not Your Girl?* (Chrysalis F2-21952) is hardly the first album of standards and showtunes by a rocker, nor is it the most novel. But it's the first to end with a whispered attack on "the Holy Roman Empire" for the "assassination" of Jesus Christ.

In light of which you might expect O'Connor to trash the eleven numbers she does here—an eccentric assortment including "Secret Love," "Bewitched, Bothered, and Bewildered," "Scarlet Ribbons," and "How Insensitve." And it wouldn't necessarily be a bad thing if she did; it might remind us that they're just songs, not the sacred texts that bookish young cabaret performers tend to treat them as. But O'Connor sings them straight, with no real distinction, braying only occasionally and never for very long. *Am I Not Your Girl?* is too awkwardly sincere to be enjoyable as camp, even on the Betty Boopish "I Want to Be Loved by You," where O'Connor sounds as though she's still wearing the platinum wig and temptress gown she donned to sing "You Do Something to Me" in the video for *Red, Hot and Blue,* the 1990 various-artists anthology that post-modernized Cole Porter in the name of AIDS (and outed him in the bargain). Like most of the rock performers who've attempted vintage pop, she doesn't have a clue how these songs are supposed to be phrased. What's surprising, in light of rock's pride in its big beat, is that rhythm is usually the area in which its singers come up short. Swing is a foreign language to them, and O'Connor is no exception.

So what do her fans hear in her? The answer's on "Success Has Made a Failure of Our Home," an anomaly for being an old Loretta Lynn hit, not something from Broadway or Tin Pan Alley. This is the only song on which O'Connor blares like she means it, as an army of dissonant horns blares right along with her. It shows how rock obviates the need for musical theater by creating lavish theater in listeners' imaginations. (Rock concerts at their most outlandish *are* musical theater.)

Am I Not Your Girl? also includes two versions of Andrew Lloyd Webber and Tim Rice's "Don't Cry for Me, Argentina," one of them a "swinging" big-band instrumental. This mawkish number from *Evita* might seem as out of place here as the Loretta Lynn cover, except for the fact that O'Connor is twenty-five. Broadway has changed so much in the past two decades that Webber's rather than those of Rodgers and Hammerstein or Lerner of Loewe is probably the name that most people under the age of thirty now most associate with it. Webber's vulgar spectacles at least kept Broadway afloat through some

lean times; that's about all that can be said in their favor. Along
with British imports, the other new trend on Broadway in the
past twenty years has been the "jazz" musical, usually featuring
an all-black cast and built around the songs of an iconic performer of another era: Fats Waller in the case of *Ain't Misbe-
havin'*, and Duke Ellington in that of *Sophisticated Ladies*.

Two such shows had their Broadway premieres in 1992, and
there's a cast album for each. Essentially a revue, *Five Guys
Named Moe* (Columbia) celebrates—or lamely attempts to—the
influence of Louis Jordan, a singer and alto saxophonist whose
hit records of the 1940s, which included "Is You Is or Is You
Ain't (Ma' Baby)" and "Choo Choo Ch' Boogie," hilariously
translated country homilies into urban jive and laid the ground-
work for rhythm and blues in the process. Jordan's songs are
as evocative of their period as a zoot suit, but they also represent superior musicianship of a kind that's timeless. You'd
never guess this from *Five Guys Named Moe*. The title song was
written for Jordan by Larry Wynn, who explains in the liner
notes that the phrase "five guys named Moe" popped into his
head one day as he was trying to remember the names of the
lesser-known musicians on a recording date with Billie Holiday, Roy Eldridge, Teddy Wilson, Don Redman, and Georgie
Auld. The five nonentities in this Broadway revue might as well
all be named Moe, so indistinguishable are they in their cheery
oversell of two dozen of Jordan's slyest numbers.

Jelly's Last Jam (Mercury) is something else altogether: more
ambitious and more effective as theater, but mean-spirited and
manipulative in its portrayal of its subject. Written and directed
by George C. Wolfe, and starring Gregory Hines, the show tells
the story of Jelly Roll Morton, the New Orleans "Creole of
color," who claimed to have "invented" jazz—and whose tangos, stomps, and variations on ragtime and blues practically did
originate jazz composition. Unfolding mostly in flashbacks after
having deposited Norton and his immortal soul in the Jungle
Inn, "a lowdown club somewheres 'tween Heaven and Hell,"

Jelly's Last Jam is simultaneously the most lavish of Broadway's black musicals and a withering critique of the genre. It breaks new ground in acknowledging the social disorder from which its subject evolved, and in incorporating lighting and stage techniques associated with the shoestring avant-garde into what's essentially a mainstream, big-bucks extravaganza. But it plays Morton for a sucker, putting him on trial for being a light-skinned opportunist who formulated his music from the experiences of people darker and lower on the social ladder than himself, whom he persisted in thinking of as his inferiors. Some of the charges might be true, but you get the feeling that Wolfe, by changing the rules on Morton and questioning whether he was "black" enough by today's standards, is using Morton to work out his own conflicts regarding color and class. The most unforgivable part of it is that *Jelly's Last Jam* stacks the cards against Morton by never letting us hear his music in anything resembling its original form. The titles of his pieces have been changed to conform to Susan Birkenhead's didactic lyrics, and Luther Henderson's unsympathetic arrangements reduce Morton's idiosyncratic rhythms to generic 1920s doo-wacka-doo.

Jazz once derived much of its repertoire from Broadway, but owing as much to changes within jazz as to a decline in the quality of Broadway songwriting, the process has been reversed, with shows such as *Jelly's Last Jam* and *Five Guys Named Moe* the unhappy result. In addition to the pleasures it affords in its own right, the current revival of *Guys and Dolls* is a reminder of a time when Broadway wasn't only more robust but also more autonomous.

The alto and soprano saxophonist Michael Hashim's album *Guys and Dolls* (Stash) is likewise a reminder of a time, this one approximately three decades past, when "jazz version of" LPs used to follow on the heels of the original cast recordings of most hit Broadway shows. Albums of this sort used to be plentiful: in the jazz section of used-record stores you're likely to find Teddy Wilson's *Gypsy*, Cannonball Adderley's *Fiddler on the*

Roof, even (with some luck) Eddie Costa's *Guys and Dolls Like Vibes.* The target audience for such albums was presumably a little baffled by modern jazz but willing to make the effort to understand it if musicians obliged by playing familiar songs of recent vintage. This secondary market for jazz no longer exists, and such albums have disappeared along with it.

All of which might make Hashim's *Guys and Dolls* merely an irresistible anachronism. But it's also vital contemporary jazz. Thanks to their challenging harmonic structures, Loesser's melodies lend themselves as readily to chordal improvisation as they do to singing. Hashim and his sidemen—the drummer Kenny Washington, the bassist Peter Washington, and the pianist Mike Le Donne, who worked out most of the arrangements— do justice to the melodies even while taking such liberties with them as voicing "I'll Know" slightly sharp, slowing "Fugue for Tinhorns" to a saunter, and putting the drum's brushstrokes up front on "If I Were a Bell." "My Time of Day" becomes a lonely blues wail, and "Marry the Man Today" is transformed into a semimodal march, replete with Phil Woodslike puckers at the end of Hashim's lengthier and more excited phrases. In exercising their improvisational flair, these four musicians also demonstrate the amenability of Loesser's songs to such novel approaches. A song-based improviser could hardly ask for better material.

They don't make albums like this anymore, in part because they don't stage shows like *Guys and Dolls* anymore, either. But did they ever? *Guys and Dolls* isn't just a Broadway musical. It's a down-to-earth platonic ideal of what a Broadway musical ought to be.

(MARCH 1993)

Infection

I'm so happy
I'm afraid I'll die
Here in your arms

What would you do
If I died
Like this-
Right now
Here in your arms?

So begins the first of many songs of love and death in *Passion*, the composer and lyricist Stephem Sondheim's third collaboratioin with the writer and director James Lapine, following *Sunday in the Park with George* (1984) and *Into the Woods* (1987). The show, which closed on Broadway last January, after 280 performances (including previews), was based on the Italian director Ettore Scola's 1981 film *Passione d'Amore*, although Sondheim and Lapine also drew from Scola's original source—Iginio Ugo Tarchetti's *Fosca*, an autobiographical gothic published in 1869, the year of Tarchetti's death from tuberculosis and typhus at the age of twenty-nine. All three versions of the tale, which is as much a vampire story without a caped antichrist as it is a meditation on the nature of romantic love, take place toward the tail end of the Risorgimento, in a newly unified Italy at peace after two decades of war.

Passion survives on CD, the format in which it will inspire arguments for years to come, although there will surely be many other productions. On stage, the musical begins with a handsome young soldier and his beautiful mistress in bed together nude, tangled in postcoital bliss as they sing the duet quoted above (untitled on stage, as are all of *Passion*'s individual songs, but called "Happiness" on the Angel cast album). Clara, who in the New York production was played by Marin Mazzie, is so happy she could die; Giorgio, played by Jere Shea, agrees that theirs isn't "another simple love story." Neither is the show, depite starting off like one.

On CD as on the stage, *Passion* includes no overture, nor is one needed. Military drumming followed by a stab of dissonance—what I think of as a "blood" chord—and a creeping three-note vamp reminiscent of Sondheim's music for *Sweeney Todd* blend into Giorgio and Clara's mutual declaration of love, which, with its harmonic deviations and sudden changes of tempo, foreshadows practically every subsequent number. That vamp—technically a "pedal point," or sustained notes in the bass register that remain the same as the harmonies around them change—is as sure a sign of unrest as the second *S* in *Passion*'s elegant red logo, which is reversed and joined to the first at the down curve. The tops of the letters form both a valentine heart and a mirror image, suggestive of love as something potentially aberrant, twisted, narcissistic. The lyric to this opening number works in much the same way as the music—as a sort of premonition. This will be the last song in which an allusion to death is understood to be figurative.

We find out later (too much later, perhaps) that Clara is unhappily married but unwilling to leave her husband, because (under nineteenth-century Italian law) to so would mean relinquishing custody of her little boy. This isn't the only thing keeping her and Giorgio apart. The luckless Giorgio, a captain decorated for saving the life of a fellow soldier on the battlefield, has received orders transferring him from Milan to a no-longer-threatened garrison in a provincial town in the northern mountains. This is where he falls prey to Fosca, his commanding officer's plain and sickly cousin, a hysteric already half in the grave. Giorgio's imagination and sensitivity set him apart from the camp's other soldiers, and Fosca recognizes him as a kindred spirit on the basis of these very qualities. "'They hear drums, we hear music,'" she sings to him at one point; and though her outburst alludes to those military cadences that open the show, the fevered rhythmic pattern to which her words are set echoes Giorgio's earlier declaration of his and Clara's "love that fuses two into one."

Fosca clutches at Giorgio, so obsessed with him that she pursues him without fear of humiliation. As many in the audience were, Giorgio is appalled by her manipulativeness and self-pity. Even so, he finds himself drawn to her, eventually concluding that her love for him—love "as pure as breath, as permanent as death, implacable as stone," in the words of the show's most haunting song—is superior in kind to any he's ever known: specifically, Clara's.

Fosca wins Giorgio's heart by convincing him that she would die for him. Someone hearing the CD for the first time, and unfamiliar with Tarchetti's novel or Scola's movie, might sneer that this isn't much of a sacrifice, given that Fosca is near death anyway. You need to read *Fosca* (available in English as *Passion*, in a new translation by Lawrence Venuti) in order to comprehend that a night of abandoned lovemaking will kill her.

Contemporary drama can be a teacher and his female student on opposite sides of a desk (David Mamet's *Oleanna*) or three men chained to a wall (Frank McGuinness's *Someone Who'll Watch Over Me*), but musicals are now admired for leaving nothing to the imagination. The most popular of them are feasts of conspicuous consumption, with the salient talking point for audiences being the cost of tickets in ratio to the size of the chorus lines and the immensity of the sets and special effects.

Passion wasn't only an anomaly by these standards, but as deliberate an affront as Sondheim and George Furth's *Merrily We Roll Along* (1981), which in lieu of costumes featured its young cast in sweatshirts that said who their characters were supposed to be. The newer show's only chorus line was a Greek chorus of uniformed soldiers who, marching in tight formation, misinterpreted Giorgio's motives in being kind to Fosca. Its primary sets were Adrianne Lobel's muted backdrops and scrims, which, an art historian friend of mine pointed out, were possibly intended to evoke the Macchiaioli, a school of mid-nineteenth-century Italian impressionists familiar *only* to art historians. This is a chamber musical in which a voluptuous actress who bares her breasts in the opening scene and there-after strolls across stage reading her lover's letters in a succession of elaborate and brightly colored period hoopskirts and bustles is upstaged by another actress in drab, colorless dresses to her ankles, with a large wart glued to her face and her hair drawn back in a spinster's bun. Tarchetti's real-life model for Fosca was an epileptic. Skin and bones in an era in which obesity was a badge of both prosperity and health, the novel's Fosca might today be diagnosed as anorectic. What ails the musical's Fosca is never specified: described by the camp physician as "a kind of medical phenomenon, a collection of many ills," she seems to be suffering from generic nineteenth-century woman's dis-ease—she faints a lot and is given to emotional outbursts. She's supposed to be hideously ugly, but the woman onstage in the New York production was no worse than homely. If this had been Andrew Lloyd Webber, there might at least be a show-stopping prosthesis.

Passion opened last May to mixed reviews, some of them frankly antipathetic. It received four Tony Awards, including one as the season's best new musical, though many in the theatrical community gossiped that this top honor was bestowed grudg-ingly and against not much competition. The show was a "hit" only in that it enjoyed a fairly long run, in part because it was relatively inexpensive to stage (it broke even at two-thirds capacity, and did better than that only occasionally).

Sondheim has described his score for *Passion* as "one long love song, one long rhapsody," and the show in its entirety—two hours long, with no intermission, no breaks for applause between numbers, and no postmodernist winking by the actors at the expense of their characters—as "a large one-act," "an opera in attitude," and "the world's first humorless musical." Ten years ago, when *Sunday in the Park with George* was new, Sondheim was frequently likened to the painter Georges Seurat, the show's protagonist, whose immersion in his canvases distanced him from the other characters in much the same way that Sondheim has increasingly distanced himself from Broadway audiences. Such are the demands that *Passion* makes on an audience—not just willing suspension of disbelief, but undivided attention to a score that circles back on itself endlessly—that Sondheim could also be likened to Fosca, who unreasonably demands Giorgio's love. To judge from the audiences I saw it with last summer, there could be a sign dangling from that reversed *S* on the Plymouth Theatre's marquee trumpeting *Passion* as THE NEW HIT MUSICAL NOBODY LIKES!

This wouldn't be completely true, of course, because there are many who admire the show immensely, including me. Sondheim's champions see him as Broadway's last remaining link to the grand songwriting traditions of George Gershwin and Jerome Kern. Some of us, again including me, regard him as this country's greatest active composer, regardless of genre. I'm not one of those people who adore everything he does, and *Passion* hardly strikes me as his richest score. It lacks *Company's* satiric vitality, *Sweeney Todd's* bigness and wicked cackle, the ill-fated *Merrily We Roll Along's* bounty of memorable songs. But coming as it does after the ostentatious *Sunday in the Park with George* and the trivial *Into the Woods* and *Assassins*, it marks a return to form. A double paradox in that it's a period musical whose characters express opera-size emotions conversationally, in lyrics as spare and direct as any its composer has ever set to music, *Passion* also achieves an ideal Sondheim has been pursuing with varying success at least since *Company*—that of the Broadway score as a kind of symphony of voices, an integrated work in which individual songs are anagramatic movements.

Sondheim has said as much. "To me, it's important that a score be not just a series of songs—that it should in some way be developed, just the way [a show's] book is," he told Stephen Schiff, the author of a *New Yorker* profile published in 1993, when *Passion* was in the planning stages. The most frequent complaint against Sondheim is that audiences don't leave the theater humming his melodies, the way they did Gershwin's and Kern's. Sondheim—who was Oscar Hammerstein II's protégé but also studied with the "serious" composer Milton Babbitt, the author of a 1958 article variously published as "The Composer as Specialist" and "Who Cares If You Listen?"—has often gone to perverse lengths to ensure that audiences won't hum the show on their way to the exits. The loveliest song in *Merrily We Roll Along*, for example, was "Good Thing Going," a love song that (in context) also becomes a song about the widening rupture between two men, a theatrical composer and his lyricist, who also happens to be his best friend. First sung by the lyricist accompanied by the composer on piano at a party for potential backers, the song is touted as a real beaut by the team's hostess (this is Sondheim setting a dare for himself). The most foolproof way to get an audience humming, as Sondheim has caustically observed in more than one interview, is to reprise ad infinitum throughout your show. "Good Thing Going" is instantly reprised by popular demand of those at the party—but the second time around the lyricist, reluctant to sing it again so soon, is joined by his hammy partner, and their voices are eventually drowned out by the jabbering partygoers (this is after the only partygoer so moved by the song that he hums along with it is shushed). Because the show moves backwards in time, when we next hear "Good Thing Going," it's offered as an example of the songwriting team's juvenilia, taken at a nervous uptempo and saddled with awkward lyrics about the drawbacks of living in New York. The song received yet another trouncing in a wonderful revival of *Merrily We Roll Along* staged with Sondheim's blessing Off-Broadway earlier this year (a cast recording is now available on Varese Saraband). It was sung as a teasing bump-and-grind by a sequined actress flanked by chorus boys in suspenders and derbies, in a devilish send-up of Bob Fosse. For that matter, the first time we heard "Good Thing Going" in this new production, Frank Sinatra was singing it. His 1981 recording was pressed into service to set up a TV interview with the song's "composers," who, in the show's present tense, are as sick of their hit song as they are of each other.

The original production of *Merrily We Roll Along*, which closed after just sixteen performances in 1981, flopped, I think, because Sondheim incorrectly assumed that audiences were becoming as disenchanted with Broadway's excesses as he was. The songs in *Passion* don't have similar alienation devices built into them, but they discourage humming along in quite another way. John Simon in a review in *New York* magazine complained that all of the score's songs sound alike. Heard on CD, they do; but therein lies both their integrity and the root of the problem that theatergoers and reviewers had with them.

The songs are so much of a piece thematically that it's difficult even for someone like me, who saw the show more than once and has practically memorized the CD, to sing a few bars of one of them—literally or in the mind's ear—without another two or three intruding. Not that it's ever easy to extract a Sondheim melody from its harmonic crisscross, anyway— melody is his equivalent of Henry James's figure in the carpet. (Sondheim is the first important American songwriter untouched by the blues, which might explain why so few jazz musicians have chosen to interpret his songs. Yet he might also be the only contemporary Broadway composer who writes songs much the way the typical jazz musician does, starting off with the chords and letting the melody emerge from them, instead of the other way around. His body of work has enormous jazz potential, but it goes unfulfilled on the new *Color and Light: Jazz Sketches of Sondheim*, a misguided all-star affair produced by Miles Goodwin and Oscar Castro Neves for Sony Classical. It also went unfulfilled on the Trotter Trio's chichi *A Passion for Jazz*, on Varese Saraband.

No matter how taken you might be with them on first hearing, these songs don't replay themselves in your head for the next few hours. They're part of a score that gets under your skin and that could almost be a metaphor for a show in which one of the characters virtually infects another with her love: Giorgio's attitude toward Fosca softens only after he contracts a fever as a result of carrying her unconscious body back to the garrison in the rain, when he could have left her to die.

Sondheim's melodies, no less than his lyrics, evolve out of situation and character. Yet in his shows, music clearly takes precedence over everything else, including story. He tends to be the favorite Broadway composer of those who feel that a show is finally only as good as its score, and because he's such an effective dramatist in his own right, his shows lose remarkably little on their cast albums. The *Passion* compact disc differs from most in not having a few seconds of silence encoded between bands; as in the theater, where applause after songs was actively discouraged, nothing is permitted to disrupt the show's alternating moods of intellectual contemplation and romantic swoon.

The disc actually improves on the show in one way: Jonathan Tunick's orchestrations of Sondheim's score is fuller and more vibrant as a result of two dozen additional strings. Yet the moment on the disc that best captures show's peculiar, dreamlike visual atmosphere features just woodwinds—what sounds like a trio of them—playing gaunt and wishful triads to begin a song titled "I Wish I Could Forget You." This figure, heard fleetingly throughout the score, often underneath and in counterpoint to another melody, serves as Fosca's theme.

In its utter simplicity more like film music than like a Broadway underscore, the theme here suggests a candle in a curtained room—burning brilliantly but close to the wick's bottom. Weakened by Giorgio's rejection of her, Fosca takes to bed with a fever. At the request of the camp physician, who's conducting what turns out to be a premature death watch, Giorgio spends the night in Fosca's room, hoping to comfort her by humoring her. She asks him to take a letter, and though Giorgio blanches when she starts to dictate and he realizes that it's to be a letter from him to her, he reluctantly obeys. The song that follows begins as if it's going to be a duet, but as Fosca sings of what she would have Giorgio feel for her, the only line of hers he echoes is "that doesn't mean I love you"—not the next line, in which Fosca has him wishing he could.

On stage, this scene fuses the score's most arresting song to an especially imaginative gambit by Lapine. Faithful to its sources, *Passion* is an epistolary musical: much of the time its three major characters sing letters they're writing or have just received, often in duet or trio and at a physical remove from one another. But this particular letter isn't in Tarchetti, and though Giorgio does write such a letter at Fosca's bidding in the movie, its contents aren't revealed and nothing more is made of it. In *Passion*, the letter assumes tremendous importance. Implying a physical intimacy Giorgio and Fosca haven't yet shared, it winds up in the hands of Fosca's cousin, who challenges Giorgio to a duel. Giorgio is too much the gentleman, too much the man of honor, to tell the colonel the truth, because to do so would confirm that the unlovely Fosca was incapable of arousing such deep and protective feelings in a man.

This is the stuff of melodrama, nothing more. But the song that sets these events in motion lends them resonance, if only because an epistolary musical is quite another matter from an epistolary novel. *Passion*'s stage characters literally give *voice* to one another's thoughts. The letter is an emotional forgery, an utter fabrication. Yet when Fosca—putting words in Giorgio's mouth, though we hear them from hers—has Giorgio realize that her love for him is deeper than any he has ever known, she's displaying an element of telepathy: he'll eventually decide this for himself.

Nothing short of beautiful in its melodic descent, "I Wish I Could Forget You" requires Donna Murphy, as Fosca, to swoop below the staff—a strategy by which Murphy and Sondheim manage to convey the character's shortness of breath while aligning her with Garbo's Camille and other seductive, sepulchral-voiced movie vamps. The first time I saw *Passion*, I left the theater thinking that there was a bit too much of the Broadway Baby in Murphy's singing—an excess of pizzazz at odds with her frail and gasping character. Listening to the CD, I think I was wrong: the song is Murphy's finest moment. In an earlier song, Fosca tells the captain that, unlike him, she doesn't read to learn—she reads to live. Fosca is a woman who's experienced most pleasures vicariously, and Sondheim gives her songs that, more than most, require Murphy to merge acting and singing. She portrays Fosca as a woman with a blazing inner life— someone who, in this context, *sings* to live.

Thirty-four years ago in Frank Loesser's *How to Succeed in Business Without Really Trying*, Robert Morse cunningly performed "I Believe in You" while staring at himself in a mirror. The song, extolling the virtues of "a seeker of wisdom and truth" has enjoyed a life outside its show; it's usually interpreted as an uptempo love song, an ode to an irresistible idealist. Nobody remembers that mirror.

One of the songs Barbra Streisand performed during her HBO special last summer was Sondheim's "Not While I'm Around," which she dedicated to her grown son, who was in the audience. In *Sweeney Todd*, this odd lullaby, which begins "Nothing's gonna harm you," was sung to Angela Lansbury by a street urchin powerless to prevent her death or his own. Yet there was nothing amiss in Streisand's motherly reinterpretation, because this is another song removable from its original context. Though it would make a good torch song, I can't imagine Streisand or anybody else singing "I Wish I Could Forget You" away from its show. The problem wouldn't be the lyric's indeterminate point of view. It would be those lines I quoted earlier about a love "as permanent as death," and a final verse that begins "and if you die tomorrow," which couldn't withstand a pronoun change on account of its rhyme scheme. The song is inextricable from the show; it's what the show's about. Fosca tells Giorgio that her sickness "is as normal to me as health is to you." A few days after seeing *Passion* for the second time, I was hospitalized with a 104-degree temperature, a symptom of what was ultimately diagnosed as a serious bacterial infection. In a situation in which part of my role as a good patient was to monitor my moods and bodily functions and dutifully report even the slightest change, I no longer saw Fosca's morbid self-absorption as quite so absurd. Fosca's love for Giorgio is supposed to be superior to Clara's by virtue of not being carnal. At least that was what Sondheim and Lapine said in interviews. But I don't think they know what their show is about. One thing that works against their interpretation is that Clara is portrayed much too sympathetically for us to believe that her love is only skin-deep. (Besides which, it would be impossible to find someone who sings Sondheim as gorgeously as Marin Mazzie does wanting in any respect.) And at the end, when Giorgio sings of having recognized in Fosca, "love without reason, love without mercy, love without pride or shame," you want to shake him and remind him of his earlier question to Fosca: "Is this what you call love? This endless and insatiable smothering . . . ." He's merely submitting to Fosca's dementia, and neither he nor the show's creators seem to recognize the difference. Regardless of Sondheim and Lapine's original intentions, the dichotomy represented on stage wasn't between body love and soul love, but between health and infirmity, the pang of happiness and the unaccountable lure of death. On Broadway, the pink of Clara's nude flesh in the opening scene contrasted as dramatically with Fosca's coffin pallor as the two women's songs did in major and minor keys.

Passion takes place in the world of the sick—not a place Broadway audiences in the mood for uplift particularly want to go. They still want to be told they'll never walk alone. As drama, the show will always be something of a muddle, but it's moving because the score is. New York audiences had trouble accepting Giorgio's final change of heart. It struck them as illogical, and it is—but that wasn't why they left the theater unsatisfied (who goes to the theater for logic?).

The problem isn't confined to a stage production. It's musical. The song with which Giorgio expresses his love for Fosca isn't ablaze with the rest of the score's sixteenth-note rhythms and sustained chords. It's inorganic. So is "Loving You," the show's big take-out ballad, in which Fosca tells Giorgio that he's become her reason for living. This song, which has Barbra Streisand written all over it, was added to the score at the last minute, in order to make Fosca more sympathetic. It's a pretty song, but it doesn't belong in this score.

If one responds to *Passion* at all, it's because of Sondheim's music, which is what newcomers will find on CD. Robert Brustein, in his favorable review of the show in *The New Republic*, said that he found himself "sobbing uncontrollably" at the end. I think the implausible story got to him only because the music did. I was similarly shaken by the new production of *Merrily We Roll Along* last summer. By the final curtain I realized that, quite without meaning to, I had conducted my personal life and my career in such a way as to betray both my closest friends and my highest ideals. Then I realized that I had done nothing of the sort; Sondheim's recurring bass figures had rubbed me raw, making me an easy mark for the book's burned-out, middle-aged blues.

More than any of Sondheim's previous shows, *Passion* embraces the concept of the "integrated" or "organic" stage musical—one like *Oklahoma!*, in which songs illuminate character and advance the plot—and takes the next logical step, to the Broadway score as a feat of extended composition. This is the sense in which Sondheim is the greatest heir of Jerome Kern, who attempted something of the same thing in his score for *Show Boat*, although this is often overlooked amid the praise for it as the first show in which music and book served a unified end.

Sondheim's dilemma is that such musical innovation is generally lost on today's Broadway audiences, who ask for nothing more from a show (and nothing less!) than vulgar spectacle and a few sentimental melodies; a patina of social consciousness is optional. In "Who Cares If You Listen?" Milton Babbitt recommended as the ideal strategy for the serious composer "voluntary withdrawal from [the] public world to one of private performance and electronic media with its very real possibility of the complete elimination of the social aspects of musical composition." As a composer of vocal music with little taste for grand opera—however much his best scores approximate it—Sondheim is in no position to heed his former mentor's advice. He needs Broadway. What I wonder is if Broadway, which often seems to tolerate him only because it needs the occasional *succès d'estime* in order to go on thinking of itself as a thriving artistic medium, will ever realize how much it needs him. Sondheim and Broadway isn't another simple love story, that's for sure.

(MARCH 1995)

Talking Kerouac

I read *On the Road* when I was sixteen, in 1963, probably imagining myself to be one of the "frenetic young men" in search of "Kicks and Truth" described on the back cover of the original

Signet paperback edition. I say probably only because I like to think that my perception of Kerouac differed slightly from that of Signet's copywriters and my own teenage peers, as a result of having practically memorized another of his novels earlier that year.

Written in 1953 but not published until six years later, after *On the Road* had created a market for Kerouac's scraps, *Maggie Cassidy* tells a tale of "adult love torn in barely grown-up ribs" in prose as fuchsia all the way through. Set in Kerouac's hometown of Lowell, Massachusetts, during his senior year in high school, it's slight as can be. But growing up across the street from a gasworks and a lumber yard in a sooty West Philadelphia neighborhood that might as well have been a New England mill town, I found more of myself in *Maggie Cassidy* than in *The Catcher in the Rye*. I still do, though I now realize that I was confusing its idealized version of Kerouac's blue-collar, Catholic adolescence with my own.

Except for the fact that he's a varsity jock and French Canadian instead of Irish, Kerouac's Jack Duluoz could have been me. He runs track, mopes in front of the radio, plays hooky with buddies he's known since grade school, and necks with his high school sweetheart (the eponymous Maggie) without going all the way—blaming his virginity on excess chivalry, not on inexperience, just as I did:

> In there, by the hissing radiator, on the couch, we did practically everything there is to do but I never touched her in the prime focal points, precious trembling places, breasts, the moist star of her thighs . . .

Sigh. The prose stabs with its pubescent longing, but it's written from the vantage point of a disillusioned man who knows (as I do, paging through it twenty-seven years later, and as Kerouac himself put it in *Doctor Sax*, another of his Lowell novels) that "you'll never be as happy as you are right now in your book-devouring boyhood." So no wonder I have a soft spot for Kerouac. But who reads him today? That's the question prompted by the arrival of Rhino's *The Jack Kerouac Collection*, a deluxe, three-CD boxed set reissue of the long-out-of-print spoken arts LPs Kerouac cut in 1958 and '59, two for Hanover (*Poetry for the Beat Generation*, with Steve Allen on piano; and *Blues and Haikus*, with the tenor saxophonists Al Cohn and Zoot Sims) and one for Verve (the unaccompanied *Readings by Jack Kerouac on the Beat Generation*). My guess is not even sixteen-year-olds, though he remains one of the most read *about* of American authors, thanks to the memoirs of Joyce Johnson and Carolyn Cassady, the women he and Neal didn't take on the road.

Lacking his friend Allen Ginsberg's flair for self-promotion and wisdom that the beat goes on, Kerouac was already out of favor by the time I left college in 1968, a year before his death. That fall, he appeared drunk, sweating and grossly overweight on *Firing Line*—the painful footage, with Kerouac playing the stooge to the reptilian William F. Buckley Jr. and rebuking his hippie and Vietnik progeny, is included in the documentary film *What Happened to Kerouac?* He appears fully reconciled to the lifelong Roman Catholic death wish that he had earlier snookered himself into believing was Buddhist enlightenment on the transient nature of human existence ("dead already and dead again," as he put it in "Praised Be Man," a poem included on the Rhino box).

If there's one thing that growing up Celtic teaches you it's that people who drink themselves to death seldom need a reason. Still, in Kerouac's case, the process was speeded along by the adoration of wannabes who thought of him as Dean Moriarty to their Sal Paradise, not having read him closely enough to realize that he still lived at home with Mamere and was comfortable only on the periphery of the beat subculture he named. As John Clellon Holmes once put it, Kerouac "was never famous, only notorious," and it must have broken his heart that he was idolized for his exploits rather than for writing about them.

The Jack Kerouac Collection isn't likely to sway those who refuse to take Kerouac seriously as a writer. Bombed on Tokay and onomatopoeia, he romanticizes every bum and railroad breakman as a Bodhisattva, while indulging in far too much Slim Gaillard-level jive ("Dem eggs & dem dem/Dere bacons, baby, . . . All that Luney & fruney/Fracon, acons, & beggs . . .") and sub-Joycean bullshit ("Whilst tee-kee-kee pearl the birdies and mummums murk and ululate in this valley of peaceful firewood"). But, my god, you'd need an ear as deaf to the tones of actual American speech as that of your average nineties tenured professor to resist something like this, from *Jack Kerouac on the Beat Generations*'s "Lucien Midnight: The Sounds of the Universe in My Window":

> Friday afternoon in the universe and all the directions in and out you got your men, women, dogs, children, horses, ponies, tics, perks, pots, pans, pools, pauls, pails, parturiences, and petty thieveries that turn into heavenly Buddha. I know boy what's I talking about 'cause I made the world and when I made it . . . I had Lucien Midnight for my name and concocted up a world so nothing you had forever thereafter make believe it's real . . .

This is language chasing its own tail, but its dizziness is contagious, especially as read by its author, his voice occasionally imitating Neal Cassaday's barroom cowboy drawl or Allen Ginsberg's crazed rabbinical rant, his gulps and pauses for breath making it easier for you by implying punctuation he didn't always remember to type. Kerouac's literary career was a sustained feat of anamnesis, and his triumph here—on the passage quoted above and numerous others—is in reexperiencing the rush of first putting these words down on paper years earlier. It's something like the rush you get reading him for the first time, and it's thrilling to hear him feeling it, too.

The booklet that comes with the *Collection* amounts to a

thirty-two-page mash note, with avid (if generally unilluminating) words from everybody from Ginsberg and William Burroughs to a columnist from the *Lowell Sun* and Kerouac's novelist daughter, Jan. (It also includes rare photos from the private collections of Ginsberg and others. In one, Joyce Johnson, Kerouac's girlfriend in 1957, when *On the Road* was published, is misidentified as Edie Parker, Kerouac's second wife—an inexcusable gaffe, because it's the photo Johnson used on the cover of her memoir, *Minor Characters*.) In 1990 no reissue is complete without previously unreleased material, and Rhino has unearthed some doozies, including outtakes and studio chatter from *Blues and Haikus*, Kerouac's tense readings from *Visions of Cody* and *On the Road* on *The Steve Allen Show*, and his drunken contribution to a 1957 Hunter College symposium on "Is There a Beat Generation?"

Even ignoring these extras, the *Collection* expands the Kerouac canon by including a numer of items not readily available in print—most notably his thirty-odd freestyle "American Haikus," with Cohn and Sims majestically filling the silences between each. These three-line poems present Kerouac at his best; atypically for him, they give the impression of having been worked over, compressed.

> *Well, here I am,*
> *2PM.*
> *What day is this?*

> *Blackbird!*
> *NO! BLUEBIRD!*
> *The branch still jumping.*

Unfortunately, the rest of *Blues and Haikus* (with Cohn frequently switching to piano) is an inebriated hoot that becomes downright embarrassing when Kerouac attempts to wail the blues (though he's no worse than Mark Murphy or Ben Sidran,

I suppose). But the session with Steve Allen is an unexpected success, even though Steverino doesn't curl a lick you haven't heard a hundred times before. His backing is giving and unobtrusive, and Kerouac reads his single most affecting poem (about his mother) and his single most apocalyptic one ("The Wheel of the Quivering Meat Conception"), both from the undervalued *Mexico City Blues*.

Still, I have to agree with Kerouac biographer Gerald Nicosia's liner note assertion that Kerouac's "spontaneous bop prosody" most approaches the actual rhythms of bebop when he reads unaccompanied, as on the excerpts from *The Subterraneans* and *Desolation Angels* on the Verve LP. In a way, Kerouac's unrequited love for jazz—his perception of which was clouded by his unconsciously racist view of black Americans as *On the Road*'s "happy, true-hearted, ecstatic" primitives—supplies a dramatic subtext for these recordings. The irony is that Amiri Baraka and countless other black poets in the contemporary oral tradition echo Kerouac's rhythms more than they do those of Charlie Parker or John Coltrane, the forebears they'd claim.

In light of this, one of the most startling cuts on the Rhino box is Kerouac's lengthy, unaccompanied reading of "Fantasy: The Early History of Bop." This 1959 magazine piece is riddled with factual errors (Kerouac has the vibraphonist Lionel Hampton "wailing his tenor saxophone," for example), but however dubious it is as history, it now amounts to prophecy:

> Bop is the language from America's inevitable Africa. . . .
> And you can't believe that bop is here to stay. Or modern music, call it what you will. . . . And figure it with histories and lost kings of immemorial tribes and jungle and *fellaheen* town. . . .
>   He is here at last. His music is here to stay. His history has washed over us. His imperialistic kingdoms are coming.

Jack Kerouac, folks, a white man with no fear of a black planet. Even if his readings fail to convince you that there was more
to him than met the eye, this ought to.

(AUGUST 1990)

Toons

The plan was that a month before the single was
released, Michael would have Frank Dileo [then his
manager] begin planting stories in the tabloid press
that [Jackson] and Prince were bitter enemies and
rivals. . . .
Then, at the height of the controversy, the "Bad" single and video would be released. In the video, Michael
and Prince would square off against one another, taking turns vocalizing and dancing—Prince doing his
James Brown steps, and Michael doing his trademark
moonwalk—in order to determine once and for all
who was "*bad*." It was an exciting premise.
When Michael telephoned Prince and told him of
his idea, Prince was not enthusiastic. . . . "Prince thinks
Michael is a wimp," said Max Hart, one of Prince's
associates. "He didn't want to be in a video with him.
He thinks Mike is silly."

–J. Randy Taraborrelli,
Michael Jackson: The Magic and the Madness

Even without having recorded together, Michael Jackson and Prince will forever be linked as the two male pop stars most emblematic of the 1980s—a decade in which a performer's songs often served as little more than background accompaniment to mass speculation about his or her private sexual identity. Along with Madonna, who's their most obvious female counterpart, Jackson and Prince transformed eighties pop into an elaborate guessing game. The question surrounding a new release by any of these gender-benders wasn't just whether the song was any good but what it could be interpreted to reveal about the singer.

As cultural constructs, decades seldom begin or end on schedule. What we now refer to as "the sixties," for example, really began in the dark winter months between November 22, 1963, and the Beatles' first appearance on *The Ed Sullivan Show* the following February, and lasted well into the 1970s. In many ways the eighties are still with us, and so are Michael Jackson and Prince, each of whom released a new album toward the end of last year. Jackson's *Dangerous* (Epic) made the headlines, though not for its music. According to *Entertainment Weekly*, whose tally will have to be accepted on faith now that the offending footage has been snipped, Jackson reached for his "private parts" thirteen times in the original version of the video for "Black or White," the first song from *Dangerous* to be released as a single. Most of his clutching and stroking occurred during a silent four-minute code in which he also smashed the windows of a parked car and hurled a garbage can through a storefront, in what some guessed was an homage to the character played by Spike Lee in his *Do the Right Thing*.

The video amounted to a brilliant publicity stunt. It got everyone talking about Michael Jackson again, just as his new album was due to arrive in the stores. What amused me about the fuss was that *Entertainment Weekly* and other publications actually bothered to keep count of how many times Jackson reached for his Pee-Wee Herman. It reminded me of growing up Catholic three decades ago, when boys and girls like me were taught that confessing that you had "touched" yourself (or disobeyed your parents or taken the Lord's name in vain) wasn't good enough—in order to receive the proper penance, you were expected to remember how often you had committed each foul deed, which required a certain amount of sedulousness even while succumbing to temptation. But those parents of small children who identify themselves as "parents," as though this were a political affiliation, were unamused by Jackson's shenanigans. Didn't Jackson, who cultivates a childlike image and whose new best chum seems to be Macaulay Culkin, the eleven-year-old star of *My Girl* and *Home Alone*, realize that he was setting a bad example with his "wilding"? What seemed most significant about the uproar was its implicit acknowledgment that preteens are the only ones who still take Michael Jackson seriously. Everybody else has outgrown him.

Much was riding on *Dangerous*, Jackson's first album in four years, which the record industry—in a slump, along with the rest of the economy—hoped would lure consumers back into the stores, just as Jackson's *Thriller* had in 1982 and 1983. But *Thriller*, still the largest-selling album in history, racked up its phenomenal figures (more than 38.5 million copies sold worldwide) as part of a package with Jackson's groundbreaking videos, his electrifying dancing on a 1983 Motown TV special, and his Neverland androgyny. In buying *Thriller*, pop fans were buying the new Michael Jackson, the former lead singer of the Jackson 5 grown up exotic.

That was nine years ago, which is practically a millennium in pop music—roughly the span from Elvis Presley to the Beatles, or from *Sgt. Pepper's Lonely Hearts Club Band* to punk and *Saturday Night Fever*. As Timothy White, the managing editor of the music tradepaper *Billboard* and the author of *Rock Lives* (which contains one of the very few in-depth interviews Jackson has ever granted), observed during a recent conversation we had about Jackson, it's difficult for a pop star to reinvent himself once he's become commonplace in millions of people's lives. Although *Dangerous* entered the charts at number one—not just in the United States but in England, Australia, Finland, Spain, and Switzerland—its sales (to Christmas-shopping parents?) somehow seemed as irrelevant as Presley's did after the summer of love.

Reflecting Jackson's determination to show that he still has what it takes to unify divergent tastes, as he did with *Thriller*, *Dangerous* sounds like it was crafted for compatibility with radio playlists rather than for the satisfaction of the home consumer. Remember "Billie Jean"? In "Who Is It," *Dangerous* has a new song just like it, right down to the driven beat and Jackson's shivered vocal interjections. For album-oriented rock stations, there's "Give in to Me," a heavy-metal ballad with Slash, from Guns 'N Roses, on guitar. "Heal the World," a big showbiz anthem about saving the environment and such, ends with a duet between Michael and a little girl in which her voice blends into his. The chorus swells and modulates just as in "We Are the World." In the mood for some gospel? Take your pick, "Will You Be There" or "Keep the Faith."

Beginning a minute too soon (with an excerpt of an uncredited orchestral performance of Beethoven's Ninth) and ending a minute too late (with Jackson's spoken ruminations, delivered in an embarrassing sob), "Will You Be There" typifies the album's excesses. *Dangerous* is almost salvaged by the seven (out of fourteen) tracks that Teddy Riley had a hand in writing and producing. Riley is a maven of "new-jack swing," a light-on-its-feet pop style that applies sophisticated studio techniques to hip-hop and rap. Some early reviews of *Dangerous* chastised him for upstaging Jackson's songwriting with his computer-generated beats and his streetwise *musique concrète*—car horns, shattering glass, and the like. This misses the point. What's important in contemporary black pop isn't songs per se but melodic hooks that can be isolated and extended to double as dance grooves; a "finished" song is raw material for a producer like Riley. He lends Jackson some badly needed street credibility, which is presumably the job he was hired for, and you have to wonder why Jackson made the insipid "Black or White," not a Riley track, the album's first video and single.

As catchy as the numbers co-produced by Riley are, the emotions Jackson expresses on them never seem remotely genuine. He sounds vexed and divided, and not just because Riley frequently plays his voice off against itself by having a chorus of buoyant Michael Jacksons repeat a song's hook ad infinitum, in opposition to the Michael Jackson we hear delivering the rest of the lyrics through clenched teeth. The strangest, if most compelling, of these tracks is a heterosexual love song inexplicably called "In the Closet," which takes the form of a dialogue between Jackson and an unidentified "mystery girl" rumored to be Madonna. Playing on our knowledge of Jackson's rumored asexuality, the song has such a narcissistic edge to it that at first I assumed the second voice was Jackson's, slightly speeded up to raise its pitch. On "Why You Wanna Trip on Me?," which Jackson had no role in writing, he admonishes the media for speculating about his personal life rather than addressing genuine social issues such as drug addiction, illiteracy, homelessness, world hunger, and "strange diseases [for which] there is no cure." In addition to failing to convince us that he has more than an elementary interest in or understanding of any of these problems (given a few minutes in front of a TV, the little girl on "Heal the World" could probably have come up with an identical list), he fails to acknowledge that our preoccupation with what seem to be his efforts to undo his race and gender through cosmetics and plastic surgery (plus whatever sympathy we might extend to someone so obviously uncomfortable inside his own skin) supplies what little emotional pull there is in "Why You Wanna Trip on Me?" or any of his other new songs.

Without endorsing the offensive notion that blackness is something that has to be earned, it's possible to understand the point of view of a black writer like Gary Dauphin, who, in reviewing the "Black or White" video in the *Village Voice*, expressed disgust with Jackson for his "trip about his face, something that instead of conjuring up a smooth cyberpunk universe, suggests Porcelana fade cream, conks, and of course, lynchings." In the video, the most admired of the special effects with which Jackson and the director, John Landis, show off their $4-million budget is a fifty-second "morphing" sequence that some reviewers have interpreted as a reference to Jackson's own metamorphosis. In this sequence the faces of thirteen different people of various races and ethnicities—including a Sumo wrestler and a Rasta—blend into one another in rapid succession. More significant, in their own way, are the special effects that land Jackson in the African bush and the Old West and enable him to sing and dance in the Russian snow, on an industrial highway, and in the Statue of Liberty's torch. These grant him a mobility heretofore granted on screen only to the casts of Looney Tunes and Merrie Melodies, kinship with whom now seems to be his chosen destiny.

What used to appeal to listeners, both black and white, about black performers like James Brown, Ray Charles, Aretha Franklin, and even such Motown smoothies as Marvin Gaye and Smokey Robinson was their "authenticity," the perceived realness of their music and the cultural values it embodied. By comparison, recent black performers, including the comic-strip militants Public Enemy, have transformed themselves into self-caricatures as insubstantial as the "Toons" in the 1988 movie *Who Framed Roger Rabbit?* (Ironically, the movie's Toons were understood to be standing in for blacks.) A glance at practically any heavy-metal video should be enough to persuade us that black performers aren't contemporary pop's only Toons. But because pop music plays such a large part in shaping both black self-image and white perceptions of black culture, more is at stake in the persona of a performer who's black. As a group, pop stars aren't even the worst offenders. That distinction belongs to those NBA players (even the dignified Julius Erving) who permit themselves to be sterotyped in commercials as overgrown homeboys with nothing on their minds besides sneakers, soft drinks, and Big Macs.

The video of "Remember the Time," the second single from *Dangerous*, features the Pharaoh Ramses II and Nefertiti. Its depiction of ancient Egypt is pointedly Afrocentric, as if to deflect charges that Jackson is out of touch with his own people. A joke making the rounds is that it features an all-black cast, except for the star. Jackson conforms to two embarrassing sterotypes—that of a black man altering his features in order to "pass," and that of the Negro as a white child's plaything. At this point, he has a complexion as pale as that of the man in the moon and a pert little reindeer nose like Annette Bening's. No one in any field, black or white, seems more the product of an animator's inkwell than this thirty-three-year-old man who would be America's inner child, a singer whose video tells us that we're all the same without acknowledging that some of us have to make ourselves over from scratch to get that way.

With his lanky hair, doe eyes, and horsy jaw, Prince (whose full name is Prince Rogers Nelson) looks like a cartoon centaur; his fondness for baring his jutting, little-man's torso in his videos and on his album jackets reinforces the effect. But he's a Toon with what Pauline Kael, in her review of *Purple Rain* (the first and best of his four vanity-project movies), aptly described as "a knowing, parodistic edge." Although his recording career began in 1978, Prince's big year was 1984, when *Purple Rain* opened in theaters and its soundtrack album stayed at number one for twenty-four weeks. A few years earlier, on the song "Controversy," from the album of the same name, he had posed the questions "Am I black or white?/Am I straight or gay?" In point of fact, both his parents were black, although the role he gave himself in *Purple Rain* (and in *Graffiti Bridge*, the silly, 1990 sequel) helped to foster the myth that he was the offspring of an interracial marriage—which, in terms of combining elements of funk and hard rock, he was, and much more so than Jackson. And given his eye for buxom leading ladies and back-up singers, and his rumored sexual involvement with most of them, it's probably safe to assume that he's straight (besides, in the closeted world of pop, heterosexuals are generally the only ones who can afford to indulge in public gender-bending).

By raising such questions about himself at a time when similar questions were beginning to be raised about Jackson, Prince emerged as the anti-Michael—a racially and sexually ambiguous superstar for those who preferred their heroes with a knowing, parodistic edge. It helped that Prince, a guitarist who also plays a number of other instruments, was a better musician than Jackson, and didn't hurt that he was almost as fluid a dancer.

Prince is the composer of a song called "Jerk U Off," and another called "The Cross." Without his musicianship—and without his irony—he might be Jim Morrison in eyeliner, another messianic satyr preaching orgasmic salvation. But his songs tend to be comically smutty instead of pretentiously so; they're great fun even (or maybe especially) at their most sophomoric. His major influences as a bandleader and record producer would seem to be James Brown, Sly Stone, and George Clinton—a modern funk triumverate whose influence is universal. But I bet that Prince's record collection also includes "party" albums of the sort that used to be clandestine best sellers in black neighborhoods and on fraternity row, by the likes of Rudy Ray Moore, Blowfly, and Doug Clark and the Hot Nuts.

In some ways Prince is now even more outdated than Jackson. For one thing, the hedonism espoused in his lyrics risks making his songs seem like remnants of the disco era, the era before mainstream America became conscious of AIDS. For another, his albums, including last year's *Diamonds and Pearls*

(Paisley Park/Warner Bros.), featuring his latest band, the New Power Generation, strive for the sound of a performance on stage—a hard-rock ideal antithetical to the current trends in black dance music exemplified by Jackson and Riley's collaboration on *Dangerous*.

Yet *Diamonds and Pearls* shows a vitality utterly lacking on *Dangerous*, thanks to Prince's sense of himself as a pop savant and his ability to synthesize everything from 1960s psychedelia to rap while sounding deliriously contemporary instead of archly postmodern. The psychedelic touches include a sitarlike guitar line on a mock gospel song called "Thunder" and a wonderfully incongruous string section (reminiscent of those on the Beatles' *Magical Mystery Tour* and the Rolling Stones' *Their Satanic Majesties Request*) that fades in briefly on "Push," a slice of energetic new-jack swing that puts Jackson and Riley to shame. The New Power Generation's resident rapper is Tony M., who captures the style's street rush far better than Heavy D. and L. T. B., the rappers enlisted by Jackson. Rosie Gaines, NPG's big-voiced backup singer, also raps convincingly here and there, as does Prince himself—most notably on a randy little ditty called "Gett Off" whose hook (about "twenty-three positions in a one-night stand") is impossible to shake once you've heard it.

The cheesy organ sound that pop fans of my generation are lifelong suckers for (remember "96 Tears" by ? and the Mysterians, from 1966?) surfaces on "Daddy Pop," which also boasts falsetto and bass vocal trade-offs, à la Sly and the Family Stone, and a girl-group chorus by Gaines. The girl-group stuff appears again on "Cream," which reuses and toughens a riff from "Bang a Gong," a 1971 hit by glam rocker Mark Bolan and his group, T Rex. At this point, Prince is even able to recycle himself to good advantage, as on "Money Don't Matter 2 Night," a moody ballad that borrows its melody from "When Doves Cry," but avoids unflattering comparison by speeding up as it goes along. "Insatiable" and the title track poke gentle fun at the falsetto love declarations of the Stylistics and other virginal-sounding early seventies "sissy" soul vocal groups. The references to do-it-yourself camcorder porno in the lyrics of "Insatiable" would be confirmation enough that this wasn't the Stylistics, but so would the Frank Zappalike chord progressions and the flashes of heavy metal in "Diamonds and Pearls." The only track that misfires is "Strollin'," Prince's condescending take on lounge jazz, replete with George Benson-style guitar licks.

Prince has made a number of dumb career moves, including his three movies after *Purple Rain* (*Sign o' the Times*, the best of them, was a great concert film, but nothing more), and his decision not to release *The Black Album*, a 1987 album considered to be his best work by some of those who have heard bootlegged copies of the tapes. No longer the pop figure of the moment, he appears to be settling into a phase of his career in which he'll continue to sell hundreds of thousands of copies of each new release and still be taken for granted: *Diamonds and Pearls* reached the Top 10, but unlike *Purple Rain* (or, for that matter, *Dangerous*) wasn't greeted as a pop event. Even so, nobody his age in pop matches Prince's all-around skills as a singer, instrumentalist, producer, bandleader, and image manipulator. Miles Davis, who recorded a few unreleased sides with Prince in 1987, said that he has the potential to be "the new Duke Ellington of our time, if he just keeps at it." That's going much too far. But say this for Prince: he doesn't sound at all presumptuous when, on "Gett Off," he samples a few lines from an old record by James Brown and has the temerity to sing along.

(APRIL 1992)

Black Skin, Black Masks

Rock and roll has outlived its usefulness to most of us who grew up with it. The current hits aren't about us anymore, but that's all right—we're no longer the ones crowding the clubs and record stores. Pop has always existed primarily for the young, the only ones who have time for it. The source of our disenchantment is in realizing that the songs of our high school and college years are no longer about us either—they reflect where we were in our lives then, not where we are now.

This may be why so many of my friends have developed a sudden interest in country, a style of pop whose subject matter is less often adolescent sensuality than adult wreckage. And unless you buy the argument that Cole Porter is one of the finer things you develop a taste for in your forties, along with cognac and cigars, it may also explain why so many aging rock singers, on finding themselves in a reflective mood, have turned to songs given their definitive interpretations by Frank Sinatra in the 1950s, when our parents were our current age. With notable exceptions, including Neil Young, Richard Thompson, and Loudon Wainwright III, the pop singers of our own generation have given us no clue how grown-ups of our day are supposed to feel and behave as they enter middle age. This is because these pop singers know no better than we do. Bob Dylan sings to us now in the voice of a grizzled old prospector—not his voice but that of an unconvincing fictional character. And Bruce Springsteen's operas on the turnpike no longer give the illusion of having an unseen cast of thousands; they could be taking place now in the driveway of his and his fashion-model wife's Hollywood mansion.

I sense, too, that the first full generation after ours—the grandchildren of Marx and Coca-Cola, to extend something

Jean-Luc Godard said about us in *Masculine Feminine* to its logical conclusion—might be more disenchanted with rock than
we are; between their favorites and ours exists no clear line of
demarcation like the one that existed between the crooners our
parents had enjoyed and our yowling idols. (Not that today's
kids haven't come up with an alternative to rock. It's called . . .
alternative rock. Not even the flannel shirts are new.) Pop today,
in other words, has something to alienate everyone: people in
their late thirties and older, that it's not just theirs anymore;
younger people because it never was just theirs.

No other subgenre of pop alienates as many people as rap
does, despite what I sense to be a suspicion—even on the part
of those who profess to find rap indistinguishable from random
gunfire—that rap is the only thing happening right now, the
only kind of pop with the sort of larger cultural significance
taken for granted of pop since Woodstock.

By the time a rap song first made the national charts—
"Rapper's Delight," by the Sugar Hill Gang, in 1979—rap was
already something of an old story, having started about five
years earlier as an underground offshoot of disco. Its origins as
a dance music are hinted at in its other name, "hip-hop," which
is preferred by those for whom it's not just music but a look, an
attitude, and a lifestyle, although even they frequently use the
terms interchangeably. The "rap" is the lead vocal or vocals;
"hip-hop" is the vocal plus everything else on the record—the
background chants and disjunct instrumental sounds that initiates call "the beats," which are sometimes supplied by live
singers and musicians but are more frequently the result of a
disc jockey's sampling or tape-looping bits and pieces of other
records.

In the beginning, the rap was optional. Hip-hop's first
heroes, in Harlem and the Bronx dance clubs in the early
1970s, were its DJs, turntable artists who provided a nonstop
groove for dancers by isolating, electronically boosting, and
repeating ad infinitum bass lines and drum breaks from seven-

ties funk and glam-rock hits. Although vilified by some as pla-
giarists and scavengers, these hip-hop DJs (Grandmaster Flash
and Afrika Bambaataa became the most famous of them) were
essentially grass-roots successors to Phil Spector, Brian Wilson,
and George Martin, the 1960s rock producers who pioneered
the use of the recording studio as an instrument in its own
right. A sociological study that attempted to link the rise of hip-
hop to the decreased availability of musical instruments in public schools since the 1970s would be right on target. In the
meantime, what needs to be acknowledged about hip-hop,
apart from its paradoxical origins as a roots music dependent on
electronic technology, is its remarkable staying power. It's out-
lasted graffiti, break-dancing, and every other manifestation of
the black-teen Zeitgeist of which it was initially seen as only
one component.

Rap remains dance music, despite the diminished role of
DJs, increased public scrutiny of its lyrical content, and the distrust that some hard-core rappers seem to have of contemporary dance culture. ("It represents the gay scene, it's separating
blacks from their past and their culture, it's upwardly mobile,"
Chuck D, of the group Public Enemy, says of the dance music
called "house," pretty much echoing the complaints of rock and
rollers and soul fans about disco in the 1970s. Needless to say,
Chuck D can't dance.) On the most basic level, a catchy rap
song wins you over in much the same manner any good pop
song does: by virtue of its hooks—those vocal refrains and stupid instrumental riffs you can't get out of your head, no matter
how embarrassed you are to find them there. The most imaginative of the record producers who have succeeded the DJs—
Teddy Riley (Wreckx-N-Effects, Kool Moe Dee, and Heavy D.
and the Boys), Prince Paul (Queen Latifah, Big Daddy Kane,
3rd Base, and De La Soul), and Hank Shocklee (Ice Cube and
Public Enemy)—are responsible for the only formal innovation
in pop since the punk minimalism of Talking Heads and the
Ramones in the late 1970s.

The controversy surrounding rap, however, usually concerns its lyrics, not its hooks or its merits as dance music. In Michael Small's informative 1992 rap scrapbook, *Break It Down* (Citadel Press), Afrika Bambaataa includes on his list of rap's possible antecedents African call and response, the insult game called the dozens, Cab Calloway, chitlin-circuit comedians, bebop scat singing, black nationalist oratory, Jamaican dance-hall "toasts," and the "political awareness rap" of the Last Poets, a spoken-word group popular in the 1970s. Others have mentioned jive-talking black radio disc jockeys, the singing poet Gil Scott-Heron, and the jump-rope game double dutch.

Rap can also be compared to 1950s a cappella or doo wop, with which it shares a street-corner male ethic, a delight in onomatopoeia, and an ingenuity in making do with very little. The difference is that doo wop's young singers were forever trying on courtly feelings much too large for them, on already popular songs such as "Red Sails in the Sunset" and "A Sunday Kind of Love." Rap has no dreamy side—unless you accept, as an indication of how much times have changed, a song like Ice Cube's "It Was a Good Day," from his recent CD *The Predator*, in which Ice Cube enjoys marathon sex, gets drunk without throwing up, doesn't get stopped and searched by the police, doesn't have to attend the funeral of any of his homies, and goes the entire day without having to fire his AK-47. As if to show us what a fantasy all this is, the video for the song ends with Ice Cube in a Los Angeles SWAT team's crosshairs.

Ice Cube, a founding member of a group called N.W.A ("Niggas With Attitude"), epitomizes "gangsta," probably the most popular style of rap right now, and certainly the most truculent and ghettocentric—the style people have in mind when they condemn rap for its comic-book Afrocentrism, its monotonous profanity, its Uzi-brandishing, its anti-Semitism and intolerance of Asians, its homophobia and crotch-grabbing misogyny, its nigger-this and nigger-that, and the seeming determination of many of its performers to fulfill every negative black sterotype. According to gangsta's apologists in the music press, these objectionable characteristics are symptoms of black disempowerment. It's difficult to argue with this at face value—difficult not to feel, on being subjected to a musical drive-by from a Jeep whose back seat has been torn out and replaced with speakers, that what one is hearing is the death rattle of Martin Luther King Jr.'s dream.

Usually it's just some kid letting the world know that he's alive and has a car. Just as there's something called alternative rock, which nobody in the music business seems quite able to define except by example, there's something called alternative rap—perhaps best exemplified by the group Arrested Development. Musically, the difference between gangsta and alternative is that alternative tends to be more playful, both in its rhymes and in its sampling. But the *perceived* difference between the two styles has almost nothing to do with music. One gains a sense of what both gangsta and alternative have come to stand for by listening to "People Everyday," a song from Arrested Development's platinum album, *3 Years, 5 Months & 2 Days in the Life of*. . . . Speech, Arrested Development's leader, is spending the afternoon in the park with his girlfriend, when along comes "a group of brothers" swigging forty-ounce bottles of malt liquor, "goin' the nigga route" and "disrespecting my black queen." Speech at first ignores them, but after they make fun of his "colorful" garb (an Afrocentric variation on thrift-shop chic, to judge from the album cover) and start "squeezing parts of my date's anatomy," he springs into action. "I ain't Ice Cube," Speech tells us, "but I had to take the brother out for bein' rude."

It takes "three or four" cops to pull Speech off of the gangsta (who evidently survives the encounter), and the story becomes one of "a black man, acting like a nigga and [getting] stomped by an African." But Speech, who tells us on another of the album's songs that he's "a bit shorter than the average man," and on yet another that "brothers" in possession of automatic weapons "need to learn how to correctly shoot them, [to] save those rounds for a revolution," has more in common with Ice Cube than he may care to admit. A machismo fantasy's still a machismo fantasy, even if it takes the form of an appeal to black pride rather than a call for retribution against the police. And shouldn't a songwriter praised for leading one of the few sexually integrated rap groups know better than to put a woman on a pedestal as his "black queen"? At least she's not his "bitch" or his "ho," as she might be on a gangsta record. And at least Speech's politics are slightly more sophisticated than those of the gangstas, many of whom claim Malcolm X as their role model, although what they seem to find most admirable about him is that he was once a thug with the gift of gab, just like them.

Beyond complaining that rap isn't really music because so few of its performers play instruments or "sing" in the conventional sense of the word, middle-class whites who grew up dancing to Motown's three-minute integration fantasies seem to be most alienated by what they take to be rap's black-separatist agenda. (During Reconstruction, before its members switched to hooded robes, the Klan used to wear white facemasks on its midnight raids. Rap is a form of blackface in much the same way: an attempt not to disguise one's race but to idealize it by exaggerating it—an attempt to wage war with it.)

A deeper source of frustration might be a sense on the part of middle-aged whites that rap's tacit off-limits sign is generational, not racial. But at whose young is rap aimed? In a nasty little cover story on rap in a 1991 issue of *The New Republic*, David Samuels argued that the audience for rap now consists in large measure of white middle-class teenagers turned on by rap's "evocation of an age-old image of blackness: a foreign, sexually charged, and criminal underworld against which the norms of white society are defined and, by extension, through which they may be defiled." The cover of Ice-T's recent *Home Invasion*, which depicts a white tousel-top surrounded by the

books of Malcom X, Donald Goines, and Iceberg Slim, listening to music (this very album?) on headphones as he fanatsizes
that his mother is being ravished and his father is being beaten
to death by muscular black intruders, suggests that there's some
merit to Samuels's argument. As does L.L. Cool J's observation,
on listening to Da Lench Mob's "Fuck You and Your Heroes,"
that "That's a song for white folks. If you want to shock niggas,
you gotta say, 'fuck Malcolm X, fuck Martin Luther King.' "

But so what? Rap's young white fans are hardly the first of
their race to get off on black music. The problem with focusing
on what percentage of rap's audience is white and whether the
militancy of some of its performers panders to white sexual
fantasies is that such questions leave black adults out of the
equation. Reading any of those recent trendy books and magazine articles contrasting the tastes and values of Boomers with
those of their offspring, you might think that generation gaps
were an exclusively white phenomenon. Yet a visit to a record
store in which you'll find one section for rap and another for
soul should be proof that black America has its own generation
gap, of which differing tastes in music are only the tip. As the
essayist Gerald Early has pointed out,

> Each new generation [of African-Americans] views its
> elders with suspicion, thinking them failures who com-
> promised and accommodated themselves in order to
> survive among the whites. And each generation, in
> some way, wishes to free itself from the generation that
> produced it.

African-Americans now in their late thirties or early forties,
already resentful of their marginalization by mass media that
tend to present black culture only in terms of new directions in
jive, must sometimes feel as though everything they grew up
believing in is under attack in some of the music their children
are listening to. "When we first started, everything was black-

this and black-that—the whole positive black thing," Easy E, the former drug dealer who was a founder of N.W.A, once explained to an interviewer. "We said fuck that—we wanted to come out in everybody's face. Something that would shock people."

Parents are forever mocked for being convinced that their children are emulating poor role models and headed straight for trouble. But given such grim statistics as the one showing that black teenage males have a greater chance of serving prison sentences than of attending college, today's black parents are justified in thinking that their children genuinely are at risk. And this particular generational clash is exacerbated by class friction of a sort seldom experienced by whites. In *Juice*, an otherwise forgettable 1992 action movie directed by Ernest Dickerson (Spike Lee's cinematographer), a young man named Quincy who is an aspiring hip-hop DJ from the projects introduces himself as "Q" (his street name) to the estranged husband of the older woman he's been sleeping with. "What, did names like Mustafah and Akbar become too hard to spell?" the husband sneers. His equal disdain for the African or Islamic names given to children by roots-conscious black parents in the 1970s and for the breezy street names many of those kids have since adopted is a tip-off that this man in a suit is a member of the black bourgeoisie, or at least aspires to it. Both kinds of names reek of the ghetto to him, and this makes him an unsympathetic character in the movie's scheme of things. But what gives the scene its surprising complexity is the glimpse it provides of the alienation felt by many middle-class African-Americans at a time when the ghetto street culture celebrated in rap is increasingly viewed as the only authentic black experience (apparently even by a black achiever like Dickerson).

My own feelings about rap are so conflicted that I hardly know how to answer when somebody asks (usually incredulously) if I'm a fan. I'm not, exactly. The first requisite for being a fan of anything is to think of it somehow as *yours*, and I no longer feel entitled to think of any pop music as "mine," rap least of all. Yet I listen to a fair amount of rap out of a combination of professional obligation and curiosity, and wind up enjoying much of what I hear—though even that often saddens or troubles me. The rapper most admired by my colleagues is Chuck D, of the group Public Enemy, who has, in effect, put a beat to the bluster of the Black Panthers and the Nation of Islam. Marshall Berman, a professor at the City University of New York, and the author of *Everything That Is Solid Melts into Air*, an influential text on modernism, has likened Public Enemy's "breakthroughs" in rap to "Picasso's in painting, Eliot's and Pound's in poetry, Faulkner's and Joyce's in the novel, Parker's in jazz." If you say so, professor. All I hear in Chuck D is a rapper whose delivery is too sententious to be convincing and whose worship by the pop intelligentsia is evidence of the extent to which black racism is now deemed a legitimate response to white oppression.

The rap performers I enjoy are those who emphasize production values, songcraft, and that quality of playfulness endemic to all good pop. These include P.M. Dawn, Neneh Cherry, De La Soul, and a new group from Los Angeles called The Pharcyde. Another new group, the Digable Planets, are nothing if not playful in attempting to fuse rap with elements of bebop, but what finally turns me off about them is their reduction of jazz to walking bass lines, finger-snaps, and bohemian vogueing.

These performers (I'll add Arrested Development, if only for their "Tennessee," an evocation of the agrarian South as a place filled with both idyllic as well as harrowing memories for black Americans) suggest the wide range of approaches possible in a genre as seemingly inflexible as rap. My very favorite among all recent pop albums is one generally spoken of as an example of alternative rap, though it might not be if the young performer responsible weren't black and didn't employ sampling and other hip-hop studio conventions.

Michael Ivey is the leader of a group called Basehead,

which—at least on its debut album, *Play with Toys*—turns out
not to be a group at all but just Ivey on guitar and vocals, a
drummer named Brian Hendrix, and a handful of other musicians drifting in and out of the studio. Ivey sings in a small voice
as uvular as any we've heard since Donovan. When he isn't
singing, he's speeding up and slowing down the tape in order
to alter his speaking voice: what are presented as arguments
between him and his friends are actually Ivey's stoned interior
monologues. Although "basehead" is street slang for someone
who freebases cocaine, the illegal substance of choice in Ivey's
songs is marijuana, and even it takes second place to beer—Ivey
or one of his imaginary buddies is always popping the top off a
cold one.

Ivey is a musical as well as a verbal ironist who delights in
subverting both rock and gangsta-rap conventions. His guitar
riffs demonstrate pop's boomerang effect: played a little faster
and with more thunder, they could be the riffs that Led Zep-
pelin and other British protometal bands appropriated from
Delta bluesmen. The bass-heavy sound mix on *Play with Toys* is
similar to those favored by the gangstas, but Ivey turns the tables
on them by sampling N.W.A's "8 Ball" on a song called (what
else?) "Ode to My Favorite Beer."

Ivey's melodies are slightly woozy and doggedly minimalistic: a key change is a big event. Not much happens in his lyrics,
either, and that's probably what I like about them. "It's the exis-
tential hero—what I like to call 'a man and his room' stories,"
the film director Paul Schrader once said of his screenplays for
American Gigolo, Light Sleeper, and Martin Scorsese's *Taxi Driver,
Raging Bull,* and *The Last Temptation of Christ.* Schrader would
love Ivey, who recently graduated from Howard University
with a degree in film and who opens and closes *Play with Toys*
leading an imaginary country band called Jethroe and the Gram
Crackeres in a redneck honky tonk, but otherwise never seems
to leave his apartment (rendering moot the question of his
street credibility, I guess). Ivey drinks beer, writes songs, broods

over breaking up with his girlfriend, and frets over his own future and the fate of other young black men as he watches the evening news. Although compared by critics to the aimless postadolescents in Richard Linklater's movie *Slacker*, Ivey can no more be said to represent a type than his music can be reduced to sociology.

Basehead's new *Not in Kansas Anymore* is a disappointing follow-up on which Ivey—whose cult listenership is mostly white, to judge from the audience that turned out for a show he gave in Philadelphia last winter—makes what sounds like a deliberate attempt to blacken up, at least in terms of his lyrics. Leaving his apartment for a change, he's treated as a potential shoplifter in a clothing store and stopped and frisked by the police for no apparent reason other than that he's young and black, and therefore assumed to be armed and dangerous. Though I don't doubt for a minute that Ivey is writing from experience, his touch is almost too light to convey his indignation.

This turf belongs to the gangstas, whose ghetto narratives forcefully express the rage a middle-class monologist like Ivey can hardly bring himself to feel. What gives a song like Ice T's "Cop Killer" or Paris's "Coffee, Doughnuts & Death" its troubling power is the performer's sense and ours that he isn't speaking just for himself. Such songs are the only ones on the radio now in which more seems at stake than a position on next week's charts. But their social significance doesn't allow us to overlook all that's reprehensible about them; issues are rarely that simple, and neither is pop.

I'm someone whose tolerance of—no, *enthusiasm* for—such violent films as Quentin Tarantino's *Reservoir Dogs*, Carl Franklin's *One False Move*, and Abel Ferrara's *Bad Lieutenant* renders him vulnerable to charges of practicing a racial double standard in feeling such dismay over rap's bloodlust. And I do admit that rap troubles me in a way that movies rarely do. But there are differences between movies and pop music, the most obvious of which is that movies, by their very nature, are capable of presenting multiple points of view. In *Reservoir Dogs*, for example, Tarantino stops just short of showing us a cop having his ear sliced off by a sadistic, razor-wielding hood played by Michael Madsen. This is a scene that sickens some moviegoers and sends others stumbling for the exits, either in fear of what they're about to see or in fear of their response to it. The camera follows Madsen throughout the scene, and it's difficult not to become caught up in his delirium as he turns up the volume on the radio, does a series of graceful little dancesteps to Stealers Wheel's "Stuck in the Middle with You," and closes in on his defenseless, screaming captive. "Was that as good for you as it was for me?" Madsen asks the cop afterward. Then he douses him with gasoline and pulls out his lighter. Madsen might as well be asking those of us who sat through the scene without averting our eyes if it was good for us—the embarrassed answer would be yes. But along with Madsen's dancesteps, what stays in the mind are the cop's screams and his dazed reaction to his mutilation and imminent death.

Pop songs are theoretically as capable as film of representing this kind of emotional and moral complexity. Randy Newman and Lou Reed are among the pop songwriters who have provided it, or at least come close. Rap is strictly first-person singular at this point. Its young performers have yet to develop the artistic (and moral) gift of empathy. Maybe when they grow up, if this isn't asking too much of pop.

(OCTOBER 1993)

Index

■ Index ■

■ Index ■

■ Index ■